First World War
and Army of Occupation
War Diary
France, Belgium and Germany

7 INDIAN (MEERUT) DIVISION
20 (Garhwal) Indian Infantry Brigade
London Regiment
1/3 Battalion London Regiment (City of London)
and Leicestershire Regiment 2nd Battalion.
9 August 1914 - 2 December 1915

WO95/3945/1

The Naval & Military Press Ltd
www.nmarchive.com
Published in association with The National Archives

Published by

The Naval & Military Press Ltd

Unit 10 Ridgewood Industrial Park,

Uckfield, East Sussex,

TN22 5QE England

Tel: +44 (0) 1825 749494

www.naval-military-press.com

www.nmarchive.com

This diary has been reprinted in facsimile from the original. Any imperfections are inevitably reproduced and the quality may fall short of modern type and cartographic standards.

© **Crown Copyright**

Images reproduced by permission of The National Archives, London, England, 2015.

Contents

Document type	Place/Title	Date From	Date To
Heading	WO95/3945/1 1/3 Battalion London Regiment		
Heading	Meerut Division Garhwal Brigade 1/3rd London Regt Feb-Oct 1915		
Heading	3 London 10th February To 31 May 1915		
Miscellaneous	British Salonika Force War Diary		
Miscellaneous	Cover For Documents. Nature Of Enclosures.		
Heading	War Diary of 1/3rd Battalion The London Regiment From 10th February 1915 To 31st May 1915		
Miscellaneous	1/3rd London Regiment		
Miscellaneous	1/3rd Battalion The London Regiment (Territorials)	01/09/1914	01/09/1914
Miscellaneous	1/3rd Battalion The London Regiment	10/02/1915	10/02/1915
Miscellaneous	Operation Orders		
Miscellaneous	Special Operation Order S By Lieut-Col A. Anthony Howell Cmdg 1/3rd Battalion The London Regiment	18/04/1915	18/04/1915
Miscellaneous	1/3rd Battalion The Lesson Regt.	11/04/1915	11/04/1915
Miscellaneous	Operation Orders By Lieut-Col. A. Anthony Howell Cmdg 1/3rd Battalion The London Regiment.	18/04/1915	18/04/1915
Miscellaneous	Operation Orders By Lieut-Col. A. Anthony Howell Commanding 1/3rd Battalion The London Regiment	23/04/1915	23/04/1915
Miscellaneous	Operation Orders By Lieut-Col. A. Anthony Howell	27/04/1915	27/04/1915
Miscellaneous	Operation Orders By Lieut-Col. A. Anthony Howell	01/05/1915	01/05/1915
Heading	3 London June 1915		
Miscellaneous	British Salonika Force War Diary 26th Division		
Heading	War Diary of 1/3rd Battalion The London Regiment From 1st June 1915 To 30th June 1915		
War Diary	Paradis	01/06/1915	01/06/1915
War Diary	Vieille Chapelle	02/06/1915	07/06/1915
War Diary	Richebourg St. Vaast	08/06/1915	18/06/1915
War Diary	Trenches	19/06/1915	20/06/1915
War Diary	Trenches Albert Rd.	21/06/1915	27/06/1915
War Diary	Trenches	28/06/1915	28/06/1915
War Diary	Les Lobes	29/06/1915	30/06/1915
Miscellaneous	Operations Order By Lieut-Col A. Anthony Howell Cmdg 1/3rd Bn The London Regt	14/06/1915	14/06/1915
Miscellaneous	Operations Order By Lieut-Col A. Anthony Howell Cmdg	14/06/1915	14/06/1915
Miscellaneous	Operations Orders By Lieut-Col.A. Anthony Howell Cmdg 1/3rd Battalion The London Regiment.	18/06/1915	18/06/1915
Miscellaneous	Special Operations Orders By Lieut-Col.A. Anthony Howell Cmdg 1/3rd Bn The London Regt	18/06/1915	18/06/1915
Miscellaneous	1/3rd Battalion, The London Regiment	21/06/1915	21/06/1915
Miscellaneous	3rd Battalion The London Regiment	23/06/1915	23/06/1915
Heading	3 London July 1915		
Miscellaneous	Cover For Documents. Nature Of Enclosures.		
Miscellaneous	British Salonika Force War Diary		
Heading	War Diary of 1/3rd London Regiment From 1st July 1915 To 31st July 1915		
War Diary	Les Lobes	01/07/1915	04/07/1915
War Diary	Richebourg	04/07/1915	10/07/1915
War Diary	Les Lobes	11/07/1915	12/07/1915

War Diary	Le Sart	15/07/1915	15/07/1915
War Diary	L'Epinette	16/07/1915	22/07/1915
War Diary	M.17.c.7.3.	23/07/1915	31/07/1915
Miscellaneous	Operation Order by Lieut Col A. Anthony Howell C.M.C. Cmdg 1/3rd Battalion The London Regiment	04/07/1915	04/07/1915
Miscellaneous	Operation Order by Lieut Col A. Anthony Howell C.M.C. Commanding 1/3rd Battalion The London Regiment	10/07/1915	10/07/1915
Miscellaneous	Operation Orders by Major P.W. Beresford Commanding 1/3rd Battalion the London Regiment	14/07/1915	14/07/1915
Miscellaneous	Operation Orders by Major P.W. Beresford Commanding 1/3rd Battalion the London Regiment	07/07/1915	07/07/1915
Miscellaneous	Operation Orders by Major P.W. Beresford Cmdg 1/3rd London-Regiment	22/07/1915	22/07/1915
Heading	3 London August 1915		
Miscellaneous	Cover For Documents. Nature Of Enclosures.		
Miscellaneous	British Salonika Force War Diary Vol. No. 14		
Heading	War Diary of 1/3rd London Regiment From 1st August 1915 To 31st August 1915		
War Diary	Estaires	01/08/1915	01/08/1915
War Diary	Pont Du Hem	02/08/1915	08/08/1915
War Diary	La Gorgue	09/08/1915	16/08/1915
War Diary	M.17.c.5.0	17/08/1915	27/08/1915
War Diary	Neuf Berquin	28/08/1915	28/08/1915
War Diary	Neuve Chapelle	29/08/1915	31/08/1915
Miscellaneous	Operation Orders by Lieut Col A. Anthony Howell C.M.G. Commanding 1/3rd Battalion the London Regiment	01/08/1915	01/08/1915
Operation(al) Order(s)	Operation Orders No.23 by Lieut Col A. Anthony Howell C.M.G. Commanding 1/3rd Battalion the London Regt	08/08/1915	08/08/1915
Miscellaneous	Operation Order No. 24 by Lieut Col A. Anthony Howell C.M.G. Commanding 1/3rd Battalion the London Regt	09/08/1915	09/08/1915
Miscellaneous	Operation Order No. 25 by Lieut Col A. Anthony Howell C.M.G. Commanding 1/3rd Battalion the London Regt	16/08/1915	16/08/1915
Operation(al) Order(s)	Operation Order No. 26 by Lieut Col A. Anthony Howell C.M.G. Commanding 1/3rd Battalion the London Regt	27/08/1915	27/08/1915
Operation(al) Order(s)	Operation Order No. 27 by Lieut Col A. Anthony Howell C.M.G. Commanding 1/3rd Battalion the London Regt	28/08/1915	28/08/1915
Heading	3 London Sept 15		
Miscellaneous	British Salonika Force War Diary 26th Division		
Heading	War Diary of 1/3rd London Regiment From 1st September 1915 To 30th September 1915		
War Diary	Neuve Chapelle	01/09/1915	01/09/1915
War Diary	La Gorgue	02/09/1915	12/09/1915
War Diary	Trenches M.35.b.7.7.	13/09/1915	18/09/1915
War Diary	La Gorgue	19/09/1915	24/09/1915
War Diary	Trenches M.35.b.7.7	25/09/1915	25/09/1915
War Diary	Trenches	25/09/1915	26/09/1915
War Diary	Bout De Ville	27/09/1915	30/09/1915
Miscellaneous			
Operation(al) Order(s)	Operation Order No 29	01/09/1915	01/09/1915

Operation(al) Order(s)	Operation Order No 23 by Lieut Col A. Anthony Howell C.M.G. Commanding 1/3rd Battalion the London Regt	10/09/1915	10/09/1915
Operation(al) Order(s)	Operation Order No 30 by Lieut Col A. Anthony Howell C.M.G. Commanding 1/3rd Battalion the London Regt	17/09/1915	17/09/1915
Operation(al) Order(s)	Operation Order No 31 by Lieut Col A. Anthony Howell C.M.G. Commanding 1/3rd Battalion the London Regiment	24/09/1915	24/09/1915
Diagram etc	Diagram		
Operation(al) Order(s)	Operation Orders No.32 by Lieut Col A. Anthony Howell C.M.G. Commanding 1/3rd Battalion the London Regiment	23/09/1915	23/09/1915
Operation(al) Order(s)	Operation Orders No.33 by Lieut Col A. Anthony Howell C.M.G. Commanding 1/3rd Battalion the London Regiment	30/09/1915	30/09/1915
Heading	3 London October 1915		
Miscellaneous	Cover For Documents. Nature Of Enclosures.		
Heading	British Salonika Force War Diary 26th Division Period From 1/3/15 To 31/3/15 Vol. No. 17		
Heading	War Diary of 1/3rd London Regiment From 1st October 1915 To 31st October 1915		
War Diary	L'Epinette	01/10/1915	03/10/1915
War Diary	Loisne	04/10/1915	11/10/1915
War Diary	Gorre	13/10/1915	20/10/1915
War Diary	Richebourg	21/10/1915	29/10/1915
War Diary	Richebourg St. Vaast	30/10/1915	31/10/1915
Operation(al) Order(s)	Operation Order No 34 by Lieut Col A. Anthony Howell C.M.G. Commanding 1/3rd Battalion the London Regiment	02/10/1915	02/10/1915
Operation(al) Order(s)	Operation Order No 35 by Lieut Col A. Anthony Howell C.M.G. Commanding 1/3rd Battalion the London Regiment	10/10/1915	10/10/1915
Operation(al) Order(s)	Operation Order No 36 by Major P.W. Beresford Cmdg 1/3rd London-Regiment	15/10/1915	15/10/1915
Miscellaneous	1/3rd London Regiment	15/10/1915	15/10/1915
Operation(al) Order(s)	Operation Orders No 37 by Major P.W. Beresford Commanding 1/3rd Battalion The London Regiment	18/10/1915	18/10/1915
Heading	WO95/3945/2 2 Battalion Leicestershire Regiment		
Heading	7 Ind Div 20 Bde Meerut Division Garhwal Brigade 2nd Bn Leicesters 1914 Aug-1915 Nov		
Heading	War Diary of 2nd Bn Leicester Regiment From 9.8.14 To 2.12.14 Volume I		
Heading	War Diary Leicestershire Regt Period 9 August 14 To 2nd Dec 1914 (26 Sheets)		
Heading	Meerut Division Aug-Dec 1914 2nd Bn Leicester Regt		
Diagram etc	Sets Of External Gable Sheeting		
War Diary	Ranikhet	09/08/1914	15/08/1914
War Diary	Bareilly	16/08/1914	05/09/1914
War Diary	Karachi	08/09/1914	08/09/1914
War Diary	Rest Camp Karachi	11/09/1914	11/09/1914
War Diary	Karachi	15/09/1914	21/10/1914
War Diary	Orleans	26/10/1914	26/10/1914
War Diary	Lillers	28/10/1914	20/11/1914
War Diary	Special	20/11/1914	30/11/1914
War Diary	(Sea Sheet 26)	01/12/1914	02/12/1914

Type	Description	Start	End
Miscellaneous		03/12/1914	03/12/1914
Heading	War Diary of The 2nd Bn Leicestershire Regiment From 3rd December 1914 To 7th January 1915		
War Diary		03/12/1914	07/01/1915
Miscellaneous	The following received from Corps Commanding. Appendix B	19/12/1914	19/12/1914
Miscellaneous		07/01/1915	07/01/1915
Heading	War Diary of 2nd Bn Leicestershire Regiment From 7th January 1915 To 3rd March 1915		
War Diary		23/01/1915	25/01/1915
War Diary	Ecquedecques	01/01/1915	21/01/1915
War Diary	Calonne	22/01/1915	22/01/1915
War Diary	La Couture	23/01/1915	03/02/1915
Miscellaneous		04/03/1915	04/03/1915
Heading	War Diary of 2/Leicestershire Regiment From 4th March 1915 To 31st March 1915		
War Diary		04/03/1915	31/03/1915
Operation(al) Order(s)	Operation Orders No.25 by Brigadier General C.G. Blackader D.S.O. Commanding Garhwal Brigade	09/03/1915	09/03/1915
Miscellaneous	Table A		
Operation(al) Order(s)	Operation Order No. 25 by Brigadier General C.G. Blackader D.S.O. Commanding Garhwal Brigade		
Miscellaneous	A Form Messages And Signals.		
Miscellaneous	Operation Orders by Lieut Colonel H. Gordon D.S.O. Comdg Leicestershire Regt.	09/03/1915	09/03/1915
Miscellaneous	Special Order	09/03/1915	09/03/1915
Miscellaneous	A Form. Messages And Signals.	11/03/1915	11/03/1915
Operation(al) Order(s)	Operation Order No. 26 by Brig Genl C.G. Blackader D.S.O. Commanding Garhwal Brigade	13/03/1915	13/03/1915
Miscellaneous	Operation Orders by Lieut Col H. Gordon D.S.O. Comdg Leicestershire Regt	13/03/1915	13/03/1915
Miscellaneous	Special Order of The Day By Brigadier General L.G. Blackader D.S.O. Commanding Garhwal Brigade	14/03/1915	14/03/1915
Miscellaneous	Appendix J		
Miscellaneous	Appendix K		
Miscellaneous	Operation Order Copy No 5		
Miscellaneous	Operation Order by Lieut Col H. Gordon D.S.O. Comdg Leicestershire Regt	24/03/1915	24/03/1915
Miscellaneous	Operation Order by Lieut Colonel H. Gordon D.S.O. Comdg Leicestershire Regt	29/03/1915	29/03/1915
Heading	War Diary of 2/Leicestershire Regiment From 4th April 1915 To 30th April 1915		
War Diary		04/04/1915	30/04/1915
Map	Map		
Heading	War Diary With Appendices Of 2nd Leicesters From 1st May 1915 To 31st May 1915		
War Diary		01/05/1915	31/05/1915
Map	Map		
Miscellaneous	Operation Order by Lieut Colonel H. Gordon D.S.O. Comdg Leicestershire Regt	07/05/1915	07/05/1915
Miscellaneous	Operation Orders by Lt Col H. Gordon D.S.O. Comdg Leicestershire Regt	15/05/1915	15/05/1915
Operation(al) Order(s)	Operation Order No. 40 by Brigadier General C.G. Blackader D.S.O. Commanding Garhwal Brigade	07/05/1915	07/05/1915
Miscellaneous	Operation Order by Brigadier General C.G. Blackader D.S.O. Commanding Garhwal Brigade	13/05/1915	13/05/1915

Type	Description	Date	Date
Diagram etc	Diagram		
Operation(al) Order(s)	Operation Order No. 43 by Brigadier General C.G. Blackader D.S.O. Commanding Garhwal Brigade	19/05/1915	19/05/1915
Operation(al) Order(s)	Operation Order No. 44 by Brigadier General C.G. Blackader D.S.O. Commanding Garhwal Brigade	24/05/1915	24/05/1915
Miscellaneous	Report On Operation From 10 To 16 May 1915	19/05/1915	19/05/1915
Heading	War Diary Appendices Tactical Progress Reports 20th To 31st May 1915		
Miscellaneous	Tactical Progress Report	20/05/1915	20/05/1915
Miscellaneous	Tactical Progress Report	21/05/1915	21/05/1915
Miscellaneous	Tactical Progress Report	22/05/1915	22/05/1915
Miscellaneous	Tactical Progress Report	23/05/1915	23/05/1915
Miscellaneous	Tactical Progress Report	24/05/1915	24/05/1915
Miscellaneous	Tactical Progress Report	25/05/1915	25/05/1915
Miscellaneous	Tactical Progress Report	26/05/1915	26/05/1915
Miscellaneous	Tactical Progress Report	27/05/1915	27/05/1915
Miscellaneous	Tactical Progress Report	28/05/1915	28/05/1915
Miscellaneous	Tactical Progress Report	29/05/1915	29/05/1915
Miscellaneous	Tactical Progress Report	30/05/1915	30/05/1915
Miscellaneous	Tactical Progress Report	31/05/1915	31/05/1915
Heading	Garhwal Brigade War Diary Appendices Operation Orders		
Operation(al) Order(s)	Operation Order No. 39 by Brigadier General C.G. Blackader D.S.O. Commanding Garhwal Brigade	04/05/1915	04/05/1915
Operation(al) Order(s)	Operation Order No. 43 by Brigadier General C.G. Blackader D.S.O. Commanding Garhwal Brigade	19/05/1915	19/05/1915
Operation(al) Order(s)	Operation Order No. 44 by Brigadier General C.G. Blackader D.S.O. Commanding Garhwal Brigade	24/05/1915	24/05/1915
Operation(al) Order(s)	Operation Order No. 45 by Brigadier General C.G. Blackader D.S.O.	26/05/1915	26/05/1915
Operation(al) Order(s)	Operation Order No. 46 by Brigadier General C.G. Blackader D.S.O. Commanding Garhwal Brigade	26/05/1915	26/05/1915
Operation(al) Order(s)	Operation Order No. 47 by Brigadier General C.G. Blackader D.S.O. Commanding Garhwal Brigade	31/05/1915	31/05/1915
Heading	Garhwal Brigade War Diary Appendices Operation Orders		
Operation(al) Order(s)	Operation Order No. 29 by Lieutenant General Sir C.A. Anderson K.C.B. Commanding Meerut Division	04/05/1915	04/05/1915
Miscellaneous	Headquarters Jullundur Bde	05/05/1915	05/05/1915
Miscellaneous	A Form Messages And Signals.	19/05/1915	19/05/1915
Miscellaneous	A Form Messages And Signals.		
Operation(al) Order(s)	Operation Order No. 32 by Lieutenant General Sir Charles Anderson K.C.B. Commanding Meerut Division	18/05/1915	18/05/1915
Operation(al) Order(s)	Operation Order No. 35 by Brigadier General W.H. Southey C.M.G. Commanding Bareilly Brigade	19/05/1915	19/05/1915
Miscellaneous	A Form Messages And Signals.		
Operation(al) Order(s)	Operation Order No. 34 by Lieutenant General Sir Charles Anderson K.C.B. Commanding Meerut Division	21/05/1915	21/05/1915
Miscellaneous	A Form Messages And Signals.		
Operation(al) Order(s)	Operation Order No. 35		
Miscellaneous	Advanced Meerut Division	22/05/1915	22/05/1915
Operation(al) Order(s)	Operation Order No. 36 by Lieutenant General Sir Charles Anderson K.C.B. Commanding Meerut Division	23/05/1915	23/05/1915

Miscellaneous	A Form Messages And Signals.	23/05/1915	23/05/1915
Miscellaneous	A Form Messages And Signals.	25/05/1915	25/05/1915
Miscellaneous	A Form Messages And Signals.	23/05/1915	23/05/1915
Operation(al) Order(s)	Brigade Order No. 31	31/05/1915	31/05/1915
Miscellaneous	Garhwal Brigade War Diary Appendices Operation Orders		
Miscellaneous	Headquarters, Meerut Division	06/05/1915	06/05/1915
Operation(al) Order(s)	Operation Order No. 30 by Lieutenant General Sir Charles Anderson K.C.B. Commanding Meerut Division	06/05/1915	06/05/1915
Diagram etc	Flags For Marking Position Of Advanced Troops		
Map	Map		
Miscellaneous	Headquarters, Meerut Division	07/05/1915	07/05/1915
Miscellaneous	A Form Messages And Signals.		
Miscellaneous	Headquarters, Meerut Division	07/05/1915	07/05/1915
Miscellaneous	Artillery Time Table		
Miscellaneous	Headquarters, Meerut Division	03/05/1915	03/05/1915
Miscellaneous	A Form Messages And Signals.		
Operation(al) Order(s)	Operation Order No. 42 By Brigadier General C.G. Blackader D.S.O. Commanding Garhwal Bde	15/05/1915	15/05/1915
Miscellaneous	A Form Messages And Signals.		
Map	Map		
Operation(al) Order(s)	Operation Order No. 31 by Brigadier General C.W. Jacob Commanding Dehradun Bde	06/05/1915	06/05/1915
Operation(al) Order(s)	Operation Orders 32 by Brigadier General C.W. Jacob Commanding Dehradun Brigade	07/05/1915	07/05/1915
Operation(al) Order(s)	Operation Order No. 32 by Brigadier General W.M. Southey C.M.G. Commanding Bareilly Bde	08/05/1915	08/05/1915
Miscellaneous	A Form Messages And Signals.		
Miscellaneous	A Form Messages And Signals		
Operation(al) Order(s)	Operation Order No. 31 by Lieutenant General Sir Charles Anderson K.C.B. Commanding Meerut Division	14/05/1915	14/05/1915
Operation(al) Order(s)	Correction To Operation Order No. 31	15/05/1915	15/05/1915
Miscellaneous	G.O.C. Garhwal Brigade	15/05/1915	15/05/1915
Miscellaneous	6th Infantry Brigade	14/05/1915	14/05/1915
Operation(al) Order(s)	Operation Order No. 42 by Br Gen W.G. Walker V.C. Comdg Sirhind Bde	14/05/1915	14/05/1915
Miscellaneous	H.Q. Sirhind Bde	15/05/1915	15/05/1915
Operation(al) Order(s)	Operation Order No. 43 by Br General W.G. Walker V.C. C.B. Comdg Sirhind Bde	15/05/1915	15/05/1915
Operation(al) Order(s)	Brigade Operation Order No. 34 by Brigadier General W.M. Southey C.M.G. Commanding Bareilly Brigade	16/05/1915	16/05/1915
Miscellaneous	A Form Messages And Signals		
Miscellaneous	Commander		
Miscellaneous	A Form Messages And Signals		
Heading	Garhwal Brigade War Diary Appendices-Operation Orders Issued 7th, 13th And 15th May		
Operation(al) Order(s)	Operation Order No. 40 by Brigadier General C.G. Blackader D.S.O. Commanding Garhwal Brigade	07/05/1915	07/05/1915
Miscellaneous	A Form Messages And Signals.		
Operation(al) Order(s)	Operation Order No. 41 By Brigadier General C.G. Blackader D.S.O. Commanding Garhwal Bde	13/05/1915	13/05/1915
Operation(al) Order(s)	Operation Order No. 42 By Brigadier General C.G. Blackader D.S.O. Commanding Garhwal Bde	15/05/1915	15/05/1915
Miscellaneous	A Form Messages And Signals.		

Heading	War Diary of 2nd Leicester From 1st June 1915 To 30th June 1915		
War Diary		01/06/1915	30/06/1915
Heading	War Diary of 2nd Leicesters From 1st July 1915 To 31st July 1915		
War Diary		01/07/1915	31/07/1915
Heading	War Diary of The 2nd Bn. Leicestershire Regiment From 1st August 1915 To 31st August 1915		
War Diary		01/08/1915	31/08/1915
Miscellaneous Map	Map		
Miscellaneous Map	Map		
Map	Bois Du Biez		
Map Miscellaneous		01/09/1915	01/09/1915
Heading	War Diary of 2nd Battalion Leicestershire Regiment From 1st September 1915 To 30th September 1915		
War Diary		01/09/1915	16/09/1915
Diagram etc	Diagram		
War Diary		17/09/1916	30/09/1916
Heading	War Diary of 2nd Battalion Leicestershire Regiment From 1st October 1915 To 31st October 1915		
War Diary		01/10/1915	31/10/1915
Heading	War Diary of 2nd Bn Leicestershire Regiment From 1st November 1915 To 30th November 1915		
War Diary		01/11/1915	02/12/1915

Heading	War Diary of 2nd Leicester From 1st June 1915 To 30th June 1915		
War Diary		01/06/1915	30/06/1915
Heading	War Diary of 2nd Leicesters From 1st July 1915 To 31st July 1915		
War Diary		01/07/1915	31/07/1915
Heading	War Diary of The 2nd Bn. Leicestershire Regiment From 1st August 1915 To 31st August 1915		
War Diary		01/08/1915	31/08/1915
Miscellaneous Map	Map		
Miscellaneous Map	Map		
Map	Bois Du Biez		
Map Miscellaneous		01/09/1915	01/09/1915
Heading	War Diary of 2nd Battalion Leicestershire Regiment From 1st September 1915 To 30th September 1915		
War Diary		01/09/1915	16/09/1915
Diagram etc	Diagram		
War Diary		17/09/1916	30/09/1916
Heading	War Diary of 2nd Battalion Leicestershire Regiment From 1st October 1915 To 31st October 1915		
War Diary		01/10/1915	31/10/1915
Heading	War Diary of 2nd Bn Leicestershire Regiment From 1st November 1915 To 30th November 1915		
War Diary		01/11/1915	02/12/1915

WO/95/3945/1

113 Battalion London Regiment
(City of London)

Meerut Division
Garhwal Brigade.
1/3rd London Regt.
Feb — Oct. 1915

To 167 Bde
56 DIV

Garhwal Rifles
Meerut Div

3 London

10ᵗʰ February to 31ˢᵗ May

April

1915

Garhwal Rifles
Meerut Div

Volume No. _____

BRITISH SALONIKA FORCE

WAR DIARY.

L. of C.

Vol. No.	Unit	PERIOD From	To
25.	No. 4. Advanced Park Co. R.E.	1.11.17	30.11.17
7.	33rd Base Park Co. R.E.	1.11.17	30.11.17
24.	114th Rly. Cons. Co. R.E.	"	"
10.	264th Rly. Cons. Co. R.E.	"	"
24.	270th Railway Labour Co. R.E.	"	"
16.	19th Railway Oper. Co. R.E.	"	"
10.	33rd Railway Oper. Co. R.E.	"	"
27.	37th Army Troops Co. R.E.	"	"
14.	420th West Lancs. Field Co. R.E.	"	"

W. 15517—M. 141. 250,000. 1/16. L.S.& Co. Forms/W 3091/2.   Army Form W. 3091.

Cover for Documents.

Nature of Enclosures.

Notes, or Letters written.

Serial No. 197.

121/5799

WAR DIARY
OF
1/3rd Battalion, The London Regiment
from 10th February 1915 to 31st May 1915.

1/3rd LONDON REGIMENT

Went out to Malta September 1914, moved to France January 1915; G.H.Q. Troops 4th February 1915; *attached to Ferozepore Bde: 10.2.'15,* joined Garhwal Brigade, Meerut Division 19th February 1915; transferred to Dehra Dun Brigade, same division 4th November 1915; to 139th Brigade 46th Division 6th November 1915; to 142nd Brigade, 47th Division 16th November 1915; to 167th Brigade, 56th Division 9th February 1916; to 173rd Brigade, 58th Division 31st January 1918 and amalgamated with 2/3rd Battalion.

2/3rd LONDON REGIMENT (A).

Went out to Malta January 1915; to Egypt August 1915; to Gallipoli September 1915, joined 88th Brigade, 29th Division 24th September 1915. Battalion moved to Egypt January 1916; to France, arriving 21st April 1916; disbanded June 1916.(? May).

2/3rd LONDON REGIMENT (B)

(Originally 3/3rd, renumbered in June 1916). Went out to Western Front with 173rd Brigade, 58th Division 22nd January 1917; amalgamated with 1/3rd Battalion, 31st January 1918.

3905

TO (7 MEERUT) DIVISION, 20 (IND) INF BDE
1915 FEB

1/3rd BATTALION THE LONDON REGIMENT (TERRITORIALS).

1914.

September.   Appendix.

1st.   The Battalion leaves the Railway
                Line for London, and is
                billetted in the Y.M.C.A.

2nd.   Complete Medical examination is
                held; 200 men are cast, and 200
                fresh Recruits enlisted. 6
                Officers also join to complete
                establishment.

4th.   Battalion leaves Waterloo at 11 pm
                for Southampton to embark for Malta.

5th.   The 1st London Brigade leaves
                Southampton for Malta in three
                Transports the horses being
                conveyed in another ship, the
                whole being convoyed by H.M.S.
                "Aphrodite". Battalion is split
                into three portions, two double
                Companies and Headquarters being
                on the S.S. "Nevassa" with the
                2nd Battalion, and one double
                Company on each of the other
                Transports. Colonel Howell as
                senior Colonel on S.S. Nevassa,
                is appointed in command of Troops,
                and Captain and Adjutant G.E.
                Hawes is appointed Ship's Adjutant.

9th.   Convoy arrives at Gibraltar after
                experiencing somewhat rough
                weather in the Bay of Biscay.
                The men rapidly get accustomed
                to their new experience of life on
                board ship.

13th.   Convoy arrives at Malta after
                beautiful passage from Gibraltar
                Orders are received that the 3rd
                Battalion is to be quartered at
                Imtarfa Barracks, which are
                situated about 7 miles from
                Valetta, almost exactly in the
                middle of the Island on the top
                of a hill.

14th.   The Battalion disembarks from
                the 3 Transports, and meets at
                10 am at Spencer's Monument just
                outside Valetta, and marches,
                conducted by Captain Kelly,

1914.

September.   Appendix.

14th.   Adjutant K.O.M.R.M., to
(Ctd).   Imtarfa Barracks. The Barracks
             at Imtarfa are of fairly modern
             construction, very convenient in
             every way, situation is
             delightful, and views over Malta
             are very beautiful indeed.
             The next 3 months in Malta are
             occupied in Preliminary
             Training, Company Training, and
             Musketry.

December.

17th.   Orders received that the 2nd, 3rd
             and 4th Battalions will leave
             Malta for destination unknown
             on or about January 1st, and are to
             be relieved by their respective
             Reserve Battalions.

1915.

January.   The 2nd, 3rd, and 4th Battalions
             embark on the Transports "Neuralia"
2nd.   and "Avon," and sail at 3 p.m. At
             4 p.m. a cypher message is handed
             to the Ship's Adjutant (Capt. G.E.
             Hawes, R.F.) despatch from the War
             Office, and worded as follows:-
             "The 2nd 3rd and 4th Battalions,
             The London Regiment (Territorial
             Force) will disembark at Marseilles".

5th.   After a fairly good passage the
             Battalion arrives at Marseilles,
             and is moored alongside the Quay
             hired by the British Government
             for disembarkation of Imperial
             Troops.   Orders are received
             that the Battalion will entrain
             for some destination unknown on
             the following day.

6th.   The Battalion disembarks and
             entrains at 8.15 p.m. at the
             Gare d'Arenc.

7th.   Train passing through valley of
             the Rhone. The scenery is
             very fine and the journey is a
             most interesting one. The French
             people are very enthusiastic to
             see the English Troops, and at
             the Railway Stations much
             enthusiasm is shewn, the local

1915.

January.   Appendix.

7th.   inhabitants giving the men
(Ctd).   chocolates, oranges, and
                newspapers, in return for
                badges etc. The Battalion
                are determined to do the
                thing properly, and whenever
                they get near a Station make
                a point of singing "Tipperary",
                and "The Marseillaise", as a
                compliment to our Allies. At
                Tournus the local bugle Band
                is formed up on the Platform
                and plays a selection of music
                in our honour.

8th.   News is received that the
                destination of the Battalion
                is the seaside town of Etaples,
                about 12 miles South of
                Boulogne. The Battalion
                detrains about 5.30 pm at Etaples
                and is conducted to a Camping
                Ground near the sea. The Camp
                is not completely pitched, and a
                few other tents have to be put up
                this evening to temporarily
                accommodate the Battalion. The
                weather is very cold, and we all
                feel it more after the warm
                climate we have left.

9th.   A terrible day of wind and rain.
                Unable to do anything to tidy
                up Camp or make ourselves comfortable.
                Everybody very well and cheery.
                The Colonel and the Adjutant
                interview Colonel Miller, the
                Camp Commandant, in the morning,
                and receive certain instructions
                with regard to the Troops.

10th.   A beautiful day; warmer, and
                there is sunshine. Camp is
                pitched on sandy sloping ground
                which quickly absorbs the rain,
                and is wonderfully dry for the
                time of year. It is surrounded
                on two sides by Pine Woods, and
                on the other side by the Etaples-
                Boulogne road, and sand dunes
                stretching away to the sea. The
                Camp is repitched and thoroughly
                cleaned up. Arrangements are
                made for the issue of warm
                clothing, rifles, equipment, etc.

1915.

January.   Appendix.

10th.
(Ctd).   No news has yet been
                received as to when we shall
                leave Etaples, or where our
                destination will be.

11th.   Nothing of interest to relate.
                Issue of equipment is
                proceeded with, and the
                Companies all go out for
                Company Route marches. Everybody
                is very well and cheery. There
                is very little sickness, and
                practically no colds which
                is surprising considering the
                very abrupt change of climate,
                to which we have all been
                subjected.

12th.   Battalion continues to draw
                equipment and companies parade
                daily at 7.30 am. for run
                lasting 20 minutes, and at
                9.30 am. for route marches.
                Orders are received to re-adopt
                the four company system.
                Further efforts are made to
                persuade the men to be inoculated,
                but without very much success up
                to the present. 197 have been
                inoculated once or twice.

13th.   The Battalion is organised in
                4 companies as follows:-

                No.1 Coy.   Captain Pulman.
                No.2 "   "   Reeves
                No.3 "   "   Livingston
                No.4 "   "   Moore.

                The health of the battalion
                continues to be excellent. There
                is practically no sickness except
                a certain amount of Diarrhoea
                which is probably partly caused
                by carelessness in cleaning
                cooking utensils.

14th.   No further equipment has been
                issued today. The health of
                the men keeps very good. The
                Adjutant lectured to Captains
                on the platoon in attack.
                Coys. afterwards practiced
                platoon drill.

15th.   Nothing special to report.
                Weather continues very cold.

1915.

January.   Appendix.

16th.   Equipment not yet arrived.
             Shall probably leave for
             our destination in the course
             of the next three days if issues
             are complete.

17th.   Sunday. 3rd & 4th Battalions
             attend Church Parade in the open.
             Very short service. Weather
             bitterly cold. No equipment yet.

18th.   Large consignment of equipment
             arrives. Rifles, web equipment,
             valises, etc. are issued. The
             battalion parades at 9.30 a.m.
             under the adjutant and practices
             battalion in attack. Results
             very satisfactory.

19th.   Weather much milder. About
             8.20 a.m. an Aeroplane was
             seen coming over, at considerable
             altitude. It circled two or
             three times and then headed
             straight for the Camp, and
             was seen to have the Union Jack
             and English sign painted underneath.
             The Machine came to ground just
             at the end of our lines. The
             Aviator, Lieut. Morgan of the
             Royal Army Flying Corps,
             breakfasted with the Officer.
             He had started out at 5.30 am.
             from Dunkirk, flown to Ostend
             where he dropped some bombs,
             and had then lost his way in
             the clouds, and was consequently
             much relieved to see the Bell
             Tents of the English Camp. About
             9.15 a.m. he left for St.Omer,
             the Headquarters of the British
             Army. The Battalion marched to
             the Station with Kit Bags all
             of which with Officers Baggage,
             except Valises, is being despatched
             to England by Messrs. Cox & Co.

20th.   Weather much milder. Companies
             went for Route March in their
             new equipment. Many of the belts
             too small. Applied for larger
             issue. The Transport arrived
             under Lieut. Moreing by road
             from Abbeville in the course of
             the afternoon.

1915.

January.   Appendix.

21st.   Execrable weather: poured
                night and day without ceasing.
                All parades had to be
                cancelled. Two Companies
                marched to the Fish Market,
                and to the Gas Works, and
                washed in pails of warm water
                supplied by the Municipality.

22nd.   Beautiful day - cold, sunny
                and bright. The remainder of
                the Battalion completed their
                washing in the Fish Market
                and the Gas Works. In the
                afternoon Route Marches in
                full marching order to accustom
                men to packs. Received
                information that we are to be in
                the 28th Division under General
                Bulfin. Destination at present
                unknown. Still no news as to
                date of leaving. 2nd.Lt.
                Garrard and Abbott joined for
                duty. Promoted from the ranks
                from the 4th Battalion, The
                London Regt. 2nd Lt. Garrard
                attached to No.2 Coy, and 2nd.
                Lt. Abbott attached to No.3
                Coy.
                Interesting report in "Daily
                Mail" of this date stating
                that enemy's airman flew over
                town and hovered over Goods
                Yard long enough to drop
                two bombs. This referred to
                the visit of the English Airman
                who breakfasted with us on the
                19th inst.

23rd.   Beautiful day - cold, frost and
                sunny. A further consignment
                of stores arrived, but still not
                sufficient large belts to fit all
                men with web equipment. It has
                been decided to equip the
                Officers with Web equipment,
                but there is not sufficient
                large belts to fit them all out.

1/3rd Battalion, The London Regiment.

DIARY FROM DATE OF JOINING THE INDIAN ARMY CORPS, FEBRUARY 10th 15.

Feb. 10th.   Arrived at Ham-en-Artois from Witte at 1.0pm and attached to Ferozepore Brigade, Lahore Division.

11th.   Inspected by Lieut-Gen. Willcocks, G.O.C. Indian Corps.

12th.   Witnessed night attack by 2/8th Gurkhas.

16th.   Left Ham for St. Venant where we were billetted one night.

17th.   Left St. Venant for Vieille Chapelle, where battalion was attached to the Garhwal Brigade, Meerut Division.

21st.   "B" & "D" Coys. went into trenches at Rue de l'Epinette.

25th.   "A" & "C" Coys. relieved "B" & "D" Coys. in the trenches.

28th.   The battalion left trenches for Les Lobes, arriving there about 6.0pm, and was billetted. Our casualties from 21st to 28th amounted to 14.

Mar. 1st. to 8th.   Most of time spent on route marching whilst at Les Lobes.

8th.   Battalion left Les Lobes for La Couture at 8.0pm.

9th.   Battalion left at midnight for brestworks behind Port Arthur.

10th.   Bombardment of enemy's trenches at 7.30am. Trenches taken 9.0am. Charge by "C" & "D" Coys. Total casualties for battalion - 8 officers and 160 other ranks.

13th.   Left trenches at 8.0pm and marched to Les Lobes, where we were billetted.

16th.   Battalion inspected by Lieut-Gen. Anderson, G.O.C. Meerut Division.

17th.   Battalion inspected by Lieut-Gen. Willcocks, G.O.C. Indian Corps.

24th.   Battalion left Les Lobes for Vieille Chapelle arriving there at noon, and billetted.

29th.   Left Vieille Chapelle for Calonne, where battalion was billetted until April 9th. Most of the time here was spent on route marching, company drill and arms drill.
Battalion attended an open air service held by the Bishop of London on Good Friday afternoon.

April 10th.   Battalion left Calonne for Paradis at 9.30am.

12th.   Left Paradis for La Couture, reaching new billets at noon. Remained here until the 18th, during which time, a few cases of measles occurred in the battalion.

19th.   Battalion left La Couture at 7.0pm for trenches. Hdqrs. established at "96 Piccadilly=" on the Rue du Bois, the battalion occupying the Crescent and Orchard trenches. Fairly quiet all the time.

28th.   Battalion came out of the trenches and marched to La Couture.

P T O

continued.   -2-   DIARY

April 29th.   Battalion marched from La Couture to Croix Barbee at
                7.0pm where it was billetted until May 8th.

May 1st.   Heavy German bombardment of Rue Du Bois at 5.0am.
                We received orders to "Stand to" but "Broke away" at 7.0am

    9th.   Battalion moved into trenches just outside Croix Barbee
                at 2.0am. Heavy bombardment of enemy's trenches at 5.0am.
                We were ordered to advance to A.1 redoubt at 11.0am and
                thence to Crescent and Orchard trenches. Whilst passing
                through the brestworks on the Rue du Bois, and in the
                communication trenches, we were subjected to a very heavy
                shell fire and suffered about 30 casualties. We occupied
                these trenches until Sunday, May 16th.

    16th.   Took part in an assault on enemy's trenches by 2nd
                Leicesters and Garhwal Rifles. Attack failed.
                Battalion left the trenches at 7.0pm for Croix Barbee.

    17th.   Battalion ordered to move into A.1 redoubt at 12.0noon
                and was temporarily attached to the Barielly Brigade.
                Weather wet and ground consequently very muddy. Remained
                in A.1 until May 19th.

    19th.   Battalion moved into the Crescent and Orchard trenches
                from A.1 at 7.0pm. Hdqrs. established on Rue du Bois.
                Battalion remained in the trenches until May 24th, and during
                this time, we experienced some periods of heavy shelling
                by the enemy. Weather generally fine.

    24th.   Battalion, with the exception of "A" Coy. which remained
                in the Orchard trench, moved back to Croix Barbee at 8.0pm,
                and were accommodated in the trenches outside Croix Barbee.

    27th.   "B"Coy. relieved "A"Coy. in the Orchard trench.
                Battalion generally engaged on cleaning up after spell in
                trenches.

    30th.   "B"Coy. relieved in the trenches by Manchester Regt.

    31st.   Orders received to move from CROIX BARBEE to PARADIS
                via VIEILLE CHAPELLE AND FOSSE. battalion parading at
                2.30pm. Settled in billets at PARADIS about 5.0pm.

                                                    Capt & Adjt.
                                            1/3rd Bn. The London Regt.

B.E.Force. France.
    May 27th 15.

It is understood that the normal report will not contain at any one time information on all the above points. Reports should be as concise as possible, only embodying such information as is clearly of importance.

Reports may be sent in by messenger or by telephone (preferably the former) and MUST be in by the time stated, as Battalion reports, based on company reports, have to be rendered to the Brigade one hour after the above times.

Apl. 18th 15.

George Hawes
Capt & Adjt.
1/3rd Bn. The London Regt.

To O.C. Coye.

Operation Orders

The following reports will be rendered by you daily to Battalion Headquarters whilst in the trenches:—

1. 6 a.m. — Report on situation and any occurrences of the night. "No change" if nothing has occurred.

2. 8 a.m. — Casualty Report.

3. 4 p.m. — Report on situation. "No change" if nothing has occurred.

4. 4.30 p.m. — Tactical Progress Report for previous 24 hours.
    Headings.
    1. (a) Action by our own troops
       (b)   "   " enemy   " including sniping, shelling, flares etc.

    2. Information, including
       (a) Alteration of enemy's obstacles
       (b) State of ground (including natural obstacles and change in height of water level)
       (c) Hostile aircraft seen
       (d) Hostile M. guns located
       (e) Hostile Batteries   "
       (f) Identification of enemy's troops
       (g) Damage done by our fire
       ~~(h) description of ground between us & enemy~~
       (h) Action of patrols sent out
       (i) Any other information
    3. Work done.

5. At any time — Any abnormal situation or activity by the enemy, such as hostile shelling.

SPECIAL OPERATION ORDERS BY
Lieut-Col. A. Anthony Howell,
Cmdg 1/3rd Battalion, The London Regiment.

April 18th 15.

(1) DRESS.

Dress for parade tomorrow will be, Marching Order, great coats. The Waterproof sheet will be carried in the valise. Care is to be taken that valises are not overpacked.

(2) TRANSPORT.

The 1st Line Transport will move into the billets now occupied by the 1st Line transport of the 2/8th Gurkhas at 8.0pm tomorrow.

(3) BLANKETS.

All blankets will be +O. valises packed on blanket waggons which ~~stacked at the Q.M. Stores~~ by 2.0pm tomorrow. *will be at Coy Head quarters*

(4) RATIONS.

One days rations will be carried on parade tomorrow. On subsequent days, O.C.Coys. will send ration parties to "WINDY CORNER" by 10.0pm daily to fetch rations.

(5) WATER.

Men will parade with filled water bottles. On subsequent days O.C.Coys. will send men carrying waterbottles by 10.0pm daily to refill at "WINDY CORNER."

(6) CHARCOAL.

Each Coy. will arrange to carry a proportion of charcoal into the trenches tomorrow night.

(7) TOOLS.

Tools on charge of the battalion will be handed over to the 2/8th Gurkhas by the Quartermaster tomorrow night, and a receipt taken. The battalion will take over the tools now on charge of the 2/8th Gurkhas now in the trenches.

Geo Hawes
Capt & Adjt.
1/3rd.Bn. The London Regiment.

1/3rd Battalion, The London Regt.   SECRET.

OPERATION ORDERS NO. 5. BY LIEUT-COL. A. ANTHONY HOWELL CMDG.

April 11th 18.

In the event of the battalion being required to move, the word "MEET" will be sent round to all concerned.

On the word "MEET" being passed round, the battalion will parade on the Alarm Post. (The field behind the white house opposite the entrance to "B"Coy. billet)

(a) If the battalion is "INLYING, it must be ready to move off 15 minutes after receipt of the word "MEET."

(b) At other times it must be ready to move within one hour.

CONCENTRATION.

The battalion and 1st Line Transport, less water carts and Cooks carts, will move off with the head of the column at the cross roads opposite battalion Hdqrs. facing EAST, and march on VIEILLE CHAPELLE, falling in behind the Leicester Regt. facing NORTH at Cross roads R.26.d.

Lieut. Edwards will report at Brigade Hdqrs. at Road Junction R.26.d. when the battalion arrives at its appointed place.

BOUNDS.

Men are on no account to leave the vicinity of their billets. Great care should be taken in placing kits in billets, so that each man is able to get at his kit as quickly as possible, and without confusion.

All ranks must sleep in boots and puttees during the time the battalion is "INLYING."

(Sgd) F.D.Samuel.Major.
1/3rd Bn. The London Regt.   a/Adjt.

OPERATION ORDERS BY
LIEUT-COL. A. ANTHONY HOWELL CMDG.
1/3rd Battalion, The London Regiment.

Copy No. 6.

Reference Maps:-
1/40000 BETHUNE SHEET.
Special Sketch Map.

April 18th 15.

(1) Lieut-Col. A. Anthony Howell cmdg.
    1/3rd Bn. The London Regt.
    2 Coys. 2nd Leicesters.
    1 Coy. Garhwal Rifles.

Will relieve the troops in the trenches at 8.0pm on the night of 19/20th April 1915.

(2) PARADE.
The troops will parade at 7 P.M. on the 19th inst. with head of column facing S.W. at cross roads X.5.a.9.3., in the following order of march:-

    1 Coy. Leicestershire Regt.
    1/3rd Bn. The London Regt. in the following order:-
        "D" Coy.
        B "C" "
        C "B" "
        "A" "
    1 Coy. Leicestershire Regt.
    1 "   Garhwal Rifles.

(3) DISTRIBUTION.
Companies will take over trenches as indicated on sketch map. One Coy. Leicestershire Regt. will take over the left section of Work A.1 and one Coy. Garhwal Rifles will take over the right section of Work A.1

(4) RATIONS.
Battalions will make their own arrangements for rationing their own companies, and for providing them with water.

(5) AMMUNITION, ETC.
150 rounds of ammunition per man will be carried. O.C. Coys. will take over all spare ammunition, rifle grenades, Very pistols and any spare tools etc. from the Coys. they relieve in the trenches, giving a written receipt for same and keeping a duplicate copy.

(6) MEDICAL ARRANGEMENTS.
The First Aid Post will be established at "WINDY CORNER".

(7) BOMB PARTIES.
Bomb parties will parade with their Coys.

(8) MACHINE GUNS.
Arrangements for Machine Guns will be under the direction of the Brigade Machine Gun Officer.

(9) COMMUNICATION.
All arrangements for communication will be under the direction of Lieut. C.J. Page, 1/3rd London Regiment.

(10) ORDERLIES.
After taking over the trenches, O.C. Coys. will detail one orderly per Coy. to report to Bn. Hdqrs., where he will remain. These orderlies must know the way from their respective Coy. Hdqrs. to Battalion Hdqrs.

(11) HEADQUARTERS.
Battalion Hdqrs. will be as indicated on sketch map.

OPERATION ORDERS
by
Lieut-Col. A. Anthony Howell.
Cmdg. 1/3rd Battalion, The London Regiment.

Reference map:-   April 23rd 15.
BETHUNE SHEET.1/40000.

(1)   The 1/3rd London Regt. less "B"Coy. and half battalion of 2nd Leicestershire Regt., will be relieved on the night 24/25 April. Times will be notified later.
      "B"Coy. 1/3rd London Regt. and one company Garhwal Rifles in A.1 will be formed up in the RUE DES BERCEAUX, clear of the entrance to the redoubt at 8.30pm on April 23rd 15. When the relieving troops have occupied the redoubt, these companies will march via CROIX BARBEE, and FOSSE to CALONNE.

(2)   The 1/3rd London Regt. less "B"Coy. and half battalion 2nd Leicestershire Regt will, after relief on the 24/25 April, march by companies to A.1, and march thence under Lieut-Col. A. Anthony Howell at 1.0am via RUE DES BERCEAUX, CROIX BARBEE and M.20.c. to VIEILLE CHAPELLE. They will march thence passing ZELOBES at 12.0noon April 25th to CALONNE.

(3) RATIONS.
    Battalions will arrange for rationing their own companies.

(4) AMMUNITION ETC.
    150 rounds of ammunition will be carried. All other ammunition in trenches and in work A.1, rifle grenades and very pistol ammunition in trenches, but no other stores will be handed over to relieving units.

(5) TOOLS.
    All tools will be brought out of the trenches and will be loaded on the 1st Line transport at "WINDY CORNER".

(6) BOMB PARTIES.
    Bomb parties will parade with their companies.

(7) DRESS FOR PARADE.
    Dress for parade will be Marching Order, great coats in the valise. Water bottles to be filled.

(8) TRANSPORT
    The tool wagons of the 1st Line transport of the 2nd Leicester Regt. and the 1/3rd London Regt., will be at "WINDY CORNER" at 11.0pm 24th inst.
    The remainder of the Transport of 1/3rd London Regt. will meet the battalion at the halting place at VIEILLE CHAPELLE at 3.0am, 25th inst.

(9) MEDICAL ARRANGEMENTS.
    The Medical cart and personnel of the 1/3rd London Regt. will meet the battalion at "WINDY CORNER" on the 25th inst. at 1.0am and proceed thenceforth with the battalion.

(10) MACHINE GUNS AND SIGNALLERS.
    Machine Guns and signallers will be relieved on the night of 23/24th April under arrangements to be made by the Officer i/c.

                                                      Capt & Adjt.
                                            1/3rd Bn. The London Regt.

Copies to -
    O.C. 2nd Leicestershire Regt.   1.
    O.C.s Coys. 1/3rd London Regt.   4.
    Quartermaster 1/3rd London Rgt.   1.
    Medical Officer   "   1.

OPERATION ORDERS
by
Lieut-Col. A.Anthony Howell
Cmdg. 1/3rd Battalion, The London Regt.

REFERENCE MAP:-
BETHUNE 1/40000.   April 27th 15.

1. RELIEFS.

The 1/3rd Londons and the company of the Leicestershire Regt. now in the trenches, will be relieved on the night 28/29th April about 9.0pm.

On relief by the 6th Jats and half 9th Gurkhas, they will march via ST VAAST, road junction and CROIX BARBEE to billets in VIEILLE CHAPELLE.

On the 28th inst. the 1/3rd Londons will pass road junction R.29.d. at 8.15pm and march to RUE DES PUITS, going into Brigade Reserve in billets vacated by two companies 2nd Leicesters.

Further orders will be issued to "D"Coy. Leicestershire Rgt. as regards rejoining their battalion.

The troops in A.1 will be drawn up on the road west and clear of the entrance to redoubt at 9.30pm tonight, 27/28 inst. On relief by the 1st company 9th Gurkhas which arrives, the company of Garhwalis will march to PONT LOGY where they will be met by a guide of the 4th Seaforths, who will lead them to their position in "C" Sub section, where this company will relieve a company of the 4th Seaforths.

The company of the Leicesters from A.1 will march, on arrival of the 2nd company of 9th Gurkhas, to rejoin their battalion in billets.

2. DETAIL

As companies are relieved they will march out, carrying all tools on charge of companies, and proceed independently to WINDY CORNER, where all tools will be stacked in tool wagons, and from thence independently to VIEILLE CHAPELLE, following above route.

3. AMMUNITION ETC.

150 rounds of ammunition will be carried per man.
Very pistols and very pistol ammunition will be taken out.
All other stores in trenches will be handed over to relieving companies and receipts taken.

4. BOMB PARTIES.

Bomb parties will parade with their companies.

5. DRESS.

Marching Order. great coats in the valise, will be worn.

6. TRANSPORT

Tool wagons and cooks wagon of the 1st Line Transport of the 1/3rd Bn. The London Regt. will be at WINDY CORNER at 9.0pm on the 28th inst

7. MEDICAL ARRANGEMENTS.

The medical cart and personnel of the 1/3rd London Regt. will remain at WINDY CORNER until the last company has passed, and then proceed to VIEILLE CHAPELLE by the same route.

8. MACHINE GUNS AND SIGNALLERS.

Machine Guns and Signallers will be relieved under arrangements to be made by the Officers in charge

Capt & Adjt
1/3rd Bn. The London Regt.

Copies to :-
O.C. 2nd Leicesters.
O.C.Coys. 1/3rd Londons.
Q.Master   "
Medical Offr.   "
O.C. A.1 redoubt.
O.C. "D"Coy. Leicesters

OPERATION ORDERS BY
LIEUT-COL. A. ANTHONY ROWELL. CMDG 1/3rd LONDON REGT.

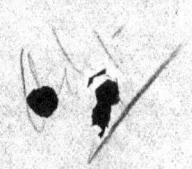

....

May 1st 15.

In the event of the battalion being required to move up into the firing line from Reserve billets, the following procedure will be adopted :-

1. PARADE

The battalion will fall in by companies outside the company billets at once, ready to move off in a quarter of an hour after receiving orders for parade.

2. DRESS.

Dress - Marching order, great coats in the valises.

3. WATER BOTTLES ETC.

Waterbottles must be kept filled. The Emergency ration in the haversack and field dressing complete.

4. AMMUNITION.

If time, the 150 rounds of ammunition carried will be made up to 300 per man.

5. The ammunition animals and one S.A.A.Cart will come up to battalion Hdqrs. at once from the 1st Line Transport.

6. TRANSPORT.

The 1st Line Transport will await orders from Brigade. Meantime they will saddle up and harness in horses.

7. Medical Arrangements.

The M.O. and personnel less Medical cart, will parade with battalion and go forward to fix an Aid Post.

8. COMMUNICATION.

The Signallers will disconnect all telephones on the order to do so being given by the Commanding Officer, and will march behind the first company, remaining always with Battalion Hdqrs. until distributed by the officer i/c Signallers.

9. BOMB PARTIES AND STRETCHER BEARERS.

Bomb parties and Stretcher bearers will parade with their Coys.

10. CYCLE ORDERLIES.

One cyclist will accompany the C.O. The remainder will join the 1st Line Transport.

11. DETAILS.

All details left in billets will join the 1st Line Transport at the earliest opportunity and will be under the Sergt Major for orders.

12. BLANKETS, COOKERS ETC.

The Cooks and Coy. Q.M.Sergts. will remain in billets and pack up blankets etc. The cookers will join the 1st Line Transport.

Capt & Adjt.
1/3rd Bn. The London Regt.

OPERATION ORDERS BY
LIEUT-COL. A. ANTHONY HOWELL. CMDG 1/3rd LONDON REGT.

....

May 1st 15.

In the event of the battalion being required to move up into the firing line from Reserve billets, the following procedure will be adopted:-

1. PARADE

The battalion will fall in by companies outside the company billets at once, ready to move off in a quarter of an hour after receiving orders for parade.

2. DRESS.

Dress - Marching order, great coats in the valises.

3. WATER BOTTLES ETC.

Waterbottles must be kept filled. The Emergency ration in the haversack and field dressing complete.

4. AMMUNITION.

If time, the 150 rounds of ammunition carried will be made up to 300 per man.

5. The ammunition animals and one S.A.A.Cart will come up to battalion Hdqrs. at once from the 1st Line Transport.

6. TRANSPORT.

The 1st Line Transport will await orders from Brigade. Meantime they will saddle up and harness in horses.

7. Medical Arrangements.

The M.O. and personnel less Medical cart, will parade with battalion and go forward to fix an Aid Post.

8. COMMUNICATION.

The Signallers will disconnect all telephones on the order to do so being given by the Commanding Officer, and will march behind the first company, remaining always with Battalion Hdqrs. until distributed by the Officer i/c Signallers.

9. BOMB PARTIES AND STRETCHER BEARERS.

Bomb parties and Stretcher bearers will parade with their Coys.

10. CYCLE ORDERLIES.

One cyclist will accompany the C.O. The remainder will join the 1st Line Transport.

11. DETAILS.

All details left in billets will join the 1st Line Transport at the earliest opportunity and will be under the Sergt Major for orders.

12. BLANKETS, COOKERS ETC.

The Cooks and Coy. Q.M.Sergts. will remain in billets and pack up blankets etc. The Cookers will join the 1st Line Transport.

Capt & Adjt.
1/3rd Bn. The London Regt.

Army Form W. 3091.

Cover for Documents.

Nature of Enclosures.

3 London
June 1915

Notes, or Letters written

(4497) W. 4884/M680 250,000 8/16 McA. & W., Ltd. (Est. 279) Forms/W 3091/3.   Army Form W. 3091.

Cover for Documents.

Nature of Enclosures.

Notes, or Letters written.

Volume No.

BRITISH SALONIKA FORCE

WAR DIARY.   26th Division.

Vol No. Unit Headquarters, General Staff

18. From 1st To 30th April, 1917.

18. Headquarters; Administrative. From 1st to 30th Apl. 1917.

Serial No. 197.

121/6/28

WAR DIARY OF

1/3rd Battalion The London Regiment.

From 1st June 1915 To 30th June 1915.

Army Form C. 2118.

WAR DIARY
or
INTELLIGENCE SUMMARY.
(Erase heading not required.)

Instructions regarding War Diaries and Intelligence Summaries are contained in F. S. Regs., Part II. and the Staff Manual respectively. Title pages will be prepared in manuscript.

Place	Date	Hour	Summary of Events and Information	Remarks and references to Appendices
PARADIS	June 1st	7.0pm	Battalion marched to VIEILLE CHAPELLE AND WAS BILLETED.	
VIEILLE CHAPELLE	2nd and 5th.		Issue of new clothing and kit where necessary and arrangements made for baths at the brewery.	
"	6th.	8.15am.	Battalion Church Parade. Holy Communion at 10.15am.	
"	7th.	9.0am.	Inspection of battalion by the Commanding Officer.	
		5.0pm.	Battalion march off by companies to bivouacs south of LA COUTURE. Battalion headquarters established at farm X.6.a.8.7. Weather very warm. In Brigade reserve.	
RICHEBOURG ST.VAAST.	8th.	8.0pm.	The whole battalion under Capt. A.J.Aglus paraded for working party to dig a communication trench.	
"	9th.	3.0am.	Battalion returned to bivouacs. One casualty, wounded.	
		8.30pm.	Battalion paraded for working party to complete work commenced last night.	
"	10th.	3.0am.	Battalion returned to bivouacs. No casualties.	
"	11th.	1.0pm.	24 N.C.O.s and men rejoined unit from hospital.	
		8.15pm.	Battalion paraded for working party.	
"	12th.	2.30am.	Battalion returned to bivouacs. No casualties.	
"	13th.	8.15pm.	Working party of 60 men and proportion of N.C.O.s paraded under 2nd Lt. E.A.Lloyd and 2nd Lt. XXXXXXXX S.E Brady.	
"	14th.	2.0am.	Working party returned to bivouacs. No casualties.	

Army Form C. 2118.

WAR DIARY
or
INTELLIGENCE SUMMARY
(Erase heading not required.)

Instructions regarding War Diaries and Intelligence Summaries are contained in F.S. Regs., Part II. and the Staff Manual respectively. Title pages will be prepared in manuscript.

Place	Date	Hour	Summary of Events and Information	Remarks and references to Appendices
	JUNE			
RICHEBOURG ST. VAAST.	14th.	6.0pm.	Battalion paraded for working party under Capt. Agius.	
"	15th.	2.0am.	Working party returned to bivouacs. No casualties.	
"	16th.	3.0am.	Driver Rankin, A.S.C. killed in La Couture by shell and one horse killed, one wounded.	
"	17th.	9.0am.	G.O.'s inspection of bivouacs. CROIX BARBEE shelled by enemy. Lieut. T. Reeves took over command of "B" Cy from 2nd Lt. Lloyd.	
"	18th.	8.30pm.	Battalion marched off by companies at 5 minutes interval to take over trenches vacated by 2nd Leicesters. Battalion Headquarters established in ALBERT ROAD. Two Companies of the 2/8th Gurkhas attached to our nit. Distribution of troops as follows :- "A" "C" & "D" Coys. in front line. "B" Coy. and No. 4 Coy. 2/8th Gurkhas in Support. No. 1 Coy. 2/8th Gurkhas in local reserve.	
Trenches.	19th	8.50pm	"C" "B" & "D" Coys. working on new trench. Casualties, one killed and one wounded.	
"	20th.		40000 rounds loose ammunition collected from trenches, sorted and returned to Brigade Hqrs. Work die same as for last night.	

Army Form C. 2118.

WAR DIARY
or
INTELLIGENCE SUMMARY.
(Erase heading not required.)

Instructions regarding War Diaries and Intelligence Summaries are contained in F.S. Regs., Part II. and the Staff Manual respectively. Title pages will be prepared in manuscript.

Place	Date	Hour	Summary of Events and Information	Remarks and references to Appendices
Trenches Albert Rd.	June 21st		Redistribution of troops as follows :- Front Line "C" & "D" Coys. Supports "A" & "B" Coys. Local reserve, Two companies 2/8th Gurkhas.	
"		10.0pm.	Captain C.E.Rochford wounded whilst in charge of working party in front line.	
"	22nd.	11.0am.	F.G.C.M. at Garhwal Bde Hdqrs. for the trial of Pte Stone.P.G.	
"	23rd	4.0pm.	4 killed and one wounded by H.E.shell. All "B"Coy.	
"		10.0pm.	"D"Coy. relieved by a company of Garhwal Rifles, moved to front line trenches between the right of the Orchard and HAZARA communication trenches. "C"Coy. relieved by 2nd Gurkhas, moved to grid iron trenches opposite "96 Piccadilly". "A" & "B" Coys. moved to grid iron trenches opposite "96 Piccadilly" and from thence "A" Coy. took over the orchard front trench and "B"Coy. the front trench of the orchard.	
"	25th.	11.0am.	Thunderstorm, heavy rain, causing a great deal of mud to form in the trenches.	
"		3.0pm.	"A" "B" & "D" Coys. working on trenches. 3000 sand bags received.	
"	26th.	9.0pm.	4000 sandbags received. "A" B" & "D" Coys. working on trenches.	
"	27th.	8.30am.	Heavily shelled by enemy for about 30 minutes, by H.E. shells. Casualties,one killed,2 wounded.	

T2134. Wt. W708—776. 500000. 4/15. Sir J. C. & S.

Army Form C. 2118.

WAR DIARY
or
INTELLIGENCE SUMMARY.
(Erase heading not required.)

Instructions regarding War Diaries and Intelligence Summaries are contained in F. S. Regs., Part II. and the Staff Manual respectively. Title pages will be prepared in manuscript.

Place	Date	Hour	Summary of Events and Information	Remarks and references to Appendices
	June			
Trenches	28th	10.0pm.	Battalion relieved by Bareilly Bde. and marched to billets in LES LOBES. Settled in billets by about 1.30am. 29th. Battalion headquarters established at K.2.a.2.2.	
Les Lobes.	29th.		Lieut.R.D.Sutcliffe, 2nd Lt. T.Reeves and 2nd Lt. E.N.Wilcox proceeded to United Kingdom on seven days leave.	
"	30th.	9.0am.	Experiment with Chlorine gas carried out at Les 8 MAISONS. All officers (except 2nd Lt. Minshull) and 50 N.C.O.s attended. Smoke helmets proved very effective.	

June 30th 15.

[signature]
Capt & Adjt.
1/3rd London Regiment.

OPERATIONS ORDERS BY
LIEUT.COL. A. ANTHONY HOWELL CMDG. 1/3RD BN. THE LONDON REGT.

....

June 14th, 1915.

In the event of the Battalion being required to move up into the Firing Line from Reserve Bivouacs, the following procedure will be adopted :-

1. PARADE.
On the word "MEET" being sent round, Coys. will fall in as a Battalion within 20 minutes, behind "A" Coy. Trenches on the right of the Line.

2. DRESS.
Dress - Marching Order, great coats in the valises.

3. WATER BOTTLES. ETC.
Waterbottles must be kept filled. The Emergency Ration in the haversack and field dressing complete.

4. AMMUNITION.
200 rounds of ammunition per man will be carried.

5. TRANSPORT.
The 1st Line Transport will await orders from Brigade. Meantime they will saddle up and harness in horses.

6. MEDICAL ARRANGEMENTS.
The Medical Officer and personnel, less the Medical Cart, will parade with the Battalion, and go forward to fix an Aid Post. The Medical Cart will join the Battalion Cookers.

7. BOMB PARTIES AND STRETCHER BEARERS.
Bomb parties and Stretcher Bearers will parade with their Coys.

8. SIGNALLERS.
The Battalion Signallers will be under the orders of the Officer in charge.

9. CYCLE ORDERLIES.
One Cyclist will accompany the C.O.

10. DETAILS.
All Headquarter Staff, and any other Details not hitherto mentioned, will join the Battalion Cookers at POPLAR FARM, and await orders. They will be under the Serjeant Major.

11. BLANKETS COOKERS ETC.
The Cooks and Coy. Q.M. Sergts. will remain in Bivouacs and pack up blankets etc, and await further orders.

Captain & Adjutant,
1/3rd Bn. The London Regiment.

Copies to -
O.C. Coys.
Q. Master.
Medical Officer.
Signalling Officer.

Copy
To Colonel
& to be Answered

June 14th 15.

OPERATION ORDERS BY LIEUT-COL. A. ANTHONY HOWELL CMDG.

(1) The Battalion,(less 60 men of "B"Coy. under 2nd Lt. Lloyd and 2nd Lt. Ainsworth,)will parade at 8.15pm tonight, behind "A"Coy. trenches on the right of our line, and march under Captain Agius to Chocolate Menier Corner (to be there punctually at 9.0pm), for work on communication trenches in "C" sub-section. An officer of the 2/3rd Gurkhas will meet and direct this party to the work. All picks and shovels on charge of the battalion will be taken by this party. Dress as usual.

(2) 60 men of "B" Coy. under 2nd Lt. Lloyd and 2nd Lt. Ainsworth, will parade behind their company lines at 8.0pm, and march to Brigade Headquarters to draw 60 spades. From there they will march to the 2nd Leicesters Headquarters in ALBERT ROAD.
Dress as usual.

Capt & Adjt.
1/3rd London Regiment.

OPERATION ORDERS BY
LIEUT-COL. A. ANTHONY HOWELL,
CMDG. 1/3rd Battalion, The London Regiment.

Copy No. 12.

Reference Maps:-
1/40000 BETHUNE SHEET.
Special sketch map.

June 18TH 1915.

(1) Lieut-Col. A. Anthony Howell Cmdg.
    1/3rd London Regiment.
    2 Coys. 2/8th Gurkhas.

Will relieve the troops in
the trenches after 9.0pm
in the night of June 18TH 1915.

(2) PARADE.
The troops will parade at 6.30pm as follows on the 18TH inst. with the head of column facing S.E. on the road running through X.6.a. where the letter "a" touches the road, in the following order of march :-

1/3rd London Regt. (in the following order)
"D" Coy.
"C"
"A"
"B"

One Coy. 2/8th Gurkhas.
One Coy. 2/8th Gurkhas.

Companies will move at 5 minutes interval, starting at 6.30pm under company commanders, and proceed via RICHEBOURG to the Leicesters Headquarters in ALBERT ROAD, where they will report to O.C. 2nd Leicesters.

(3) DISTRIBUTION.
Companies will take over the trenches as indicated on sketch map. One company of the 2/8th Gurkhas will remain in reserve in the trenches near battalion headquarters. Officers commanding Coys. will report to battalion headquarters immediately reliefs are complete.

(4) RATIONS.
Battalions will make their own arrangements for rationing their own companies, and for providing them with water.

(5) TOOLS.
All tools on charge of the 1/3rd London Regt. will be stacked at battalion headquarters by 4.0 . The two companies of the 2/8th Gurkhas will carry a proportion of spades into the trenches with them.

(6) AMMUNITION ETC.
200 rounds of ammunition per man will be carried. O.C.Coys. will take over in the trenches all spare ammunition, Very pistols and ammunition, sprayers and rifle grenades. Immediately after taking over, O.C.Coys. will send into Battalion Headquarters a complete list of stores, shewing numbers and amounts of ammunition etc. taken over.

(7) MEDICAL ARRANGEMENTS.
The First Aid post will be established in the RUE DES BERCEAUX, close to the junction of the RUE DES BERCEAUX and ALBERT ROAD.

(8) BOMB PARTIES.
Bomb parties will parade with their companies.

(9) MACHINE GUNS.
Arrangements for Machine Guns will be under the direction of the Brigade Machine Gun Officer.

(10) COMMUNICATION.
All arrangements for communication will be under the direction of Captain C.J.Page, 1/3rd London Regt.

(11) ORDERLIES.
After taking over the trenches, O.C.Coys. will detail one orderly per company to report to battalion headquarters, where he will remain. These orderlies must know the way from their

P T O

Continued.   Operation Orders No.12.

(their)
respective company headquarters to battalion headquarters, and vice versa.

(12) BATTALION HEADQUARTERS.

Battalion Headquarters will be in ALBERT ROAD.

                                              Capt & Adjt
                                              1/3rd London Regiment.

SPECIAL OPERATION ORDERS BY
Lieut. Col. A. Anthony Howell, Cmdg;
1/3rd Bn. The London Regt.

June 18th, 1915.

(1) DRESS.

Dress for parade tonight will be Marching Order, great coats in the Valise. The Waterproof sheet will be carried on top of the Valise.

(2) TRANSPORT.

The First Line Transport will remain in their present Bivouacs.

(3) BLANKETS.

All Blankets and Officers' Valises, will be packed on the Blanket Waggons which will arrive in the Lines at 6.0pm. this afternoon.

(4) RATIONS.

One day's Rations, which will be issued in the Lines at 5.0pm. this afternoon, will be carried.
From tomorrow, inclusive, Rations will be drawn from Railhead at the Headquarters of the 2/3rd Gurkhas in the Rue du Bois according to verbal instructions already issued.

(5) WATER.

Men will parade with filled Water-bottles.
From tomorrow, inclusive, O.C.Coys. will send parties to draw water after 9.0pm. daily to the First Aid Post.

(6) TOOLS.

All Tools on charge of the Battalion will be stacked at Battalion Headquarters by 4.0pm. this afternoon.

[signature]

Captain & Adjutant,
1/3rd Bn. The London Regiment.

(7) WATER CARTS.

Water Carts will be filled, and will proceed to the First Aid Post parading with the first Company at 8.30pm. tonight.

1/3rd Battalion, The London Regiment.

COPY NO.13.   June 21st 1915.

OPERATION ORDER BY LIEUT-COL. A. ANTHONY HOWELL CMDG.

(1) **RELIEFS.**

The following changes in the distribution of troops in "D" Sub-section will take place tonight :-

"C" Coy. 3rd Londons will take over the whole of the new trench as detailed.

"B" Coy. will move up from the old British trench and take over that part of the Front trench recently held by "C" Coy. moving up at 8.0pm.

No.1 Coy. 2/8th Gurkhas will take over that part of the old British trench hitherto held by "B" Coy. 3rd Londons, moving up at 8.0pm.

(2) **WORKING PARTIES.**

"A" Coy. 3rd Londons. will place all available men under O.C. "C" Coy. for work on new trench.

"B" Coy. 3rd Londons.   Work as for last night.

"C" Coy. 3rd Londons.   -do-

"D" Coy. 3rd Londons.   -do-

No.1 Coy. 2/8th G.R.   Work as for last night. O.C. this company will send a party to battalion headquarters at 9.0pm to draw 3000 sandbags for use of "C" Coy. 3rd Londons, and 1000 sandbags for his own use.

No.4 Coy. 2/8th G.R.   Work as detailed. O.C. this company will send 20 men to draw 1000 sand bags from Battalion headquarters for his own use at 9.0pm.

                                    Capt & Adjt.
                                    1/3rd London Regiment.

COPY NO.14.   3rd Battalion, The London Regt.
                               ───────────────────────────────

                                                 June 23rd 15.
         OPERATION ORDERS BY LIEUT-COL. A. ANTHONY HOWELL CMDG.
         ───────────────────────

(1) RELIEFS.

         The following reliefs will take place tonight at 9.0pm:-
         "A" Coy. to trenches now occupied by "B" Coy.
         "B" "   "   "   "   "   "C" Coy. Except 3 traverses.
         "C" "   "   "   "   "   "B" Coy. Plus 3 traverses
                                                      of front trench.
         "D" "   "   "   "   "   "A" Coy.

(2) WORK.

         "A" Coy. complete earthing of new front trench, continuing
on left of line. They will also find a covering party of 14
men under an N.C.O. to hold ridge in front.
         "B" Coy. As for last night.
         "C" Coy. Make parados and lateral communication trench
behind new front trench working from left end of same and
completing work as preceding.
         "D" Coy. As for last night.

                                                Capt & Adjt.
                                                1/3rd London Regiment.

Orders No. 16.   3rd Battalion, The London Regiment.

June 23rd 15.

OPERATION ORDERS BY LIEUT-COL A. ANTHONY HOWELL CMDG.

The following reliefs will take place tonight :-

"D" Coy.   will be relieved by a company of the 1/39th Garhwals about 7.0pm, and will move after relief to the Reserve trenches on the ALBERT ROAD. They will stand by there until further orders, and will subsequently move to the front line trenches between the right of the Orchard and HAZARA communication trench.

"C" Coy.   will be relieved about 11.0pm by the 2nd Gurkhas and on relief will march to grid iron trenches opposite of PICCADILLY.

"A" & "B" Coys. will move out of their present trenches, when they have received information from O.C. 1/39th Garhwals that the 2nd Gurkhas have arrived in their trenches i.e. probably about 10.0pm, and will move to the grid iron trenches opposite of PICCADILLY. From there "A" Coy. will move up and take over the Orchard front trench, and "B" Coy. will take over the front trench of the orchard.

The route to be followed by all companies in moving West from that point of the RUE DU BOIS intersected by ~~ALBERT ROAD~~ one tree, will not be along the RUE DU BOIS but along the line of trenches North of and parallel to it, until they eventually reach the grid iron trenches opposite of PICCADILLY, where O.C. Coys. will report to the Adjutant.

Companies will bring out with them 35 spades, periscopes, Very pistols and Very pistol ammunition, flares, telescopic rifles and Vermoral sprayer if one is on charge.

(Sgd) G.Hawes. Capt & Adjt.
1/3rd London Regiment.

3 London

July 1915

(6392) Wt. W6192/P875 1,500,000 4/18 McA & W Ltd (E 2815) Forms W3091/4.   Army Form W.3091.

Cover for Documents.

Nature of Enclosures.

Notes, or Letters written.

BRITISH SALONIKA FORCE.

WAR DIARY.

North Persian Force.

Vol. No.	Unit	Period From	To
3	Headquarters. 39th Inf. Bde.	1-3-19	31-3-19
3	9th Bn. Royal Warwicks.	—	—
2	7th " Gloucs. Regt.	1-2-19	28-2-19
4	44th Bty. R.F.A.	1-4-19	30-4-19

Serial No. 197. War/Recent

121/6502

WAR DIARY
OF
1/3rd London Regiment.

FROM 1st July 1915 TO 31st July 1915

Army Form C. 2118.

WAR DIARY
or
INTELLIGENCE SUMMARY.
(Erase heading not required.)

Instructions regarding War Diaries and Intelligence Summaries are contained in F. S. Regs., Part II. and the Staff Manual respectively. Title pages will be prepared in manuscript.

Place	Date	Hour	Summary of Events and Information	Remarks and references to Appendices
LES LOBES	1915. July. 1st		For Tactical purposes only, the battalion assumed a two company formation, "A" & "C" forming No.1 Coy. and "B" & "D" No.2 Coy. under the command of Major F.D.Samuel and Capt. A.J.Agius respectively.	
		2.0pm.	2nd Lts. F.C.Davis and C.S.Morley rejoined the battalion from England, off sick leave.	
		"	2nd Lt. S.J.Ainsworth deputed to meet a draft of 4th SEAFORTHS at LESTREM and conduct them to billets in PARADIS, remaining temporarily in command of them.	
	2nd.	"	2nd Lt. S.J.Ainsworth deputed to meet a further draft of 4th SEAFORTHS and conduct them to billets in PARADIS near to those previously mentioned.	
	3rd		Captain G.Hawes, (Adjutant) left for seven days leave in PARIS, 2nd Lt. D.W.L.Jones acting in his place meanwhile Major P.W.Beresford rejoined the battalion from England, having been wounded back in April.	
		8.0pm.	Ordered to provide a working party of 225 tonight, 2nd Lt.F.C.Davis in command, with four other subalterns.	
	4th.	2.0am.	2nd Lt. S.J.Ainsworth rejoined the battalion from PARADIS.	
RICHE-BOURG.		6.0pm.	Battalion paraded for marching to trenches in "D" sub Section, No.1 Coy. taking over front line and supports with No.2 Coy. in local reserve. Headquarters and Aid Post established in RUE DES BERCEAUX AT S.8.b.5.5. BETHUNE SHEET 1/40000.	
	5th.	9.0am.	14 men sent to Convalescent Camp, MERVILLE. Quiet in the trenches.	

Army Form C. 2118.

WAR DIARY
or
INTELLIGENCE SUMMARY.
(Erase heading not required.)

Instructions regarding War Diaries and Intelligence Summaries are contained in F.S. Regs., Part II. and the Staff Manual respectively. Title pages will be prepared in manuscript.

Place	Date	Hour	Summary of Events and Information	Remarks and references to Appendices
PICHE-BOURG.	July 6th	6.0 am.	5 wounded by shrapnel. Three N.C.O.s granted seven days leave to U.K.	
	7th	4.0 pm.	Capt.R.D.Sutcliffe, 2nd Lts. Reeves and E.N.Wilcox rejoined from leave.	
	8th	11.0 am.	Lord Kitchener's inspection of the First Army. Our battalion unable to line the route through LES LOBES. Major F.D.Samuel, Capt.A.M.Agius, Capt.O.J.Page and 2nd Lt. Brady granted seven days leave.	
		6.0 pm.	Received notification of the Adjutant's(Capt.G.Hawes) transfer to the Staff at G.H.Q. and wired him in PARIS to this effect.	
	9th.		Captain R.D.Sutcliffe appointed Adjutant vice Capt. Hawes to G.H.Q.	
	10th.	8.0pm.	Battalion relieved in the trenches by 4th Cavalry, afterwards marching back to billets in LES LOBES.	
LES LOBES.	11th.	5.45 pm.	Church parade. Commanding officer granted 10 days leave, Major P.W.Beresford taking over command of the battalion.	
	12th.	7.0 pm.	Three N.C.O.s granted seven days leave. Battalion paraded to march to billets at LE SART, west of MERVILLE, reaching destination about 10.30pm.	
LE SART	15th.	6.0 pm.	Battalion paraded with the 2nd Leicesters to march to billets at L'Epinette, arriving about 8.30 pm.	
L'Epin-ette.	16th.		Battalion transferred from Garhwal Bde, Meerut Division, to Sirhind Bde, Lahore Division.	

T2134. Wt. W708—776. 500000. 4/15. Sir J.C.&S.

Army Form C. 2118.

WAR DIARY
or
INTELLIGENCE SUMMARY.
(Erase heading not required.)

Instructions regarding War Diaries and Intelligence Summaries are contained in F. S. Regs., Part II. and the Staff Manual respectively. Title pages will be prepared in manuscript.

Place	Date	Hour	Summary of Events and Information	Remarks and references to Appendices
July 1915				
L'Epinette.	17th		Three other ranks granted seven days leave.	
	18th	11.0am.	Church Parade on Alarm Post.	
	19th		Three other ranks granted seven days leave.	
	20th		Companies had baths at PONT RICQUEUL between noon and 4.0pm.	
	21st.		Medical Officer and two other ranks granted seven days leave. Details had baths at PONT RICQUEUL.	
	22nd.		Two new Officers joined unit, 2nd Lt. C.D.Geage and 2nd Lt.E.F.Moseley. Battalion paraded on the ALARM POST at 7.0pm to march to trenches. Lt-Col. A.Anthony Howell in command of Left Centre Sub-Section. 57th Rifles in front line, 3rd London Regt. in "DREADNOUGHT" ERITH", and "LONELY" posts. Headquarters established on the Rue du BACQUEROT at M.17.C.7.3, BETHUNE SHEET, 1/40000. Very rainy night.	
M.17.c.7.3.	23rd.		Generally quiet.	
	24th		Four new Officers joined, 2nd Lts.H.Lloyd, A.H.Bateman, D.Lewis, and A.E.George.	
	25th		Our 1st Line Transport was shelled about 6.0pm, causing one killed, one officer wounded and eight other ranks.	
	27th		Two new Officers joined, Capts. Bailey and Newson.	

Army Form C. 2118.

WAR DIARY
or
INTELLIGENCE SUMMARY.
(Erase heading not required.)

Instructions regarding War Diaries and Intelligence Summaries are contained in F. S. Regs., Part II. and the Staff Manual respectively. Title pages will be prepared in manuscript.

Place	Date	Hour	Summary of Events and Information	Remarks and references to Appendices
M.17.c.7.3.	27th.		57th Rifles relieved in front line by 2/8th Gurkhas, Lt-Col. Morris, 2/8th G.R. taking over command of the Sub-Section.	
	28th.		Two other ranks granted seven days leave. Quartermaster returned to duty from Hospital.	
	30th.		3rd Londons relieved by the 69 Punjabis. Battalion left LONELY post at 8.0pm for billets in ESTAIRES. All settled in by 11.0pm.	
	31st.		Three other ranks granted seven days leave. Rejoined the GARHWAL BDE. MEERUT DIVISION.	

July 31st 15.

A.Mitcalfe
Captain & Adjt.
1/3rd London Regiment.

OPERATION ORDERS
by
Lieut-Col. A. Anthony Howell. C.M.G.
Cmdg. 1/3rd Battalion, The London Regiment.

No. 16.

July 4th 15.

Reference Map:-
1/20000 TRENCH SHEET

(1) RELIEF.
The 1/3rd Battalion, plus one company Leicester Regt., will relieve the 2/6th Gurkhas in the trenches, taking up the front from BOND STREET communication trench on the left to COCKSPUR STREET communication trench on the right.

(2) PARADE.
Companies will parade on their company parade grounds at 8.0pm this evening.
No. 1 Coy. under Major W.D. Samuel will march off at 8.0pm, via the trestle bridge in square X.8.f. and will cross road junction G.2.6.,3.8. at 8.35pm. They will pick up a guide at Broken Tree Corner from the 2/6th Gurkhas, and proceed to take over the front line as arranged.
No. 3 Coy. under Captain A.J. Agius will march off at 8.5pm tonight by the same route as No.1 Coy. picking up a guide at Broken Tree Corner. They will be in Reserve bivouacs NORTH and WEST of HOWARD ROAD.

(3) TOOLS.
Each company will carry 50 spades.

(4) MEDICAL ARRANGEMENTS.
The First Aid Post will be established in the RUE DES ECOLES close to the junction of the RUE DES ECOLES and ALBERT ROAD.

(5) BOMB PARTIES.
Bomb parties will parade with their companies.

(6) MACHINE GUNS.
Arrangements for machine guns will be under the direction of the Brigade Machine Gun Officer.

(7) COMMUNICATION.
All arrangements for communication will be under the direction of Captain Page, 1/3rd London Regiment.

(8) ORDERLIES.
After taking over the trenches O. C. Coys. will detail one orderly per company to report to battalion headquarters, where he will remain. These orderlies must know their way from their respective company headquarters to battalion headquarters and vice versa.

(9) DRESS.
Dress for parade tonight will be Marching order, great coats in the valises. The waterproof sheet will be carried on top of the valise.

(10) OFFICERS' VALISES, BLANKETS.
Blanket wagons will be sent to Coy. Headquarters at 8.0pm this evening to collect blankets and officers' valises, which must be ready.

(11) WATER, WATER CARTS.
Men will parade with filled water bottles. Arrangements for water will be made locally by O.C. Coys.
The water carts will be filled and proceed to the First Aid Post, moving in rear of the last party of the battalion, in company with the medical cart and officers mess cart.

P.T.O.

Operation Orders No. 10. continued.

MARCH ORDER KEY.
(11) HEADQUARTERS.
The details of Headquarters will parade with this party.

(12) BATTALION HEADQUARTERS.
Battalion Headquarters will be established in the RUE DES BORDEAUX close to the junction of the RUE DES BORDEAUX AND ALBERT ROAD.

No.12.

OPERATION ORDERS
by
Lieut-Col. A. Anthony Morell, C. M. G.
Commanding 1/3rd Battalion, The London Regiment.

Reference Map
1/40000 BETHUNE SHEET.   July 14th 1915.

(1) **MOVE.**

The battalion will be relieved in the trenches tonight by a detachment of the 4th Cavalry.

(2) **RELIEFS.**

One guide from No.2 Coy.(reporting at Battalion Headquarters on his way) will be at the FORTIFIED HOUSE at 6. pm to conduct detachment of 4th Cavalry to trenches (via WINDY CORNER and EDWARD ROAD).

As companies are relieved they will march to LES LOBES independently by the following route :-

       EDWARD ROAD.
       WINDY CORNER.
       S.5.c.
       X.6.c.
       X.4.d.
       X.3.d.
       TRESTLE BRIDGE   to LES LOBES.

Coy. Q.M.Sergts. will meet companies at the ESTAMINET, LES LOBES and conduct them to billets.

(3) **DRESS.**

Dress will be Marching order, great coats in, and waterproof sheets on top of the valise.

(4) **SPADES.**

Companies will bring out 30 spades. These tools will be carried by companies to FORTIFIED HOUSE, where they will be loaded on limbers.

Men carrying spades are to be noted and names taken of any men who do not arrive at FORTIFIED HOUSE with same.

(5) **STORES.**

Companies will bring out of the trenches the following :-

    (a) Periscopes, to be loaded on limbers at FORTIFIED HSE.
    (b) Very pistols.
    (c) Telescopic rifles.
    (d) Gas Alarm gongs.
    (e) Ten water tins.
    (f) Hand grenades and bombs.

Each man will carry 150 rounds of ammunition.

(6) **MEDICAL ARRANGEMENTS**

Latrine tins are to be emptied at 5.30pm. The Medical cart and personnel will proceed to billets behind No.2 Coy.

(7) **SANITATION.**

Trenches are to be left scrupulously clean.

                                                                P.T.O.

Continued.   -2-   OPERATION ORDERS No. AY.

(x) HEADQUARTERS.

The Headquarter party will move off at 7.apm under the Regimental Sergt-Major.

(xi) SIGNALLERS.

Orders will be issued later.

(xx) NOTICE.

The battalion will be on two hours notice in billets and form part of the Divisional Reserve.

                                              Captain & Adjt.
                                           1/3rd London Regiment.

Copies to :-
   O.C. No.1 Coy.
   O.C. No.4 "
   Medical Officer.
   Quartermaster.
   Sergt-Major.
   File.

OPERATION ORDERS   No. 46.

by

Major P.W.Beresford
Commanding 1/3rd Battalion, The London Regiment.

July 18th 16.

(1) **MOVE.**

The Battalion, with Machine Gun Section and Brigade Bomb Gun Section, will march to rest billets west of MERVILLE tonight.

(2) **PARADE.**

The Battalion will parade on the Alarm Post at 7.0pm. Machine Gun and Bomb Gun Sections will be drawn up on the road ready to move off.

(3) **DRESS.**

Dress will be marching order, great coats on and water proof sheets on top of the valise.

(4) **BAGGAGE.**

The baggage wagons will be at company headquarters at 4.30pm. All blankets, officers valises and baggage are to be loaded on wagons by 6.0pm.

(5) **MESS CART.**

The Officers Mess Cart will visit officers billets at 6.0pm to collect Mess kit.

Captain & Adjt.
1/3rd London Regiment.

No. 10.

OPERATION ORDERS

by

MAJOR F.W. BERESFORD,
Commanding 1/3rd Bn. The London Regt.

Reference Map - AIRE SHEET 4/40000.   July, 14th, 1915.

(1) MOVE.

   The Battalion will march to Billets at L'EPINETTE on the 15th July, and become affiliated with the Sirhind Brigade of the LAHORE DIVISION.

(2) PARADE.

   The Battalion will parade at 6.pm. with the head at road junction K.27.d.8.5. facing WEST. No. 1. Company in front.

(3) DRESS.

   Full Marching Order, great coats on, and waterproof sheets on top, of, valise.

(4) BAGGAGE.

   The Baggage Waggons will be at Company Headquarters at [illegible]. All Blankets, Officers' Valises, and baggage, are to be loaded on Waggons by [illegible].

(5) MESS CART.

   The Officers' Mess Cart will visit Officers' Billets at 5.0pm. to collect Mess Kit.

                                            Captain & Adjutant,
                                       1/3rd Bn. The London Regiment.

Copies to :-

   O.C. No. 1 Coy.
   O.C. No. 2 Coy.
   Quartermaster.
   Medical Officer.
   Machine Gun Officer.
   Signallers.
   Office.

No. ...

OPERATION ORDERS
by
MAJOR P. W. BERESFORD,
Commanding 1/4rd Battalion, The London Regiment.

L'EPINETTE,
JULY 27th 15.

In the event of the battalion being required to move up into the firing line from Reserve billets, the following procedure will be adopted :-

(1) PARADE.
The battalion will fall in on the alarm post ready to move off as soon as possible after the receipt of orders.

(2) DRESS.
Marching order, great coats in and waterproofs on top of valises.

(3) WATERBOTTLES. ETC.
Waterbottles must be kept filled, the emergency ration in the haversack and field dressing complete.

(4) AMMUNITION.
If time, the 120 rounds of ammunition carried will be made up to 200 per man. The ammunition animals and one S.A.A. cart will come up to battalion headquarters at once from the 1st Line Transport.

(5) TRANSPORT.
The First Line Transport will await orders from the brigade; meanwhile, they will saddle up and harness in horses.

(6) MEDICAL ARRANGEMENTS.
The Medical Officer and personnel, less medical cart will parade with the battalion and go forward to fix an Aid Post.

(7) COMMUNICATION.
The Signallers will disconnect all telephones on the order to do so being given by the Commanding Officer and will march behind the First company, remaining always with battalion headquarters until distributed by the officer i/c Signallers.

(8) BOMB PARTIES AND STRETCHER BEARERS.
Bomb parties and stretcher bearers will parade with their companies.

(9) CYCLE ORDERLIES.
One cyclist will accompany the Commanding Officer, the remainder will join the First Line Transport.

(10) DETAILS.
All details left in billets will join the 1st Line Transport at the earliest opportunity, and will be under the Sergt-Major for orders.

(11) BLANKETS, COOKERS, ETC.
The cooks and Coy. Q.M. Sergts. will remain in billets and pack up blankets. The cookers will join the 1st Line Transport.

Captain & Adjutant.
1/4th London Regiment.

Copies to :- O.C. No.1 Coy.
No.2 Coy.
Quartermaster.
Medical Officer.
Signalling Officer.
Bomb Officer.

OPERATION ORDERS   No. 34.
by
MAJOR P. W. BERESFORD,
Commanding 1/3rd London Regiment.

Reference Map:-
1/40000 BETHUNE SHEET.   July 22nd 15.

(1) MOVE.
    The battalion will relieve the SEAFORTH and ARGYLE
HIGHLANDERS on the night of the 22/23rd July.

(2) PARADE.
    The battalion will parade on the alarm post ready to move
off at 7-30 p.m.

(3) DRESS.
    Dress for parade will be marching order, great coats in
the valise. Waterproof sheets will be carried on top of the valise.

(4) AMMUNITION.
    200 rounds of ammunition will be carried on the man. This
should be made up from the S.A.A.Carts as soon as possible.

(5) TOOLS.
    Each company will take 50 spades and 15 picks. These tools
will be carried on limbers as far as the RUE DE BACQUEROT.

(6) BOMB PARTIES.
    Bomb parties will parade with their Coys.

(7) OFFICERS' VALISES.
    A wagon will be sent to Coy. Hdqrs. at 3.0 p.m. today to
collect Officers' Valises.

(8) ORDERLIES.
    After taking over the trenches O.C.Coys. will detail one
Orderly per Coy. to report to Battalion Hdqrs. where he will
remain.
    These orderlies must know their way from their respective
company headquarters to battalion headquarters and vice versa.

(9) COMMUNICATION.
    All arrangements for communication will be under the
direction of Captain Page.

(10) MEDICAL ARRANGEMENTS.
    The First Aid Post will be established in the LA FLINQUE
FAUQUISSART road M.17.d.6.4.

(11) WATER. WATER CARTS.
    Men will parade with filled waterbottles. Arrangements
for water will be made locally by O.C.Coys.
    The water carts will be filled and proceed to the First
Aid Post moving in rear of the last party of the battalion in
company with the Medical Cart.
    The details in Headquarters will parade with this party.

(12) BATTALION HEADQUARTERS.
    Battalion Headquarters will be established at LONELY POST,
RUE DE BACQUEROT.

                                        Captain & Adjutant.
                                        1/3rd London Regiment.

3 London

August 1915

(6392) Wt. W6192/P875 1,500,000 4/18 McA & W Ltd (E 2815) Forms W3091/4.   Army Form W.3091.

Cover for Documents.

Nature of Enclosures.

Notes, or Letters written.

BRITISH SALONIKA FORCE.

WAR DIARY.

Vol. No.	Unit	PERIOD From	To
14	Meteorological Section R.E.	1-1-19	~~31-1-19~~

Serial No 197.

12/6948

WAR DIARY
OF
1/3rd London Regiment

FROM 1st August 1915. TO 31st August 1915

Army Form C. 2118

WAR DIARY
or
INTELLIGENCE SUMMARY.
(Erase heading not required.)

Instructions regarding War Diaries and Intelligence Summaries are contained in F. S. Regs., Part II. and the Staff Manual respectively. Title pages will be prepared in manuscript.

Place	Date	Hour	Summary of Events and Information	Remarks and references to Appendices
ESTAIRES	1915 Aug. 1st.	7.30pm	Battalion paraded on the Alarm Post to march to billets in RUGBY ROAD square M.15d.4.0 near PONT DU HEM. In Brigade Reserve here.	
PONT DU HEM	2nd.		Quiet generally speaking. Commenced making barbed wire balls for front line.	
	4th.	2.30pm.	Battalion photographed at PONT DU HEM, under authority of India Office. 2nd Lt. C.G.Ochs and 15 other ranks joined the unit from Base. Q.M. granted weeks leave.	
		9.0pm.	Battalion on a working party to dig a support trench.	
	5th.	9.0pm.	No. 1 Coy. under Major F.D.Samuel relieved "B" Coy. 2nd Leicesters in front line, the company of 2nd Leicesters taking over billets vacated by our No.1 Coy.	
	6th.	-.0pm.	Three other ranks granted leave.	
		9.0pm.	Our No. 2 Coy. and "B"Coy, Leicesters on working party.	
	7th.		2nd. Lts. Ainsworth, Rice and Lloyd.A.E. granted 7 days leave.	
	8th.	2.0pm.	Accidental explosion in pump house behind front line trenches, injuring four of our men, two of whom were admitted to Hospital. Court of Enquiry on this is to be held by 2nd Leicester Regt. Garhwal Brigade relieved by Dehra Dun Brigade tonight. Battalion marched back to billets in La Gorgue.	
LA GORGUE	9th.	6.45pm.	Garhwal Bde in Divisional Reserve. Battalion on working party, digging in neighbourhood of NEUVE CHAPELLE.	

P T O

Army Form C. 2118

WAR DIARY
or
INTELLIGENCE SUMMARY
(Erase heading not required.)

Instructions regarding War Diaries and Intelligence Summaries are contained in F. S. Regs., Part II. and the Staff Manual respectively. Title pages will be prepared in manuscript.

Place	Date	Hour	Summary of Events and Information	Remarks and references to Appendices
LA GORGUE	1915 Aug. 10th.	7.0am.	Battalion granted use of baths at LA GORGUE FROM 7.0am to 12:0 noon.	
		6.0pm.	Battalion concert at LA GORGUE BATHS.	
	11th.		Three other ranks granted leave.	
	13th	6.45pm.	Battalion on working party under Capt. Newson.	
	14th	3.0pm.	Major Beresford and 2nd Lt. Garrard granted leave. Confirmation by Bishop Gwynne, The Bishop of Khartoum, in the Mairie, LA GORGUE.	
	15th.		2nd Lt. Winshull granted leave.	
	16th.		16 men detached for duty with Bde. Grenade Coy. making 2 officers and 20 men in all on this duty. 7 unfits inspected by the G.O.C. Meerut Division at 8.30am at ESTAIRES. Three other ranks granted leave.	
		7.0pm.	Battalion paraded on the Alarm Post to march to trenches, relieving 1/4th Black Watch in "A" Sub-Sub Section. O.C. 2/3rd Gurkhas in command of the sub-section. No 2 Coy.3rd Londons in front line and supports, and No. 1 Coy. in Reserve in LONELY POST. Headquarters established on Rue du Bacquerot at M.17.c.5.0.	
M.17.c.5.0.	17th.		Generally quiet.	

Army Form C. 2118

WAR DIARY
or
INTELLIGENCE SUMMARY.
(Erase heading not required.)

Instructions regarding War Diaries and Intelligence Summaries are contained in F.S. Regs., Part II. and the Staff Manual respectively. Title pages will be prepared in manuscript.

Place	Date	Hour	Summary of Events and Information	Remarks and references to Appendices
M.17.c.5.0.	18th.		Generally quiet all day.	
"	19th.		—do—	
"	20th.	10.0pm.	Enemy active with Machine gun fire for about 15 mins.	
"	21st.		2 platoons of the 6th Wiltshires(19th Division) attached to our battalion in the front line for experience. Enemy quiet all day.	
"	22nd.	8.0pm.	No. 1 Coy. under Major F.D.Samuel took over the front line from No. 2 Coy., the latter moving back to LONELY POST under Capt.A.J.Agius, and remaining in local reserve. Enemy quiet.	
"	23rd		Major P.W.Beresford and 2nd Lt. T.G.C.Garrard returned off leave. A further 2 platoons of the 6th Wilts. attached to our battalion to relieve the two already with us.	
"	24th		2nd Lt. Bateman attached to the Divisional Magazine at NOUVEAU MONDE for instruction in bomb making. 2nd Lt.J.L.Minshull rejoined unit off leave. A further two platoons of the 6th Wilts attached to us in addition to those already with us. One casualty in 6th Wilts. by bomb(killed)	
"	25th		Lt. Jones.D.W.L. left on leave. 3 casualties in 6th Wilts. by shell. 2 of the platoons of 6th Wilts leaving us tonight.	
"	26th		2nd Lt. C.F.Davis left on leave. One man wounded a working party early this morning.	

Army Form C. 2118.

WAR DIARY
or
INTELLIGENCE SUMMARY.
(Erase heading not required.)

Instructions regarding War Diaries and Intelligence Summaries are contained in F. S. Regs., Part II. and the Staff Manual respectively. Title pages will be prepared in manuscript.

Sept. 5th 15.

R.D.Fitz.Webb
Captain & Adjutant.
1/3rd London Regiment.

Place	Date	Hour	Summary of Events and Information	Remarks and references to Appendices
M.17.&c.5.0.	27th	8.0pm.	Battalion relieved by 12th Rifle Brigade(20th Division) and marched back to bivouacs at NEUF BERQUIN for one night only. Quiet all day.	
NEUF BERQUIN	28th	4.15pm.	Battalion paraded on the ALARM POST to march to trenches in front of NEUVE CHAPELLE, to relieve the 4th Kings Liverpools, reliefs being completed by 10.30pm. No. 2 Coy. in front line. No. 1 Coy.in local reserve, under the command of O.C. Garhwal Rifles, who was in command of "B" Sub. Section. Hdqrs. established at NEUVE CHAPELLE end of EUSTON ROAD trench.	
NEUVE CHAPELLE	29th.noon.		Draft of 45, of which 11 were sick and wounded returned to duty, joined battalion.	
		4.15pm.	Enemy bombardment causing casualties as follows :- 2 killed, 16 wounded. 3 of the latter have since died of wounds. Enemy artillery active throughout remainder of day.	
"	30th	All day	Our artillery on left heavily bombarded enemy trenches, with great success. Very little retaliation by the enemy, and five of our aeroplanes observing for our artillery, received hardly any attention from the enemy anti-aircraft guns. The draft reported as joining the battalion on the 28th, came up to join the battalion in the trenches.	
"	31st.		Generally quiet on our front. Two wounded whilst bringing up rations at night. Some machine gun activity on part of enemy at night whilst our working parties were out. No casualties.	

OPERATION ORDERS
by
Lieut-Col. A. Anthony Howell C.M.G.
Commanding 1/3rd London Regiment.

No. 22.

August 1st 15.

(1) PARADE.

The battalion will parade on the ALARM POST at 7.30pm tonight, to march to new billets.
The following Officers will be with their companies:-

No. 1 Coy.	No. 2 Coy.
Major F.D.Samuel.	Capts. A.J.Agius.
Capt. E.A.Bowman.	" F.R.Bailey.
2nd Lt. S.E.Brady.	2nd Lt.S.J.Ainsworth.
" C.R.Godge.	" A.H.Bateman.

All other officers of companies will remain with the 1st Line Transport.

(2) DRESS.

Dress for parade will be Marching Order, great coats in packs. Waterproof sheet to be carried on top of the pack.

(3) AMMUNITION.

220 rounds of ammunition per man will be carried. Deficiencies to be made up as soon as possible from the S.A.A. carts.

(4) OFFICERS VALISES.

A wagon will be sent to Officers billets at 6.0pm to collect Officers valises, which are being sent back on the wagons to the 2nd Line Transport.

(5) MESS CART.

The Officers Mess cart will call at Officers billets at 6.0pm. to collect Officers Mess kit.

(6) COMMUNICATIONS.

All communications will be under the direction of Capt. C.J.Page.

(7) WATER BOTTLES.

All waterbottles are to be filled from the water carts by 6.0pm.

(8)

The Commanding Officer will see Officers Commanding Coys. at his billet at 5.0pm today.

(9) RATIONS.

Rations will be brought up under the same arrangements as when the battalion is in the trenches, arriving tonight at the barricade at 10.30pm.

Captain & Adjutant.
1/3rd London Regmt.

Copies to :-
Commanding Officer.
Adjt.
O. C. No. 1 Coy.
O. C.   2 "
Quartermaster.
Signalling and M.Officer.

Copy No. 7

OPERATION ORDERS NO. 23.
by
Lieut-Col. A. Anthony Howell, C.M.G.
Commanding 1/3rd Battalion, The London Regt.

Reference Maps,　　　　　　　　　　　　　　　　　　　　August 6th 15.
FRANCE, sheets 36 & 36.C.

1. **RELIEFS.**

    Half battalion, The London Regt. and one company 2nd Leicester Regt. in billets at RUGBY ROAD will be relieved tonight by the 2nd Gurkhas, and will march back to billets at LA GORGUE.
    No. 1 Coy. Londons, will march to billets under orders of O.C., 2nd Leicester Regt.

2. **HAND GRENADES.**

    A limber will be at the North end of RUGBY ROAD (M.16.c) to collect grenade boxes of No. 1 Coy.
    A limber will be at the cross roads PONT DU HEM at 12.0 noon this morning to collect No. 3 Coy's hand grenades.

3. **TOOLS.**

    A limber will be at cross roads PONT DU HEM at 12.0 noon to collect all battalion tools.

4. **AMMUNITION.**

    200 rounds of ammunition per man will be carried.

5. **OFFICERS MESS CART.**

    The Officers Mess cart will be at the cross roads PONT DU HEM at 6.0pm this evening.

　　　　　　　　　　　　　　　　　　　　　　　　　Captain & Adjutant.
　　　　　　　　　　　　　　　　　　　　　　　　　1/3rd London Regiment.

Copy No.1 to O.C. 2nd Leicesters.
  "   2   O.C. "D"Coy.   "
  "   3   O.C. No. 1 Coy. Londons.
  "   4   O.C. No. 3   "   "
  "   5   Quartermaster,   "
  "   6   Medical Officer   "
  "   7   Office file.

Copy No.........

OPERATION ORDERS NO. 34.
by
Lieut-Col. A. Anthony Howell, C.M.G.
Commanding 1/3rd Battalion, The London Regiment.

August 7th 1915.

It is notified for information that the CARNWAL BRIGADE is at present in Divisional Reserve, and the state of readiness of the battalion is two hours notice.

In the event of the battalion being required to move up from Reserve billets, the following procedure will be adopted :-

1. PARADE.

    The battalion will fall in on the alarm post, (which is the field in which the 1st Line Transport is parked, immediately behind the Convent,) as soon as possible after the receipt of orders.

2. DRESS.

    Marching Order, greatcoats in and waterproof sheets on top of valises.

3. WATERBOTTLES ETC.

    Waterbottles must be filled, the emergency ration in the haversack and field dressing complete.

4. S.A.A. and Medical Carts will accompany the battalion.

5. TRANSPORT.

    The First Line Transport will await orders from the Brigade; meanwhile, they will saddle up and harness in horses.

6. COOKERS.

    Coy. Q.M.Sergts. and cooks, as well as the cookers will join the 1st Line Transport.

7. CYCLE ORDERLIES.

    One cyclist Orderly will accompany the Commanding Officer, the remainder joining the 1st Line Transport.

8. DETAILS.

    All details left in billets will join the 1st Line Transport at earliest opportunity, and will be under the Sergt. Major for orders.

Captain & Adjt.
1/3rd London Regiment.

COPY NO. 6

OPERATION ORDERS NO. 25.
by
Lieut-Col. A. Anthony Rowell, C.B.E.
Commanding 1/3rd Battalion, The London Regiment.

August 18th 15.

(1) **PARADE.**
The battalion will parade on the ALARM POST at 7.epm this evening ready to move off, to relieve the 1/4th Black Watch in the trenches.

(2) **DRESS.**
Dress for parade will be marching order, great coats in and waterproof sheets on top of, valises.

(3) **AMMUNITION.**
200 rounds of ammunition per man will be carried.

(4) **TOOLS AND BOMBS.**
Each company will take 30 spades and 16 picks, which will be carried by limber as far as the RUE DU BACQUEROT.
Bombs also be will be carried on a limber.

(5) **BOMB PARTIES AND STRETCHER BEARERS.**
These parties will parade with their companies.

(6) **OFFICERS VALISES.**
A cart will call at Officers billets at noon today to collect Officers valises, which must be ready by that time.

(7) **MESS CART.**
The mess cart will call at Officers billets at 5.epm to collect mess kit.

(8) **WATER.**
All men will parade with filled waterbottles. Arrangements for water will be made locally by O.C.Coys.
The water carts will be filled and proceed to Battalion Headquarters at LONELY POST, RUE DU BACQUEROT, moving in rear of the last party of the battalion, in company with the medical cart.
The details of headquarters will parade with this party.

(9) **MEDICAL ARRANGEMENTS.**
The First Aid post will be established at WINCHESTER POST.

(10) **COMMUNICATION.**
All arrangements for communication will be under the direction of Captain C.J.Page.

(11) **ORDERLIES.**
After reliefs O.C.Coys. will detail one Orderly per Coy. to report to Battalion Headquarters, where he will remain.

(12) **REPORTS.**
As soon as reliefs are completed O.C.Coys. will report same to Headquarters, and also state the number of Officers and other ranks in trenches or posts. Numbers in firing line, supports and reserve to be shown separately.

(13) **BATTALION HEADQUARTERS.**
Headquarters will be established at LONELY POST on the RUE DU BACQUEROT.

Capt & Adjt.
1/3rd London Regiment.

Copy No. 8

OPERATION ORDERS No. 26.
by
Lieut-Col. A. Anthony Howell, C.M.G.
Commanding 1/3rd Battalion, The London Regiment.

Reference Maps:-   August 27th 16.
1/10000, 36.S.W.No.1.
1/20000, 36.S & N 36.

1. **RELIEF.**
   The Battalion will be relieved on the night of the 27/28th inst. by the 21th K.R.R., 60th Brigade, 20th Division.

2. **ROUTES.**
   Relieving units will enter by LONELY-SMITH communication trench.
   Relieved units will depart by WINCHESTER TRENCH.
   On relief companies will march independently to billets at L.28.c.3.3. and L.22.d.3.R *, observing the following route:-
   M.16.b. - LE BIZET - Bridge G.25.c.

3. **DEPARTURE.**
   No. 1 Coy. will not pass GRANT POST until they have ascertained its relief is completed and the relieved garrison has moved out.

4. **DRESS.**
   Dress will be Marching Order, greatcoats on and waterproof sheets on top of, valises.

5. **STORES.**
   Officers to take over stores will arrive between 4.0 and 5.0pm, 27th inst. Only permanent trench stores and post stores will be handed over on relief.
   Lists in duplicate will be made out beforehand by Officers concerned, and receipts obtained when the stores have been handed over. These certificates will be sent to Sub-Section Hqrs. as soon as receipted.
   A limber will be at the near end of RUE L'EPINETTE to carry company bombs and tools.
   No. 1 Coy. will bring out three VERMOREL SPRAYERS and place them on the limber.

6. **MEDICAL ARRANGEMENTS.**
   The M.O. will inspect the trenches at 8.0pm night 27/28th. The medical cart and personnel will proceed to billets behind the 1st Coy.

7. **SANITATION.**
   The trenches are to be left scrupulously clean and latrine tins are to be cleaned, NOT buried.

8. **HEADQUARTERS PARTY.**
   The Headquarter party will move off at 6.0pm.

9. **SIGNALLERS.**
   Signallers will hand over to relieving unit at 6.0pm, leaving one man per telephone until the Commanding Officer leaves.

10. **REPORTS.**
    No. 1 Coy. moving out by WINCHESTER TRENCH will report at Sub-Section Hqrs on their way through, that their relief is complete.

P.T.O.

CONTINUED.   2.

11. BATTALION HEADQUARTERS.
        Battalion Headquarters will be established at L.28.c.5.9.
     on arrival at billets.

12. NOTICE.
        The battalion will be on two hours notice in billets.

                                              Captain & Adjutant,
                                              1/3rd London Regiment.

Copy No.1 to C.O.
     "   2. Major P.W.Beresford.
     "   3. O.C.No.1 Coy.
     "   4. O.C.No.2 Coy.
     "   5. Medical Officer.
     "   6. Capt.C.J.Page.
     "   7. Quartermaster.
     "   8. File.

        ─────────────────────

~~MESS CART.~~
        ~~The Officers Mess cart will be at near end of Rue L'Epinette
     at 5.30pm this evening, and will be ready to move off at 6.0pm.~~

OFFICERS RIDING HORSES.
        Officers Horses will be at Headquarters at 5.0pm tonight.

Copy No. 8

OPERATION ORDERS NO. 27.
by
Lieut-Col. A. Anthony Howell, C.M.G.
Commanding 1/3rd Battalion, The London Regiment.

Reference Maps:—
1/10000. 36.S.W.No.1.
1/40000. 36.a and 36.

AUG. 29th 15.

1. **PARADE.**

    The battalion will parade on the ALARM POST (which is the field adjoining the Quartermasters Stores) at 4.0pm this evening, to march to the trenches to relieve the 4th Kings, in "B" Sub-section.

    One platoon of No. 1 Coy. will be paraded with No. 2 Coy. to be temporarily attached to No. 2 Coy. whilst in the front line.

2. **DRESS.**

    Dress for parade will be marching order, greatcoats in, and waterproof sheets on top of, valises.

3. **AMMUNITION.**

    130 rounds of ammunition will be carried.

4. **TOOLS AND BOMBS.**

    Each company will take 50 spades and 15 picks which will be carried by limber. Bombs also, will be carried by limber.

5. **OFFICERS VALISES.**

    A cart will call at Officers' billets at 12.30pm today to collect Officers valises, which must be ready by that time.

6. **MESS CART.**

    The mess cart will call at Officers billets at 2.30pm to collect mess kit.

7. **WATER.**

    All men will parade with filled waterbottles. Arrangements for water will be made locally by O.C.Coys.

    Water carts will be filled and proceed to the First Aid Post moving in rear of the last party of the battalion, in company with the Medical cart.

    The details of Headquarters will parade with this party.

8. **ORDERLIES.**

    After reliefs, O.C.Coys. will detail one orderly per Coy. to report to Battalion Hdqrs, where he will remain.

9. **REPORTS.**

    As soon as reliefs are completed, O.C.Coys. will report same to Hdqrs. and also state the numbers of Officers and Other ranks in trenches or posts. Numbers in firing line, supports and reserve to be shewn separately.

10. **BATTALION HEADQUARTERS.**

    Position of Battalion Hdqrs. will be notified as soon as possible after reliefs are completed.

Capt & Adjt.
1/3rd London Regiment.

Copy No. 1 to C.O.
    2 " Major Beresford.
    3 " O.C.No.1 Coy.
    4 " O.C.No.2 Coy.
    5 " Quartermaster.
    6 " M.O.
    7 " Capt Page.
    8 " File.

3 London
Sept '15

Army Form W. 3091.

Cover for Documents.

Nature of Enclosures.

Notes, or Letters written.

Volume No. _____

BRITISH SALONIKA FORCE

WAR DIARY.

26th Division

Vol. No.	Unit	PERIOD From	To
16	77th Trench Mortar Batty.		
14	78th do	1-2-18.	28-2-18.
14	79th do		

Manual
Serial No. 197.

13/7286

WAR DIARY
OF
1/3rd London Regiment.

FROM 1st September 1915 TO 30th September 1915

Army Form C. 2118.

WAR DIARY
or
INTELLIGENCE SUMMARY.

(Erase heading not required.)

Instructions regarding War Diaries and Intelligence Summaries are contained in F. S. Regs., Part II. and the Staff Manual respectively. Title pages will be prepared in manuscript.

Place	Date	Hour	Summary of Events and Information	Remarks and references to Appendices
NEUVE CHAPELLE	1915 Sept 1st.		We are being relieved tonight by the 1st Manchesters, Jullunder Bde. Lahore Division, and companies will march back independently to billets North of LA GORGUE at L.35.c.(AIRE SHEET 1/40000)	
LA GORGUE	2nd.	9.0am	Battalion on two hours notice to move off whilst here. Kit Inspectin under company arrangements.	
"	5th.	9.0am 7.0pm	Church Parade at Hdqrs. 100 men on working party under Lt.E.A.Lloyd.	
"	6th.	9.30am	Half battalion under the Sgt.Major for company training.	
"	7th.	5.30pm	Working party of 2 Officers and 112 other ranks conveyed by carts to ROUGE CROIX.	
"	8th.	9.0am	Commanding Officer inspected the iron rations of the battalion. Lieut.T.Reeves and 2nd Lt. Minshull admitted to Hospital sick today.	
		7.0pm	Working party of 3 Officers and 179 Other ranks.	
"	9th.		Indian Corps baths at LA GORGUE allotted to the battalion from 7.0am to noon.	
		10.0am.	2nd Lt. S.J.Ainsworth sent to O. C. 107th Pioneers at 10.0am for Machine Gun Course.	
		10.30am.	9 unfits inspected by the A.D.M.S. Meerut Division	
"	10th.	11.0am.	All Officers and N.C.O.s attended gas experiment at CHELTENHAM POST(M.20.a.9.6, 1/40000 BETHUNE SHEET)	

WAR DIARY or INTELLIGENCE SUMMARY.

(Erase heading not required.)

Army Form C. 2118

Place	Date	Hour	Summary of Events and Information	Remarks and references to Appendices
	Sept.			
LA GORGUE.	10th.	3.0pm.	Companies instructed in use of tube smoke helmet.	
"	12th.	5.0pm.	Battalion paraded on ALARM POST to march to trenches near NEUVE CHAPELLE (M.35.b.7.7.1/40000 BETHUNE SHEET), relieving the 2/2nd Gurkhas. No. 1 Coy. and three platoons of No. 2 Coy. in front line and one platoon of No. 2 Coy. in support. Lt-Col.Drake-Brockman, Garhwal Rifles is O.C. Sub-section. Our 1st Line Transport moved to BOUT DE VILLE.	
TRENCHES M.35.b.7.7.	13th. 14th.		Generally quiet, all day. Our artillery very active all day. One casualty; slight wound.	
"	15th.	10.0pm.	S.A.A. reserve brought up to the Support line.	
"	16th.	3.30pm.	Enemy shelled our support line for about 15 mins. No damage done.	
		9.0pm.	One accidental casualty (bullet wound).	
"	17th.	12.0 noon.	2nd Lt. Morgan, Interpreter, joined us today. 5 unfits and under age sent to Base Rouen for discharge. Generally quiet.	
"	18th.	9.0am.	8 men departed on seven days leave. Battalion is being relieved tonight, No. 1 Coy. by 2/2nd Gurkhas and No. 2 Coy. by 1/4th Seaforths. Battalion will march back to billets at L.28.c.5.2. North of LA GORGUE.	
LA GORGUE.	19th.		Battalion on two hours notice to move off.	

Instructions regarding War Diaries and Intelligence
Summaries are contained in F.S. Regs., Part II.
and the Staff Manual respectively. Title pages
will be prepared in manuscript.

Army Form C. 2118.

WAR DIARY
or
INTELLIGENCE SUMMARY.
(Erase heading not required.)

Place	Date	Hour	Summary of Events and Information	Remarks and references to Appendices
LA GORGUE	Sept. 19th.		Divine services as follows :-	
		11.15am.	Morning Church Parade.) All held	
		Noon.	Holy Communion.) at Battalion	
		7.15pm.	Lantern Service) Hdqrs.	
			Corps baths in LA GORGUE allotted to the battalion from 3.0pm to 6.0pm today.	
"	20th.	10.30am.	Inspection of the GARHWAL BRIGADE en masse by Lord Kitchener on the PONT ROCHON road 300 yds. S.E. of road junction R.5. central, 1/40000 BETHUNE SHEET. Dress, Drill Order.	
"	21st.	8.0am.	Holy Communion at the MAIRIE, LA GORGUE.	
"	22nd.	11.0am.	F.G.C.M. held at our Hdqrs. Major P.W.Beresford President. Accused - Sergt.Woolford. F.	
"	23rd.	6.0pm.	Battalion parades on the Alarm Post to march to point of assembly: viz. BOUT DE VILLE (M.20.a.4.6) 1/40000 BETHUNE SHEET. Encountered thunderstorm en route.	
"	24th.	9.0am.	Holy Communion at Hdqrs. of 2nd Leicesters in CHELTENHAM RD.	
		5.0pm.	Battalion marched to trenches at take up their position in front line. Hdqrs. established in support line at M.35.b.7.7. (1/40000 BETHUNE SHEET) One company in "Ducks Bill" and "Neck" and one company from SUNKEN STREET to SUNKEN ROAD.	
TRENCHES M.35.b.7.7.	25th.	4.40am.	The heads of a gas battery of six cylinders were blown off by a German bomb. The gas escaped in large volumes, causing casualties in both the	

WAR DIARY
or
INTELLIGENCE SUMMARY.
(Erase heading not required.)

Army Form C. 2118.

Place	Date	Hour	Summary of Events and Information	Remarks and references to Appendices
TRENCHES	25th		contd.	

front line and support line. Very prompt action was taken to earth over the cylinders and by this method a serious disaster was prevented. There was an absence of all panic, the men being steady and working hard. The Officer in charge of the gas arrangements was badly affected and had to be evacuated. The senior N.C.O. left reported to my Officer in charge of the "Ducks Bill" (Capt.A.J.Agius) that he could not carry on as he had no instructions as to time of releasing and quantity of gas to be released, and also that he had not sufficient men. This gas in the "Ducks Bill" also affected a bombing party of the Manchester Regt. with 2 officers, who I understand had been sent to the "Ducks Bill" as a jumping off place for their attack.

The morning was wet and misty and when at "ZERO" the smoke candles were lighted a very thick heavy yellow fog was caused. I noted that when the smoke candles were first lit, a cloud or smoke floated back over our lines before taking the direction of the enemy. Even when the yellow fumes of the smoke candles cleared, there was still left an opaque white mist. The smoke was some time in dispersing, in fact for nearly an hour it was impossible to notice any action between our lines and the enemy, so that I am unable to report on the attacks delivered by our battalions on my left.

It was very noticeable how very little musketry fire could be heard during the whole morning. This also applies to bombing.

At 7.45am the Manchester Regt. on our immediate right seemed to make an attack and about two platoons lost direction and came into the "Ducks Bill", but what

P.T.O.

WAR DIARY
or
INTELLIGENCE SUMMARY.
(Erase heading not required.)

Army Form C. 2118.

Place	Date	Hour	Summary of Events and Information	Remarks and references to Appendices
TRENCHES	Sept. 25th		**contd.** further happened I do not know. They were sent back to rejoin their regiment by the senior Officer present in the "Ducks Bill." There was a heavy bombardment on our support and reserve lines from Zero (3.50am) until sunset by heavy German guns (4.2 and 5.9 high explosive). During the night the enemy were very quiet, and all day on the 26th little activity was shewn until we were relieved at 2.0pm. 26th, except that between 7.30am and 10.0am. 26th, the "Ducks Bill" was vigorously bombed from two directions. The total casualties in this action was:-	
			Officers. Other ranks. Killed. 1 5 Died of wounds. 1 Wounded. 1 27 Gassed. 18 Missing. 1 3 Total 3 52.	
"	26th.		Battalion relieved in the afternoon by 2/2nd Gurkhas, and marched back to billets at BOUT DE VILLE. Owing to heavy rain ~~communication~~ the communication trenches were in a very muddy condition, and in places over ankle deep in mud and water.	
BOUT DE VILLE.	27th		Day devoted to cleaning up generally. Battalion on two hours notice to move off. 2nd Lt. Henri.P.R. joined the battalion as reinforcement on 25th inst. and 2nd Lt. Abbott.D.L. rejoined battalion from sick leave in United Kingdom on 26th inst.	

Army Form C. 2118.

WAR DIARY
or
INTELLIGENCE SUMMARY.
(Erase heading not required.)

Instructions regarding War Diaries and Intelligence Summaries are contained in F.S. Regs., Part II. and the Staff Manual respectively. Title pages will be prepared in manuscript.

Place	Date	Hour	Summary of Events and Information	Remarks and references to Appendices
BOUT DE VILLE	1915. Sept. 28th.	11.0am.	Battalion Muster parade on the Alarm Post by order of the Brigade, when it was ascertained that the effective strength of the battalion was 24 officers and 593 other ranks. Baths at LA GORGUE allotted to the battalion from 2.0pm to 5.0pm today. Sentence of F.G.C.M. on Sergt. Woolford. F.D. promulgated at 6.0pm.	
"	29th.		Pouring rain all day.	
"	30th.		Battalion paraded on the Alarm Post & 2.0pm to march to billets at L'EPINETTE, reaching that place at 4.30pm. Headquarters established at Q.12.c.9.1 (1/40000 BETHUNE SHEET).	

R.N......
Capt & Adjt.
1/3rd London Regiment.

Appendix 4

OPERATION ORDER
by
Lt. Col. A.M. Tring Howell C.B.
Comdg. 1/4th Bn. The London Regt.

Reference Map:
Trenches 1/10,000 No.1   September 1st 1916.
1/40,000 No.5 & 5a.

1) Relief

The Battalion will be relieved on the night of the 1/2nd September by the 1st Manchesters, 42nd Division Brigade, 14th Division.

2) Route

The relief Coy will march independently to Billets at L.H. GORENE 2.35.c covering the following route:— POTIJZE tunnel — PONT DU HEM — RUE D'ENFER.

3) Dress

Dress will be Marching Order.

4) Stores

The present trench and stores will remain taken over & over 4.0 and see par. 1. but every permanent trench stores and not otherwise dealt with to be handed over on relief.

Lists in duplicate will be made out beforehand by Officers concerned, and receipts obtained how the stores have been handed over. These

(1)   P.T.O.

[illegible] will [illegible] according to [illegible] [illegible]
[illegible] as required.

O.C. [illegible] will [illegible] LEICESTER ROAD to every Company bombs and [illegible].

No 4 Coy will [illegible] out all VERMOREL SPRAYERS, and place them in the Trenches.

(c) Sanitation.

[illegible] must not be left [illegible] [illegible] [illegible] and Latrines must be cleaned out [illegible] [illegible].

[illegible] Capt
Captain & Adjutant,
[illegible] London Regt.

Copy No 1 OC No 1 Coy.
2 OC [illegible]
3 Commanding
4 File

Copy No......6

OPERATION ORDERS NO. 22
by
Lieut-Col. A. Anthony Howell C.M.G.
Commanding 1/3rd Battalion, The London Regiment.

Reference Map:-   Sept. 12th 1915.
    Trench Map.

(1) **GENERAL**.
        The battalion will relieve the 2nd Gurkhas in the trenches tonight the 12th inst.

(2) **ROUTE**.
        Reliefs will enter by SUNKEN STREET communication trench via PONT ROCHON – PONT DU HEM – ROUGE CROIX – SUNKEN STREET.

(3) **PARADE**.
        The battalion will parade on the ALARM POST ready to move off at 5.0pm.

(4) **DRESS**.
        Dress for parade will be marching order, Great coat in and waterproof sheets on top of, valises.

(5) **AMMUNITION**.
        120 rounds of S.A.A. will be carried on the men, plus one bandolier. Full bandoliers can be obtained from the Q.M. Stores.

(6) **TOOLS**.
        Each company will take in their tools. These tools will be carried on a limber as far as the RUE DU BACQUEROT.

(7) **OFFICERS VALISES**.
        A cart will call at officers billets at noon today to collect officers valises, which must be ready by that time.

(8) **WATER**.
        All men will parade with filled water bottles. Arrangements for water will be made locally by O.C. Coys.

(9) **ORDERLIES**.
        After taking over trenches, O.C. Coys. will detail one orderly per Coy. to report to Battalion Hdqrs, where he will remain. These orderlies must know their way from the respective Company Hdqrs. to Battalion Hdqrs. and vice versa.

(10) **REPORTS**.
        As soon as reliefs are complete, O.C. Coys. will same to Battalion Hdqrs. and also state the numbers of Officers and other ranks in trenches or posts. Numbers in firing line, supports and reserves should be shown separately.

(11) **BATTALION HEADQUARTERS**.
        Position of Battalion Hdqrs. will be notified later.

                                                    Captain & Adjutant.
                                                 1/3rd London Regiment.

MESS CART.   The mess cart will call at officers billets at 4.30pm this afternoon, and everything must be ready for loading by that time.

Copy No. 1 to Commanding Officer.
      " 2 " Major D.W.Beresford.
      " 3 " O.C.No.1 Coy.   Copy No. 5 to Lt.Davis & Q.M.
      " 4 " O.C.No.2 Coy.   6 " Medical Officer.
                                                                        7 " Capt. Page.
                                                                        8 " File.

Copy No. 8

OPERATION ORDERS NO. 30,
by
Lieut-Col. A. Anthony Howell, C.M.G.
Commanding 1/3rd Battalion, The London Regt.

Reference Maps :-
1/40000 sheet 36 & 36A.
Trench-Map.

Sept. 17th 15.

(1) **RELIEF.**
    The battalion will be relieved on the night of the 18/19th inst: No. 1 Coy. by the 2/2nd Gurkhas and No. 2 Coy. by the 1/4th Seaforths.
    One platoon of the 2/8th G.R. and party of the Brigade Grenade Coy. will accompany No. 2 Coy. and rejoin their unit at billets.

(2) **ROUTES.**
    On relief, companies will march independently to billets at L.26.c.4.7. and L.27.b. observing the following route :-
    ROUGE CROIX - G.31.c. - LA GORGUE.

(3) **DEPARTURE.**
    On relief, companies will depart by LAFONE TRENCH, reporting "RELIEF COMPLETE" to Battalion Hdqrs. on route.

(4) **DRESS.**
    Dress will be Marching Order, great coats in and waterproof sheets on top of, valises.

(5) **TOOLS.**
    Tools and waterbottles will be stacked at Battalion Hdqrs. by 7.0pm. No. 1 Coy will bring out three VERMOREL SPRAYERS with them.

(6) **STORES.**
    Officers to take over stores will arrive during the day. Only Permanent Trench stores will be handed over on relief. Lists in duplicate will be made out by O. C. Coys. and receipts obtained when stores have been handed over. These receipts will be sent to Battalion Hdqrs. as soon as possible.

(7) **SANITATION.**
    The trenches are to be left scrupulously clean, and latrine tins are to be cleaned, NOT buried.

(8) **SIGNALLERS.**
    Signallers will hand over to relieving unit, leaving one man per station, until the Commanding Officer leave the trenches.

(9) **BATTALION HEADQUARTERS.**
    Battalion Headquarters will be established at L.26.c.5.9.

Captain & Adjt.
1/3rd London Regiment.

OFFICERS MESS CART. This cart will be at PONT DU HEM corner at 3.30pm tomorrow, the 18th inst.

HEADQUARTERS PARTY. This party will leave the trenches at 3.0pm, 18th inst.

Copies to :-
No. 1. Commanding Officer.   No. 5. Medical Officer.
    2. Major Beresford.   6. Capt. Page.
    3. O.C. No. 1 Coy.   7. Transport Offr & Q.M
    4. O.C. No. 2 Coy.   8. File.

Copy No. 8

OPERATION ORDERS NO. 31
by
Lieut-Col. A. Anthony Howell, C.M.G.
Commanding 1/3rd Battalion, The London Regiment.

Reference Map :-
Trench Map.

CHELTENHAM ROAD,
Sept. 24. 1915.

(1) **INFORMATION**.

The First Army is resuming the offensive. Indian Corps will -
(a) Attack enemy's line between SUNKEN and WINCHESTER ROADS and establish our line along MAUQUISSART - DUCKS BILL road.
(b) Press on with its left in front, until its left gains the high ground between HAUT POMMEREAU and LA CLIQUETERIE FERME.
(c) Continue its advance from there in a South Easterly direction. The Garhwal Brigade and Bareilly Brigade will carry out the assault with the Dehra Dun Brigade in Divisional Reserve.

The assault will be preceded by -
(1) 4 days deliberate bombardment by artillery and trench mortars; rifle, rifle grenade and machine gun fire being employed to prevent the enemy repairing the damage done to his obstacles and defences by this bombardment.
(2) The explosion of a mine under the enemy's parapet at M.30.a.3.4. to take place two minutes before the gas and smoke attack commences.
(3) A gas and smoke attack immediately before the assault.
(4) Formation of thick smoke barrages on each flank of the assaulting troops.

The immediate objective of the assault is the general line of the road from M.30.a.3.4. to M.30.c.7.8 and thence due North and thence due North to the enemy's front parapet at M.30.a.7.6. and is to include the capture of all enemy's front and supporting lines.

The 19th and LAHORE divisions will hold the front of the INDIAN CORPS less that allotted to the assaulting Brigades. The 20th and LAHORE divisions will cover the flanks of the attack by fire and will advance and maintain touch with the MEERUT Division, when the latter advances beyond the enemy's front and supporting line trenches. The dividing line between the assaulting Brigades runs from centre of salient M.30.c.9.4. on a true bearing of ~~~~~~~~~~~~~~~~~~~~ (magnetic bearing 112 degrees) and passes between two solitary dead trees. They are about 4 feet apart and about 190 yards from our trenches. The line is also marked by sandbags for a few yards from our trenches.

98 degrees 26 minutes (3M.24)

(2) **INTENTION**.

(a) The Garhwal Brigade is to capture that part of the enemy's line between M.30.a.3.4. and the dividing line (vide ma). The troops are not to delay in the enemy's front line trenches but will push on and capture the supporting lines. They will not halt if portions of the line are held up but will push on towards their objective. Should the enemy's opposition be unshaken they will consolidate the position gained, pushing forward covering parties and patrols. All trenches on the right flank or forward will be double blocked and vigorous bomb attacks continued along them to maintain touch with the enemy and to find out whether he shows any sign of weakening. Should the enemy's opposition be slight the subsequent advance will be on HAUTE POMMEREAU and LA CLIQUETERIE FARM.

(b) 3rd Londons will hold the front line from SUNKEN STREET exclusive to SUNKEN ROAD inclusive and DUCKS BILL.

On the German front line being captured the 3rd London Regt. will at once continue and occupy trench along North side of the MAUQUISSART ROAD from the DUCKS BILL to the German trench, still holding the DUCKS BILL and its neck.

CONTINUED.   2.

(3) DISTRIBUTION.

No. 1 Coy.   Hold Front Line from SUNKEN STREET exclusive
Major F.D.Samuel.   to field gun emplacement.
                          3 platoons in front line.
                          1 platoon in support at extreme right of
                          company front.

No. 2 Coy.   Hold front line from field gun emplacement
Capt. A.J.Agius.   to SUNKEN ROAD exclusive and DUCKS BILL
                          and NECK.
                          1 platoon DUCKS BILL.
                          1   "   NECK.
                          1   "   from SUNKEN ROAD exclusive to field
                          gun emplacement.
                          1 platoon in earthwork leading to right
                          listening post.

(4) BATTALION BOMBERS.
    (Lieut. Garrard)
        Distribution as follows :-

            Half at base of DUCKS BILL & NECK.
            And Half - Half way down NECK.

        Battalion bombs will be carried in boxes.

(5) ACTION IN CASE OF GERMAN MINING.
        In case of a mine being blown up on our battalion front,
the crater is to be occupied at once and consolidated by No. 2 Coy.

(6) PROGRAMME OF ASSAULT.
        The approximate programme of assault is as follows. This is
liable to alteration:-

Time.
 . 3.   Explosion of a mine (BAREILLY front.)

 0.   Daylight rocket signal sent up from Report Centre, BAREILLY
         Bde. to give the time to gas and candle men not provided
         with watches.
         Commencement of gas.
         Artillery commences bombardment of enemy's fire trenches.

 0. 5.   Smoke screen on flanks begins. Smoke screen begins from
         emplacements from which no gas is being emitted.

 0. 6.   Smoke along entire front.

 0. 8.   Gas cut off. Infantry fill up actual bays of fire trench.

 0. 9.   Infantry cross parapet and form up. Artillery lifts 100 yds.

 0.10.   Assault commences.

 0.11.   Artillery lifts 100 yards.

 0.14.   Artillery lifts to German second position.

 0.15.   Smoke screen on flanks finishes but has now to disperse.

        All timings on the day of assault are from zero which will be
the hour at which the gas attack commences. Zero will be marked by
the simultaneous discharge of a bunch of red, blue and yellow daylight
rockets from a point close to Bareilly Bde Report Centre.
        Assaulting battalions will cross our parapet in front of our fire: 9 hours
counting from zero, and will form up

P.T.O.

CONTINUED.   3.

They will advance to the assault of the enemy's front trenches at
.19. hours.

NOTE.   SMOKE ON RIGHT AND LEFT FLANKS IS HARMLESS.

(7) DRESS.
Packs will NOT be carried.   Haversacks and ground sheets on
back, mess tin on belt.   Care must be taken to see that every man
has his iron ration.   Waterbottles to be filled.
All ranks will wear BALACLAVA CAPS and NOT ordinary caps.
On the day of the assault, 10 minutes before the emission of gas
they will wear the tube smoke helmet rolled up and so arranged as
to be able to be pulled down into position over the head and face
at a moments notice. *Tube helmets will also be carried by all
ranks in the usual way.*

(8) AMMUNITION.
300 rounds of S.A.A. is to be carried on the man.

(9) DEPOTS OF S.A.A & GRENADES.

In front line:- near heads of SUNKEN & SOUTH TILLELOY STREETS &
at salient N.30.C.9.4.

                        15 boxes S.A.A.   )
                       160 hand grenades.   ) In each.
                       1 box VERY pistol   )
                       1 " illuminating pistol)

LAFONE POST.)   100 boxes S.A.A.   )
COLVIN POST.)   500 hand grenades.   ) In each.
                 120 rifle grenades.)

Junction of)   350 boxes S.A.A.
LAFONE ST. &)   300 rounds Very pistol ammn.
Rue TILLELOY)

M.29.C.9.C.   )
where tramline)   1000 hand grenades.
crosses Rue   )
TILLELOY.   )

The above are marked by notice boards and direction arrows have
been erected in front line to point out the way to nearest ammunition
or hand grenade depot.
THE POSITION OF THESE DUG OUTS ARE TO BE EXPLAINED TO ALL RANKS,
and company commanders should satisfy themselves that these places
are known to the men of their Coy.

(10) PRISONERS.
Prisoners will be escorted to RUE BACQUEROT via MIN STREET and
handed over to 4th Cavalry when escort will return immediately to
its unit. Prisoners to be searched immediately for documents and
other articles as soon as possible after being captured. These must
accompany prisoners and be handed over with them.
Prisoners taken by the 3rd Londons will be handed over to the
Carnwal Rifles who will be in the original front line.

(11) DISTINGUISHING FLAGS.
Distinguishing flags will be carried to assist in showing
locations reached by our own troops. There will be two with each
grenade party and 10 per battalion. A coloured diagram of flags
used by our and other units is attached.

                                                                           P.T.O.

CONTINUED. 4.

(12) SALLY PORTS.
Sally Ports are not to be used between 0.0. hours and 0.20 hours on the day of assault.

(13) VERMOREL SPRAYERS.
The battalion will carry three VERMOREL sprayers and two refils.

(14) TRENCH TRAFFIC.
Traffic in long communication trenches must move in accordance with direction arrows.
The following are "UP":-
    SUNKEN STREET.
    SOUTH TILLELOY ST.
    COLVIN STREET.

The following are "DOWN":-
    EBENEZER STREET.
    LAPONE STREET.
    S. MOATED GRANGE STREET.
    MOATED GRANGE STREET.

Traffic rules may be broken for urgent tactical reasons ONLY.

(15) MEDICAL.
The regimental Aid Post is installed in LAPONE STREET.

(16) TIME.
ZERO will be notified secretly to all Officers later.

(17) SIGNALS.
Each assaulting Brigade will have 50 daylight rockets and a proportion of mortars for firing them.

    GARHWAL BDE..........RED.
    BAREILLY BDE.........BLUE.

They will be used in bunches or several one after another, so that they cannot be mistaken for German signals and will signify that the infantry is making a further advance.
The number, if any, allotted to battalions will be notified later.

The following signals are also in use by night throughout the INDIAN CORPS:-

(a) "ENEMY INFANTRY ATTACKING." Green rocket followed immediately by a white rocket sent up from vicinity of point attacked and repeated after half minute intervals.

(b) "HEAVY ARTILLERY OR TRENCH MORTAR BOMBARDMENT OF OUR TRENCHES." Green rocket followed immediately by a red rocket sent up and repeated in similar manner.

(c) "OUR SHELLS FALLING SHORT, LENGTHEN THE RANGE." Two red rockets sent up and repeated in similar manner.

These signals are to be considered as supplementary to and not in substitution of other means of communication such as telephone.

(18) REPORT CENTRE.
               Junction of
Battalion Hdqrs. will be established at/SUNKEN STREET and new Support line.

                [signature]
                Captain & Adjt.
                1/3rd London Regiment.

COPIES TO:- No.1 to O.C.No.1 Coy.
    2 " O.C.No.2 "
    3 " Cmdg.Officer.
    4 " Major Beresford.
    5 " File.

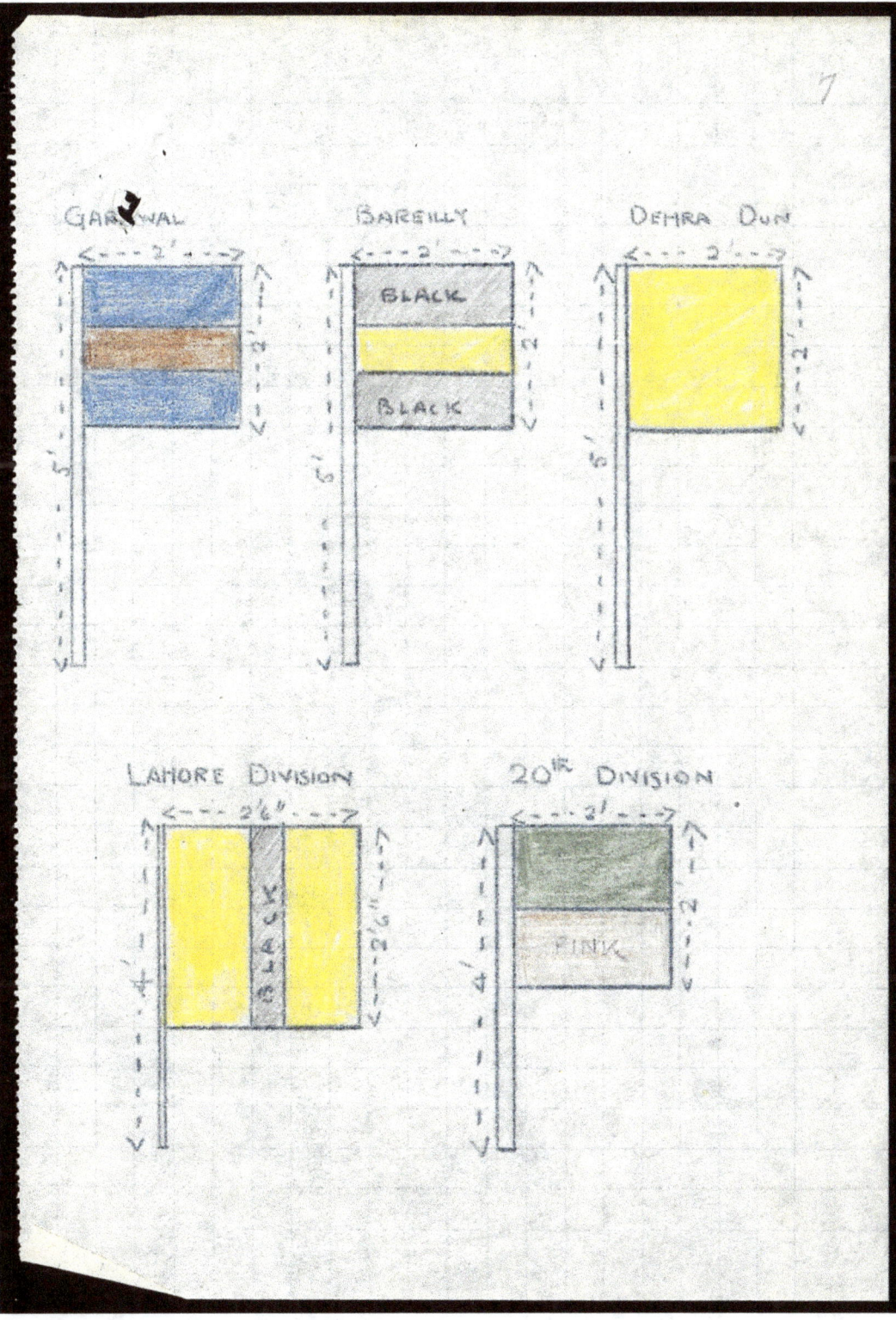

Copy No. 8

OPERATION ORDERS NO.32
by
Lieut-Col. A. Anthony Howell, C.M.G.
Commanding 1/3rd Battalion, The London Regiment.

Ref. Maps:— Sept. 23rd 15.
1/40000. sheets 36 A 36A.

(1) **PARADE.**
The battalion will parade on the ALARM POST at 6.0pm this evening ready to move off, destination being M.29.c.d.7.

(2) **ROUTE.**
The battalion will march via POT ROCHON — RIEZ BAILLEUL.

(3) **DRESS.**
Dress for parade will be Full Marching Order, greatcoats in and waterproof sheets on top of, valises.

(4) **AMMUNITION.**
200 rounds of S.A.A. per man will be carried.

(5) **OFFICERS' VALISES.**
All Officers' valises are to be at the Q. M. Stores by 5.0pm today.

(6) **WATER.**
All ranks will parade with filled waterbottles.

(7) **STATE OF READINESS.**
After 6.0pm, 24th inst. the state of readiness will be "IMMEDIATE."

Captain & Adjt.
1/3rd London Regiment.

MESS CART.
The Officers Mess cart will call at Officers billets at 5.0pm today, and all mess kit must be ready by that time.

Copies to :-
    No. 1 to Commanding Officer.
     " 2 " Major Beresford.
     " 3 " O. C. No. 1 Coy.
     " 4 " O. C. No. 2 Coy.
     " 5 " Medical Officer.
     " 6 " Capt. Page.
     " 7 " Lt. Davis & Q.M.
     " 8 " File.

Copy No. 8....

OPERATION ORDERS NO. 33
by
Lieut-Col. A. Anthony Morell, C.M.G.
Comdg. 1/3rd Battalion, The London Regiment.

BOUT DE VILLE,
Sept. 30th 15.

(1) PARADE.

The battalion will parade on the ADAM POST at 1.30pm today to march to new billets near CALONNE.

(2) DRESS.

Dress for parade will be full marching order, greet coats in and waterproof sheets on top of valises.

(3) BAGGAGE.

Baggage wagons will call at Company Headquarters at 11.0am this morning, and all Officers' valises and blankets must be ready for loading up by that time.

(4) BILLETS.

All billets must be left scrupulously clean.

(5) MESS CART.

The Officers mess cart will call at billets at 12.45pm, and mess kit must be ready packed by that time.

Captain & Adjt.
1/3rd London Regiment.

Copies :-
No. 1 to Commanding Officer.
2. Major F.D. Samuel.
3. O.C. No. 1 Coy.
4. O.C. No. 2 "
5. Medical Officer.
6. Capt. Page.
7. Q.M. & Lt. Davis.
8. File.

3 London
October
1915

(6202) W 11186/M1151 350,000 12/16 McA. & W., Ltd. (Est. 781) Forms/W 3091/3.   Army Form W. 3091.

Cover for Documents.

Nature of Enclosures.

Notes, or Letters written.

Volume No. _____

BRITISH SALONIKA FORCE

WAR DIARY.

26th DIVISION

Vol. No.	Unit	PERIOD	
		From	To
17	77th Trench Mortar Battery	1/3/18	31/3/18
15	78th do	do	do
15	79th do	do	do

Serial No 197.

Confidential
131/7601
War Diary

of

1/3rd London Regiment

Tokk St. 6-11-15

FROM 1st October 1915. TO 31st October 1915.

Army Form C. 2118.

WAR DIARY
or
INTELLIGENCE SUMMARY.
(Erase heading not required.)

Instructions regarding War Diaries and Intelligence Summaries are contained in F.S. Regs., Part II. and the Staff Manual respectively. Title pages will be prepared in manuscript.

Place	Date	Hour	Summary of Events and Information	Remarks and references to Appendices
L'Epinette.	1915. Oct. 1st.	8.30am.	Battalion parade on the Alarm Post. Coys. on route march of one hours duration from 3.0pm to 4.0pm.	
	2nd.	8.15am.	Church Parade. Holy Communion 10.0am. Companies on one hours route march from 3.0 to 4.0pm. Major P.W.Beresford rejoined unit, having been gassed.	
	3rd	12.30pm.	Battalion parade on Alarm Post ready to march to new billets at LOISNE, via PARADIS, LOCON and LE HAMEL. Meerut Division to take over new front from LA BASSEE canal to ORKNEY ROAD with two Brigades in Front Line and one in Reserve. Garhwal Bde (of which we form part) to be in Brigade Reserve. Battalion is on 45 mins. notice whilst at LOISNE.	
LOISNE	4th.	1.0am.	Great activity on our front, but this did not necessitate us moving up.	
	6th.		2nd Lieuts. Carnegie.J.W.P. and Thomas.W.S. joined unit as reinforcements. Companies on route marches from 11.0am to 12 noon and 3.0pm to 4.0pm.	
	7th.		Companies on route marches as yesterday.	
	8th.	6.0pm.	Heavy enemy bombardment and attack on our front. We received orders to "stand to" although did not move up.	
	9th.	3.0am. 6.0pm.	Situation now normal and orders received to "stand down". Cinema Show in No. 1 Coys. billet. Good attendance. P.T.O.	

T2134. Wt. W708—776. 500000. 4/15. Sir J.C.&S.

Army Form C. 2118.

WAR DIARY
or
INTELLIGENCE SUMMARY.
(Erase heading not required.)

Instructions regarding War Diaries and Intelligence Summaries are contained in F.S. Regs., Part II. and the Staff Manual respectively. Title pages will be prepared in manuscript.

2. contd.

Place	Date	Hour	Summary of Events and Information	Remarks and references to Appendices
LOISNE.	Oct. 10th.	11.0am.	Church Parade. Holy Communion 11.45am.	
	11th.	11.0am.	Battalion to parade on the Alarm Post to march to trenches, joining up with 2nd Leicesters at GORRE chateau. Under the Command of O.C. Leicesters whilst in the trenches. We are relieving the 2nd & 4th Black Watch, Bareilly Bde. 1st Aid Post established at WINDY CORNER (Sq. A.8.c.2.8. 1/40000 Bethune Sheet) 1st Line Transport and Hdqrs. will move to GORRE (Sq. F.4.b.0.3) Cmdg. Officer granted 16 days leave. Major P.W.Beresford in command.	
GORRE	13th.	10.30am.	Ordered to "Stand To" as operations were to take place on our front. Everything again Normal by 6.0pm.	
		4.0pm.	Draft of 57 other ranks arrived from Merville. All these men originally landed in France with the battalion from Malta, but had gone away sick or wounded in the meantime. Casualties today:- 2nd Lt.H.Lloyd wounded. One O.R. killed and 3,0.Rs wounded	
	14th.		Capt.R.D.Sutcliffe (Adjt) granted 7 days leave. One other rank wounded today.	
	15th.	2.0pm.	Our companies will be relieved in the front line by 2nd Leicesters and take over the following seven redoubts:-	
			No.2 Coy. SPOIL BANK. Capt.Agius & 40 O.R.S. ORCHARD FARM. Lt. Lewis & 30 " MAIRIE. Lt. E.A.Lloyd 40 "	
			No.1 Coy. HILDER. 2ndLt.Abbott. & 25 O.R.S. MOATED FARM. " Morley. & 15 " POPPY. " Ochs. & 15 " HERTS. Capt. Newson & 30 "	

Army Form C. 2118.

WAR DIARY
or
INTELLIGENCE SUMMARY.
(Erase heading not required.)

Instructions regarding War Diaries and Intelligence Summaries are contained in F. S. Regs., Part II. and the Staff Manual respectively. Title pages will be prepared in manuscript.

Place	Date	Hour	Summary of Events and Information	Remarks and references to Appendices
GORRE.	Oct. 15th.		One Machine Gunner killed in action.	
	16th.		Leave for other ranks re-opened at the rate of one per day	
	17th.	11.0am.	Morning service. Holy Communion 11.45 am.	
	19th.		Garhwal Bde. relieved by the 85th Bde. 28th Div. On relief detachments from various posts will march back to old billets in LOISNE.	
	20th.	11.0am.	Battalion paraded and marched off to garrison the following 15 posts in the forward area, Battalion Hdqrs. being established at farm Sq. S.7.d.4.4., 1/40000 Bethune sheet, and 1st Line Depot in LA COUTURE.	
			No.1 Company. No.2 Company.	
			Richebourg Post. Chocolate Post.	
			Hunter Post. Dead Cow Post.	
			Scott Post. Cats Post.	
			Dogs Post. Factory.	
			Path Post. Pall Mall Post.	
			"Z"Orchard Post Fallen Tree Post.	
			Haystack Post. Waters Post.	
			Albert Post.	
RICHEBOURG	21st		2nd Lts. Corden.G.S. and Herapeth.P.W. joined unit as reinforcements.	
	23rd		Adjutant returned off leave.	
	24th to 29th.		Weather very wet, making the redoubts very muddy and uncomfortable for the troops.	

Army Form C. 2118.

Contd. 4.

WAR DIARY
or
INTELLIGENCE SUMMARY.
(Erase heading not required.)

Instructions regarding War Diaries and Intelligence Summaries are contained in F. S. Regs., Part II. and the Staff Manual respectively. Title pages will be prepared in manuscript.

Place	Date	Hour	Summary of Events and Information	Remarks and references to Appendices
RICHEBOURG St. Vaast.	30th.	10.0am.	Major F.D.Samuels and Lieut.E.N.Wilcox proceed to England on seven days leave.	
	31st.		Morning Service at LA COUTURE (1st Line Depot) 9.15am and celebration of Holy Communion at same place 9.50am. Draft of 30 other ranks joining the battalion today, arriving at MERVILLE at 2.0pm. These consist of sick and wounded returned to duty.	
			Weather continues most inclement.	

A.Pulletts

Captain & Adjt.
1/3rd London Regiment.

B.E.Force. France.
Oct. 31st 15.

Copy No...8.

OPERATION ORDERS NO. 34.
by
Lieut-Col. A. Anthony Howell, C.M.G.
Cmdg. 1/3rd Battalion, The London Regiment.

Reference Map :-
1/40000 Bethune Sheet.

L'EPINETTE,
Oct. 2nd 15.

(1) **FRONT.**
The Meerut Division is to hold the front from LA BASSEE Canal to ORMSBY ROAD, with two Brigades in Front Line and one in reserve.

(2) **MOVE.**
The Garhwal Brigade (in reserve) will march to billets in LE HAMEL on October 3rd 1915.

(3) **ROUTE.**
The battalion will march via PARADIS - Road junctions R.25.c, 31.a, 32.c, X.7.a, X.8.c, bridge X.15.d.

(4) **PARADE.**
The battalion will parade on the ALARM POST at 12.30pm the 3rd inst.
Transport will march in rear of the battalion.

(5) **DRESS.**
Dress for parade will be full marching order, ~~great coats in and waterproof sheets on top of, valises.~~

(6) **AMMUNITION.**
120 rounds of S.A.A. per man will be carried.

(7) **BAGGAGE.**
Wagons will call at company billets at 9.00am to pick up blankets and waterproof sheets.
Officers valises will be collected at 10.00am.

(8) **OFFICERS MESS CART.**
The mess cart will call at Officers billets at 12.noon.

(9) **RATIONS.**
Rations will be issued at LE HAMEL on the 3rd inst.

Captain & Adjt.
1/3rd London Regiment.

Copies to :-
- No. 1 to Commanding Officer.
- 2   Major Samuel.
- 3   O.C. No.1 Coy.
- 4   O.C. No.2 Coy.
- 5   Medical Officer.
- 6   Capt. Page.
- 7   Q.M. and Transport Officer.
- 8   File.

Copy...2...

OPERATION ORDERS No. 35.
by
Lieut-Col. A. Anthony Howell, C.M.G.
Cmdg. 1/3rd Battalion, The London Regiment.

Reference Maps :-
1/40000 Bethune Sheet.
1/10000 Trench Map.

LOISNE,
Oct. 10th 16.

(1) **PARADE.**
The battalion will parade on the ALARM POST at 11.0am tomorrow (11th inst) and march to GORE Chateau, where they will join the 2nd Leicesters.

(2) **ORDER OF MARCH.**
The following is the order of march :-
- 1 platoon of No.1 Coy.
- 2 platoons No.2 Coy.
- 1 platoon No.1 Coy.
- 2 platoons No.1 Coy.
- 2 platoons No.2 Coy.

(3) **BAGGAGE.**
The baggage wagons will call at Coy. Hdqrs. to collect officers valises and blankets at 9.0am, which must be ready by that time.

(4) **AMMUNITION.**
120 rounds of S.A.A. per man is to be carried. This will be made up first thing tomorrow morning.

(5) **HAND GRENADES.**
All hand grenades on charge of the battalion will be taken up and kept in Battalion Reserve.

(6) **FIRST AID POST.**
The Aid Post will be established at WINDY CORNER (A.8.c.2e).

(7) **MESS CART.**
The Officers Mess cart will call at billets at 9.30am, and all mess kit must be ready by that time.
The Mess cart will not come up from the 1st Line Transport until the evening.

Captain & Adjutant.
1/3rd London Regiment.

Copies to :-
- No. 1 to C. O.
- 2 Major Beresford.
- 3 " Samuel.
- 4 O.C. No. 1 Coy.
- 5 O.C. No. 2 "
- 6 Coy.S.M. No. 1 Coy.
- 7 " No. 2 "
- 8 Quartermaster.
- 9 Transport Officer.
- 10. Medical Officer.
- 11. Capt. Page.
- 12. File.

Copy No ..8......

OPERATION ORDERS NO 36
by
MAJOR P.W. BERESFORD
Cmdg. 1/3rd London Regiment.

G O R R E,
Octr. 15th, 1915.

Reference Map
1/10,000 Trench Map.

(1) RELIEFS.

The 3rd London Regt. will be relieved by the 2nd Leicesters in the Front Line about 2.9pm. today (15th inst.).

(2) INTENTION.

On Relief Coys. will garrison Posts as follows :-

No. 2 Coy.
(SPOIL BANK   Captain Agius and 40 O.Ranks.
(ORCHARD FARM 2/Lt. Lewis and 30 O. Ranks. 2nd Lt Lewis
(MAIRIE   Lieut. E.A. Lloyd and 40 O. Ranks.

No. 1 Coy.
(HEDER POST   1 Officer and 25 O. Ranks.   2nd Lt A.L. Abbott
(HOATED FARM   1 Officer and 15 O. Ranks.   2nd Lt Cromonly
(POPPY   1 Officer and 10 O. Ranks   (2nd Lt FOCHS.)
(HERTS   Officer and 50 O.Ranks.   Capt Newman

Distribution of Officers for these posts(No. 1 Coy.) is left to discretion of Coy. Commanders.

(3) DRAFT.

The numbers necessary to complete Garrisons will be sent up first thing in the morning from the 1st Line Transport.

(4) DEPARTURE.

On relief detachments will leave via HALFMOON STREET.

(5) STORES.

Coy. Commanders will make their own arrangements to take over Stores at Posts.

(6) WATER TINS.

O.C. Coys. will arrange to bring out with them all Water receptacles on charge of the Battalion.

Major
for Captain & Adjutant.
1/3rd London Regt. (T.F.)

COPIES TO:-
No. 1 to O. C. No. 1 Coy.
 " 2 " O. C. No. 2 Coy.
 " 3 " O. C. No. 3 Coy.
 " 4 " M. O.
 " 5 " Capt. Pegg.
 " 6 " Q.Mr. & Transport Officer.
 " 7 " Adjutant.
 " 8 " File.

1/3rd London Regiment.

NOTES FOR OFFICERS COMMANDING POSTS.

(1) DEFENCE OF POSTS.

Each post is to be put into a state of complete defence all round. Wire entanglements to be used ad lib.
A doorway of wire is to be constructed to block approaches in case of emergency. If possible, beyond bombing distance.

(2) WORK IN POSTS.

Dug outs are to be made or improved to accommodate the garrison. Separate stores are to be provided -

    (a) For food.
    (b) For ammunition.

These stores are not to be lived in by the men of the garrison.
There must be a thorough cleaning up all round posts immediately. Tins and other rubbish are to be buried. Tins outside parapets give the position away.

(3) ROUTINE.

(a) All garrisons will "stand to" twice every day. Every man must be acquainted with his exact post and make himself a fire position there. Two men to be told off to block approaches.

(b) By order of the G.O.C. garrisons of posts are not available for working parties outside their post without express sanction from the Brigade Office.

(c) Machine Gun detachments are under the command of O.C. posts.

These orders are additional to Standing Orders of posts and any special orders from Officer Commanding Sub-Section.

Major for O.C.
1/3rd London Regiment.

FRANCE.
Oct. 15th 15.

TO :- Posts as below: 16/10/'15.

Gool Bank, Orchard Farm, Maine.
Hilder, Moated Farm, Poppy, Hants.

OPERATION ORDERS No. 37.   Copy No. 11
by
Major P. W. Beresford,
Commanding 1/3rd Battalion, The London Regiment

GORRE. Oct. 12th 15.

(1) **INTENTION.**

The Garhwal Brigade will be relieved on the 12th inst by the 85th Brigade, and garrisons of Posts will be relieved under the orders of Sub-Section Commanders.

On relief, detachments will march independently to billets at LOISNE.

(2) **TRENCH STORES.**

Officers in charge of Posts will render to their Sub-Section Commanders receipted lists of trench stores handed over on relief. This is most important and there must be no failure.

(3) **BOMBS.**

Any bombs in posts which are on battalion charge, must be brought out on relief. A limber is being sent up for these. See below.

(4) **OFFICERS MESS CART.**

The Officers' Mess cart and limber for battalion bombs will be at WESTMINSTER BRIDGE at 9.30am tomorrow morning, 13th inst.

(5) **MEDICAL CART.**

The Medical Cart will be at WINDY CORNER at 9.30am.

(6) **OFFICERS RIDING HORSES.**

Owing to the short distance to march, these horses will not be sent up.

Major.
1/3rd London Regiment.

Copy No. 1. to O.C. Spoil Bank.
2. O.C. Orchard Farm.
3. O.C. Mairie.
4. O.C. Hilder.
5. O.C. Moated Farm.
6. O.C. Poppy.
7. O.C. Herts.
8. Medical Officer.
9. Quartermaster.
10. Transport Officer.
11. File.

WO/95/3945/1-2

2 Battalion Leicestershire Regiment

7 (IND) DIV

20 BDE

Meerut Division Garhwal Brigade
2n Bn. Leicesters
Jan — Nov 1915

1914 Aug — 1915 Nov

To MESNOT

7 (IND) DIV
28 BDE

121/2743

War Diary
of
2nd Bn. Leicester Regiment
From 9.8.14.
To 2-12-14
Volume I
pp 1 to 26

Original

War Diary
Leicestershire Regt.

Period – 9° August 14 to 2nd Dec 1914
(26 sheets)

9.8.1914
2.12.1915

Meerut Division Aug - Dec 1914

2nd Bn Leicester Regt.

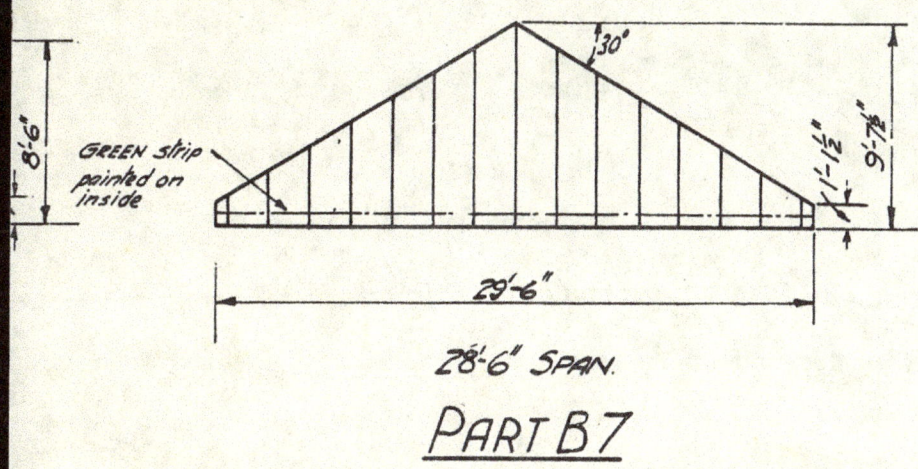

28'-6" SPAN.

PART B7

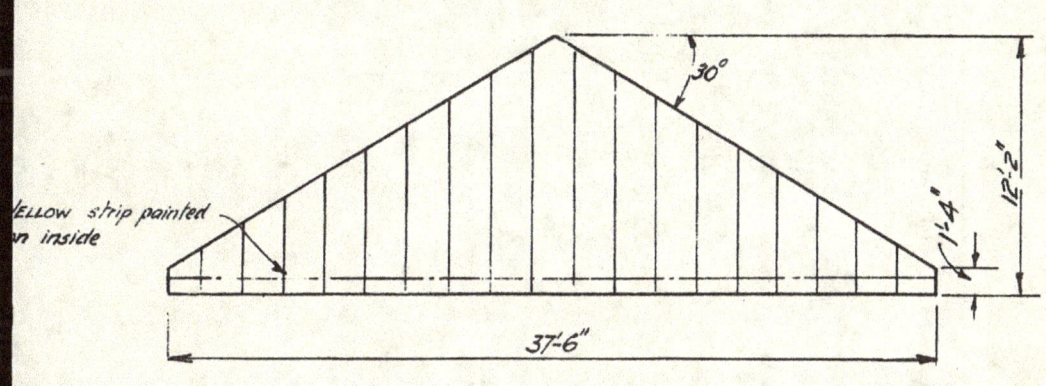

36'-6" SPAN

PART B8

SETS OF EXTERNAL GABLE SHEETING

WHEN FIXED

fixed they conform to the dimensions shown.
be clearly marked by means of a 6" coloured
indicated
× 24 gauge, & to be laid with single side laps.

AMENDED 19-10-38.

SHEETS.   DRAWING No. H. 356/37

Army Form C. 2118.

WAR DIARY
of
2nd Bn. Leicestershire Regt.
INTELLIGENCE SUMMARY.
(Volume I)
(Erase heading not required.)

From:- 9th August 1914 To:-

Hour, Date, Place.	Summary of Events and Information.	Remarks and references to Appendices
11 a.m. Ranikhet 9-8-14.	Orders from Brigade Major Bareilly Bde No. 34 & 5/7(N) issued "Mobilizing 7th War Division" Batt'n Orders ordering Mobilization published same day. Batt'n to form part of 20th Brigade. O.C. "C" Coy Delhi warned. Batt'n medically inspected. Bayonets being sharpened, boots being repaired	F.
Ranikhet 10-5-14	No. Q. 7th Divn instruct "C" Coy Delhi to be relieved by detach 3rd K.R.R. from Meerut. A.Q.S 7th Divn orders Batt'n to move to Bareilly without delay. Bde Major instructs that Govt issue Government of 10% proceed with Batt'n.	F.
Ranikhet 11-8-14	G.M.G. in India directs that troops mobilizing will take winter scale clothing with one blanket. A.G. wires - "All Officers on leave in India to be recalled." Batt'n completed at Ranikhet ready for quitting station.	F.
Ranikhet 12-8-14	Batt'n left Ranikhet and arrived Ratighat - 21 miles.	F.
13-5-14	Arrived Bhowali - 9 miles uphill.	F.

Army Form C. 2118.

WAR DIARY
or
INTELLIGENCE SUMMARY.
(Erase heading not required.)

Instructions regarding War Diaries and Intelligence Summaries are contained in F. S. Regs., Part II, and the Staff Manual respectively. Title pages will be prepared in manuscript.

Hour, Date, Place.	Summary of Events and Information.	Remarks and references to Appendices
14-8-14 Bareilly	Arrived JEOLIKOTE - 9 miles	72.
15-8-14	Arrived KATHGODAM - 13 miles. Entrained and arrived BAREILLY in two trains, 5 p.m. & 6 p.m. Marched to SOUTH CAMP. First issue of Ordnance, Accounts & Railway manuals received.	72.
16-8-14 BAREILLY	Medical Inspection of men rejoining from detached Employments. Web Equipment brought from Station.	72.
17-8-14 BAREILLY.	Mobilization progressing. The following articles not arrived hose. Component parts Machine Gun 2, 2 mules, frogs 2 pouches, web equipment, Balaklava Caps, mittens, warm coats, waterproof sheets, spare boots. Repeated Telegrams sent to Clothing, Ordnance, 2 Remounts.	72.
18-8-14 BAREILLY	Mobilization progressing. Should be ready but following not yet received. 258 pouches for web equipment. All Balaklava Caps & mitts. 160 prs Spare boots. 116 British Warms, 89 Waterproof Sheets, Component parts M. Guns. Medical Officer not yet arrived. Can only now find 15 men excluding all Batmen to Field Service Strength.	72.

Army Form C. 2118.

Instructions regarding War Diaries and Intelligence Summaries are contained in F. S. Regs., Part II, and the Staff Manual respectively. Title pages will be prepared in manuscript.

WAR DIARY
or
~~INTELLIGENCE SUMMARY.~~

(Erase heading not required.)

Hour, Date, Place.	Summary of Events and Information.	Remarks and references to Appendices
BAREILLY 19-8-14	Mobilization progressing. Reinforcements reported yesterday not yet arrived. Medical Officer not yet joined. Can now find a draft 25 men for first reinforcement, thirteen of whom arrive from RANIKHET on twenty first.	72.
BAREILLY 20-8-14	Mobilization progressing. The following still wanted. All frogs. & 250 pouches expected 22nd inst. 160 prs boots. 166 Butial Warms. A few component parts M. Guns. Medical Officer arrives. 72.	72.
BAREILLY 21-8-14	Mobilization progressing. The following still wanted. All frogs & 250 pouches expected tonight. 160 prs Spare boots. Remainder yesterdays deficiencies completed.	72.
BAREILLY 22-8-14	Mobilization completed except that 160 prs Spare Boots still required. Frogs & all pouches just arrived.	72.
BAREILLY 23-8-14	Mobilization ready to move except that 160 prs Spare Boot still required.	72.
BAREILLY 24-8-14	Telegram from ADMINSTAFF 20th BRIGADE Nr. 40 S. "No orders yet for your move." Mobilization complete. Ready to move. Arsenal wires "Boots should be supplied regimentally." This hitherto could not possibly be arranged.	72.

(4.)

Army Form C. 2118.

WAR DIARY

of

INTELLIGENCE SUMMARY.

(Erase heading not required.)

Instructions regarding War Diaries and Intelligence Summaries are contained in F.S. Regs., Part II, and the Staff Manual respectively. Title pages will be prepared in manuscript.

Hour, Date, Place.	Summary of Events and Information.	Remarks and references to Appendices
BAREILLY 26.8.14	Inspection of all Mobilizing Units in BAREILLY by MAJOR-GENERAL F. MACBEAN, C.V.O., C.B.. Units paraded at full I.S. strength without transport. Marched past in column of route. On parade :— 4th Cavalry, 20th By. R.F.A. 2/Leic: Regt, 2/ The Black Watch, 41st Dogras.	72..
BAREILLY 29.8.14	Head Quarters 20th Brigade leaves LANSDOWNE on 30-8-14. Arrives at KARACHI 2nd September. Head Quarters 7th Division leaves MEERUT and Head Quarters 21st Brigade leaves BAREILLY on same date.	72.
BAREILLY 3.9.14	Telegram from CONTROL, SIMLA ordering Battalion to leave BAREILLY for KARACHI on 5-9-14.	72.
BAREILLY 5.9.14	Battalion entrained for KARACHI. one train. departed 8.5 am	72.
KARACHI 8.9.14	Arrived 11.29 am - Quartered in REST CAMP pending orders to entrain. Strength 9 Brn on Camp - Officers (including medical) 20. W.O. 2 (including Asst Surgeon) attatched 864.	72.
REST CAMP 11.9.14 KARACHI.	Battalion inspected by Major General Keary, C.B, DSO, Comdg 20th Infantry Brigade.	72.

Gulab Singh & Sons, Calcutta—No. 22 Army C.—5-8-14—1,07,000.

Army Form C. 2118.

WAR DIARY

or

~~INTELLIGENCE SUMMARY~~

2nd Bn Leicestershire Regiment
(Erase heading not required.)

Hour, Date, Place.	Summary of Events and Information.	Remarks and references to Appendices
10.0 A.M. 15th Sept 1914 Karachi	Battalion Head Quarters and 2 Companies (C & D) embarked on S.S. "DEVANHA". Strength = Officers 10. Other ranks 437.	F.
10.0 A.M. 16th Sept 1914 Karachi	Half Battalion (A & B Companies) embarked on S.S. "ELEPHANTA". Strength = Officers 9 (including Medical) Other ranks 417.	F.
17th Sept 1914	The Battalion, although it left its Peace station at 69 hours notice, and although all requisitions were despatched immediately to complete equipment and also returning the Battalion was 4 days marching to BAREILLY, it took exactly 5 weeks to get on board ship. The men in the meantime suffered considerably in their health. At Bareilly 2 companies were put under canvas and although the C.O. urged that buildings should be requisitioned, and although being available, in order to get the men under cover from the heat and wet, this was refused by the O.C. Bareilly. It was only by dint of repeated telegrams and memorandum that the requisitions were complied with both by the Arsenal and Clothing Factory. On the 22nd August the last requisition was complied with, so had it been necessary to embark the Battalion at once, it would have gone only partially equipped.	F.
21st Sept 1914	Sailed from KARACHI.	F.
4th October 1914	Arrived at PORT SAID.	F.
6th October 1914	Sailed from PORT SAID.	F.
12 October 1914	Disembarked at MARSEILLES, and march to Ln VALENTINE CAMP.	F.
3am 20 October 1914	Entrained for Orleans	F.
6am 21 October 1914	Arrived at ORLEANS & marched into Camp.	F.

Army Form C. 2118.

WAR DIARY
or
INTELLIGENCE SUMMARY.
2nd Bn. Leicestershire Regt
(Erase heading not required.)

Instructions regarding War Diaries and Intelligence Summaries are contained in F. S. Regs., Part II, and the Staff Manual respectively. Title pages will be prepared in manuscript.

Hour, Date, Place.	Summary of Events and Information.	Remarks and references to Appendices
26-10-14 ORLEANS 9.30 p.m.	Entrained for "X" arrived at LILLERS about 7 P.M. 27-10-14. Lay in town square the night of 27.28.	
28-10-14 LILLERS	7.0 a.m. Marched to CALLONNE arrived about 11. A.M. and billeted	
29-10-14	7.0 a.m. Marched from CALLONNE. In firing line (trenches) in relief of 3rd Worcestershire. Trenches very much unimproved.	
30-10-14	Battalion under heavy shell fire. Capt Trotman and 3 men killed, and 9 men wounded. Continued digging by enemy. Strengthening of trenches, etc. commenced.	
31-10-14	Situation unchanged. Heavy shell fire and continuous sniping. 1 man killed and 1 wounded	

Army Form C. 2118.

WAR DIARY
or
INTELLIGENCE SUMMARY.
2nd Gloucestershire Regt.
(Erase heading not required.)

Instructions regarding War Diaries and Intelligence Summaries are contained in F. S. Regs., Part II, and the Staff Manual respectively. Title pages will be prepared in manuscript.

Hour, Date, Place.	Summary of Events and Information.	Remarks and references to Appendices
1-11-14	Situation unchanged. Sniping continues but slightly from our Left. Lieut Lefroi and 8 men wounded.	
2-11-14	Situation unchanged. Continued Sniping. German trench 450 yards S.E. of farm now extends across the road. 1 Sergeant and 1 man wounded. (Morning Report.)	
3-11-14	Situation unchanged. Improvement of trenches etc. continued. Three (?) enemy shells blew down parapet in Batt= trenches (five feet). now repaired. Enemy continues working front day and night via their trenches. (One of enemy's them has trenches similar to Belgian type with emplacements from front (with Loot centre) in front with German arms underneath. Private Marelle wounded.	

Army Form C. 2118.

WAR DIARY

or

INTELLIGENCE SUMMARY

2nd Bn Wiltshire Regt

(Erase heading not required.)

Instructions regarding War Diaries and Intelligence Summaries are contained in F. S. Regs., Part II, and the Staff Manual respectively. Title pages will be prepared in manuscript.

Hour, Date, Place.	Summary of Events and Information.	Remarks and references to Appendices
3-11-14	(Evening Report) Snipers fairly active. Claim about 12 German casualties including one gentleman dressed in blue with black hat. Parapet breached in three places by enemy's high explosive.	—
4-11-14	(Morning Report) Situation generally normal. Left heavily sniped during night. Two men wounded. (Evening Report) Situation normal. Snipers fairly active, apparently enemy hold trenches lightly by day and occupy in force about 6-30 p.m. Also their artillery could occasionally shell the trenches at night where they are at work so as to interfere with it.	—

WAR DIARY
or
INTELLIGENCE SUMMARY.
2 Leicestershire Regt

Army Form C. 2118.

Hour, Date, Place.	Summary of Events and Information.	Remarks and references to Appendices
5-11-14	(Morning Report) Situation Normal. At 11.30 p.m. 4-11-14 enemy's searchlight was turned 150° + N of farm opposite my centre and which artillery deliberately shell. At 11-30 p.m. heavy vehicles reported moving across our front direction unknown. At 1-30 a.m. scouts reported about 100 Germans moving across our front from centre to right and crossing road running E about 500 yds from from just to S. of right of our own position. Improvement of trenches progressing. (Evening Report) Situation normal in front also held reserve in readiness on right owing to very heavy firing on that flank, but about which nothing can be ascertained.	
6-11-14.	(Morning Report) Situation normal. Enemy digging during night in their trenches in front of my left.	

WAR DIARY
or
INTELLIGENCE SUMMARY.

(Erase heading not required.)

Army Form C. 2118.

Hour, Date, Place.	Summary of Events and Information.	Remarks and references to Appendices
6 cont. 6-11-14. M.	We worked all night at new flanking trenches on our right, not yet complete. Sending in various articles taken from dead Germans that I here days ago. (5TH JAGER MAGDEBURG BATTALION.) Casualties 3 wounded.	
7-11-14. M.	Situation normal. Small parties were unable to make any head way last night against enemy's trenches, they appear to have more men in them than ever. About 6 men advanced against my left Coy but retired immediately losing three on R. flank, but not completed yet. Should we continue work on R. flank but not completed yet. Should like to have the same party of Sappers again to night & could they bring more wood supports for loopholes all wood is exhausted here.	
E.	Situation quiet. Enemy still working at trench S.E. of my right.	
M.	Two advances against "C" Coy by 50 to 100 enemy at 4.30 a.m. & 1.30 a.m. Work on R. flank continued, some help is given will be finished tomorrow. Wire entanglements erected. At 6.15 this morning when enemy opposite my section were not firing a while I had advance parties out in front our own artillery fired a its fire of our own artillery when the enemy made no sign of attack in the section. Fighting strength 15 & 665. Casualties 1 N.C.O. killed & 1 M.E.O. 9 men wounded.	

Army Form C. 2118.

WAR DIARY
— or —
INTELLIGENCE SUMMARY.

(Erase heading not required.)

Instructions regarding War Diaries and Intelligence Summaries are contained in F. S. Regs., Part II, and the Staff Manual respectively. Title pages will be prepared in manuscript.

Hour, Date, Place.	Summary of Events and Information.	Remarks and references to Appendices
6 – 11 – 14. E.	Situation normal. At 2.10 p.m. enemy shrapnel on left of our line burst correctly in enemy's trenches, though on extreme left range appeared 150ˣ over.	
9 – 11 – 14. M.	Situation normal. Working parties hard at work night trenches but still require lot of wire. Can saw at R. Flank. 3.S.15 & Sappers help tonight. Would like more wire for R. Flank. 3.S.15 & 6.y.5. Casualties: IMCo wanted 9.	
E.	Situation normal – Enemy fairly quiet.	
M.	Casualties: IMCo killed. 3.S.13 & 6.y7. (4 sick shown as last night). Scouts went out on R. Flank – diged to feel the enemy' new trenches. a few succeeded in going on W. out, but the whole were driven back by enemy's rifle & frontal fire. Parties of enemy about 12, covered by own M.G. fire tried to cut wire on our R. Flank but did not succeed. O. left flank scouts got within 100ˣ of enemy trenches but were driven back. This report suggests mines as of motor working – this latter is also heard on R. Flank trenches in R. Flank appear to be strongly held. Enemy particularly active in throwing bombs throughout the night is still continued. One bomb dropped in our trench. Appears to be directed at working party on new trench. W.lf farm – night ouths. Working all night on improvement. Wire, sandbags, pickets all wallets required.	
10 – 11 – 14 E.	Situation on usual. Nothing to report except that enemy's trench S.E. of my section is extending.	

Gulab Singh & Sons, Calcutta—No. 22 Army C.—5-8-14—1,07,000.

WAR DIARY
INTELLIGENCE SUMMARY.
(Erase heading not required.)

Army Form C. 2118.

Instructions regarding War Diaries and Intelligence Summaries are contained in F. S. Regs., Part II, and the Staff Manual respectively. Title pages will be prepared in manuscript.

Hour, Date, Place.	Summary of Events and Information.	Remarks and references to Appendices
11-11-14 M.	Casualties:- 1 man killed, 1 officer 9 3 NCOs 9 men wounded. 4 returned (sick) from hospital. F.S. 15 & 645. Situation normal. Fire was opened on retired at 12 noon to which enemy replied. Our night Parties gave of a trench to withdraw its a redoubt. Trenches were generally improved & obstacles strengthened. Scouts report all trenches were held by the enemy during the night & were unable to get through.	
E	Situation normal. Snipers active as usual. A few small parties shown on German trenches opposite our left centre. Shelling more than usual. Germans you are aware of situation on my right.	
12-11-14 M.	Situation all quiet during the night. Pamphlets war important, obstacles made & trenches generally deepened. Scouts not returned. Casualties:- nil. F.S. 15 & 640.	
E	Shelling heavier than usual, also snipers very active. A mile not certain whether a bomb or high explosive got a trench facing east on my right centre almost in reverse causing annual casualties. If it was a shell a battery of this enemy must have moved right south. Complaint against slot Bde not falling in trenches which they evacuate, it forms a source of approach to my R. flank. San sentry in a German unexploded head. Pi.	

WAR DIARY
INTELLIGENCE SUMMARY

(Erase heading not required.)

Army Form C. 2118.

Instructions regarding War Diaries and Intelligence Summaries are contained in F. S. Regs., Part II, and the Staff Manual respectively. Title pages will be prepared in manuscript.

Hour, Date, Place.		Summary of Events and Information.	Remarks and references to Appendices
13-11-14	M.	On my right enemy strongly occupied last night long continuous trench in front of my position & also that of 21st Bde. Opposite either they appear to have a machine gun. Bomb throwers? sniping as usual. Scouts on left not returned yet. Work all night making loopholes, entanglements &c. Casualties: Killed 2 NCOs Wounded 8 NCOs & men. Plans to Casualties to date 3. J.S. 15 D 650. Sick. Returned to duty.	7.
	E.	Situation unchanged except enemy have commenced trenches recently vacated by 21st Bde.	7.
14-11-14	M.	Today. — Nothing to report except enemy appear to be reinforced.	7.
		Opposite my L front last night. A M.Gun appeared opposite my L. Centre & fired obliquely in direction of 3/3 Gurkhas. A strong searchlight appeared also opening my extreme left & played across front during whole night. Officers on my left observed effect of shell fire last night & trenches for the extreme accuracy. Scouts & patrols report hearing sounds & yells from enemy trenches. Beyond my extreme right also a small searchlight which lit up ground. Enemy left a small covering party out in front of left trench there was however a digging was heard. The trench was topped also in another place & found to be occupied. Working parties & listening patrols. Compressed into working trenches, intanglements, & harass enemy, ultimately to work & which & return towards enemy which may ultimately to use for listening patrols. Casualties? Rfl. Sgd. A. J.S. 15 D 641. H.A.C. for duties in trenches with "A" Coy.	7.

WAR DIARY
INTELLIGENCE SUMMARY.
(Erase heading not required.)

Army Form C. 2118.

Instructions regarding War Diaries and Intelligence Summaries are contained in F.S. Regs., Part II, and the Staff Manual respectively. Title pages will be prepared in manuscript.

Hour, Date, Place.	Summary of Events and Information.	Remarks and references to Appendices
14-11-14 E	Enemy is making a new trench diagonally out of the new trench on my right towards the S. face of the enclosure of the farm held by us. It looks very much as if they were starting to sap up to that face or to the Eastern face on my right.	
15-11-14 M	On my R. at 10 p.m. Officers patrol went towards ale fellow in trenches recently occupied by 2nd Bde - reported presence of about 50 men in the trench. This report was sent to left section of the Bde. This party would be about 150ᵈ from my R. flank & to the S. of it, a little further S. near the blown up barn. Germans have improved communication & dug trenches & firing was continuous practically the whole night. Scouts patrols report that Germans on E. front of my right flank are digging or sapping from the new firing towards the S. face of the farm enclosure held by us on our R. This farm is still burning. More work going on in trenches last night than usual. On my centre enemy trenches searchlights fired on the trenches half-a-dozen times during the night - this fire was not returned. In this part searchlights were continually turned on the scouts when they fired at us. On my left enemy continue to dig in their new line original line of trench.	7

WAR DIARY
or
INTELLIGENCE SUMMARY.

(Erase heading not required.)

Army Form C. 2118.

Hour, Date, Place.	Summary of Events and Information.	Remarks and references to Appendices
Cont⁴ 15-11-14 M	Scouts worked along the whole line of this trench, 50 ft enemy & heard movement & talking going on. They also had a listening patrol of about 6 men in front of their centre. During the day sand bags were filled & during the night the standing patrol in the ditch wanting towards the enemy was advanced some 60ʸ where they established themselves. Sappers was commenced & we will push further forward still. Sentries continued work all night improving loopholes, strengthening wire entanglements & pushing trenches forward to accommodate distant patrols towards the enemy. Could we be supplied with a number of those fire grates mentioned by travel G.S. to make bomb-proof shelters which I am starting for the men. Also I want more sand bags & wire as these are continually damaged by enemy's shell fire. One German killed yesterday at range of 5 yards. Casualties:- 1 wounded. H SieR G.S. 15 & 623.	
E	The R. was subjected to somewhat heavy shell fire today which did damage to parapets. On left enemy are commencing to dig an advance trench about 150ˣ in front of their land and In front R. there was no digging in the German trenches during the night. Nothing further to report. Impossible to work in the open between our night as immediately we began enemy's battery from their new position opened fire. Would	
M. 16/11/14		

Army Form C. 2118.

WAR DIARY

INTELLIGENCE SUMMARY.

(Erase heading not required.)

Instructions regarding War Diaries and Intelligence Summaries are contained in F. S. Regs., Part II, and the Staff Manual respectively. Title pages will be prepared in manuscript.

Hour, Date, Place.	Summary of Events and Information.	Remarks and references to Appendices
Cont= 16-11-14 M.	Casualties:- Killed 4. Wounded 11. Sick 3. Returned 1. P.S. 15 & 606.	Fr.
E	Have nothing further to report.	Fr.
19-11-14 M	On my extreme right all quiet. Patrols report that sap on E front has now turned N.E. and follows German trenches. On R centre nothing to report. Sappers worked at sap towards enemy. On the centre there was no sniping or searchlight. Last night two were wounded by our own guns. On left only a few rounds were fired from enemy trenches. During the night the enemy has on left sapping towards my trenches at any rate. This is a contradiction of my statement of yesterday. Work:- Brushwood collected, gangsaps & wire entanglements repairs & on left continued sap towards enemy also on return R.	
E	Casualties:- Killed 1. Wounded 5. Sick 12. P.S. 15 & 588.	Fr.
	On my right 2 centre nothing to report. On my left the standing patrol in the ditch leading up to enemy trenches was driven in, but I am pushing another forward to occupy it. On this flank R it is reported that enemy are very nearly made shields in their trenches with air holes. "B" & "C" Coys. relieved by 2 Coys of Seaforth Highrs. night 17-18th	Fr.

Gulab Singh & Sons, Calcutta—No. 22 Army C.—5-8-14—1,07,000.

WAR DIARY
or
INTELLIGENCE SUMMARY.

(Erase heading not required.)

Army Form C. 2118.

F 17

Instructions regarding War Diaries and Intelligence Summaries are contained in F. S. Regs., Part II, and the Staff Manual respectively. Title pages will be prepared in manuscript.

Hour, Date, Place.	Summary of Events and Information.	Remarks and references to Appendices
15-11-14. M.	Casualties:- Killed 1. Wounded 3. Sick 3. F.S. 15 & 1. 2 Trenches 9 & 2 & 6. On the night the Germans occupied the trenches vacated by Bareilly Bde thickly. Think that if howitzers turned on to this area sometime by night they might get a bag. On R. centre Germans served putting, as they turned searchlight continually off & on all night, and tracer in continually to bursts of fire from 3 or 4 men together at a time. Perhaps they expected an attack and thought men were up. It might be a good thing when rifle fire takes place again to turn some artillery on as certainly the trenches are more thickly held last night than usual. Party endeavoured to get out to sap but were unable as immediately discovered & driven back by rifle fire & bombs. On the left desultory sniping all night. Work done:- Saps continued. communications improved. Ammunition 430 ods pm man rest counting stray ammunition picked up in trenches.	Zn
	On my right R.centre enemy are still busy extracting their trenches. Farm house enclosure was shelled by big guns but no damage done. One German killed here. Our left scouts crawled up trench leading towards enemy and found picquet of 5 Germans sitting down behind barricade. They fire at him but he escaped bringing news when covering Sikh Bugle on out of the Germans.	Zn

Army Form C. 2118.

WAR DIARY

~~INTELLIGENCE SUMMARY.~~

(Erase heading not required.)

Instructions regarding War Diaries and Intelligence Summaries are contained in F. S. Regs., Part II, and the Staff Manual respectively. Title pages will be prepared in manuscript.

Hour, Date, Place.		Summary of Events and Information.	Remarks and references to Appendices
19-11-14	M.	Situation normal. Nothing to report. Wire entanglements repaired and communication trenches improved. Reserve Trenches for R. commenced. Wounded 3. Sick 2. F.S. 15/596 trenches 9/29. Ammunition # 30.	Z.
	E.	6 R. wing are running a trench parallel to the S. front of my redoubt. They have also extended the vacated trench of the 21st Brigade are now about 100* away from my redoubt. On the R centre nothing now to report but they are paying great attention to farm enclosure with than shells. On the left trenches appear to be strongly held from the amount of fire produced on our aeroplane today. D.E. Seaforths suggests that we be provided with searchlight. He reports also our guns made very accurate practice on enemy's trenches yesterday afternoon and he suggests they should do this most often. R. was heavily sniped till 12 M.N. when all were quite —	Z.
20.11-14	M.	Nothing to report about centre or left. In case of attack on centre suggest that the 4 haystacks near farm bgo* in front be set alight by artillery in order to light up attacking enemy. War diary:- damaged parapets repaired & communications continued also reserve trench in rear. Could we be supplied with planking & posts for overhead protection against weather, also want sandbags & wire.	

20/19

Army Form C. 2118.

Instructions regarding War Diaries and Intelligence Summaries are contained in F. S. Regs., Part II, and the Staff Manual respectively. Title pages will be prepared in manuscript.

WAR DIARY
INTELLIGENCE SUMMARY.
(Erase heading not required.)

Hour, Date, Place.	Summary of Events and Information.	Remarks and references to Appendices
cont.^d 20-11-14 M.	Left Coy Seaforths reports that yesterday a number of Gurkhas were in an empty Redout in rear of this Coy with a large fire lit while O.C. Coy thinks might attract attention of enemy. Killed 1 Wounded 5 Sick 1. Seaforth's Casualties: N.C.O.'s 0 Men J.C. 15/56. Trenches: B.I.E. 9/0 4 6 Seaforths 7/250 Ammunition 4/30. Fr.	
20-11-14 Special	Copy of letter from Lieut Waller 107th Pioneers. Sir, I beg to bring to your good notice the following incident which occurred this morning about 9.30 am. a mortar bomb from the German trenches dropped right into a portion of this trench occupied by the 107th Pioneers and exploded throwing one man right out of the trench out on to the parapet. This was witnessed by this men of the section who was at the moment working in a communication trench 20 yards behind. But one of the men of the Leicesters saw the occurrence. He ran down and departed up the trench with him and found the man moaning the other side. The man in the Leicesters was N° 9139 Pte Routin, A' Coy. Pte Routin said I am going for him, jumped out of the trench, and dragged the wounded man in. This all took place within 70x of the enemy's trenches and was done so quickly that the enemy had no time to fire. I consider it a brave act Fr. 34/- B H Waller Lt 107th Pioneers	

Army Form C. 2118.

WAR DIARY
or
INTELLIGENCE SUMMARY.

(Erase heading not required.)

Instructions regarding War Diaries and Intelligence Summaries are contained in F. S. Regs., Part II, and the Staff Manual respectively. Title pages will be prepared in manuscript.

Hour, Date, Place.	Summary of Events and Information.	Remarks and references to Appendices
20-11-14 Special	I concur in considering this act a meritorious one as it was most incumbent on Pte Barton to retain this wounded man. I desire to bring this act to your favorable notice. In Left Centre Trenches. sd/- H. J. Coney Lt. Col. Comdg. 1st Bn. 107th Pioneers. 20-11-14 Major To: Bde Major Garhwal Bde. I beg to forward the accompanying report from the O.C. Bn. 107th Pioneers. In my opinion the act of Pte Barton was a brave one, when one considers that at the present time even a movement in our trenches brings down the fire of the enemy. I recommend Pte Barton of the Bn under my command to the favourable notice of the G.O.C. (Sd) O.J. Blackader Lt. Col. 2.	
20-11-14 E	No change on my right. Digging company in most of the German trenches. They are now 50x off the S. face of the farm enclosure. Underground sap is proceeding towards the now two different directions. On the left 2 left centre enemy have commenced a new trench each side of the natural ditch running into our parapet about 70 ft from our advance trench. A Pom-Pom opened this afternoon against this face firing single shots.	

Army Form C. 2118.

WAR DIARY
INTELLIGENCE SUMMARY.
(Erase heading not required.)

Instructions regarding War Diaries and Intelligence Summaries are contained in F. S. Regs., Part II, and the Staff Manual respectively. Title pages will be prepared in manuscript.

Hour, Date, Place.		Summary of Events and Information.	Remarks and references to Appendices
20-11-14	E	If we have such an epistle on our side we would colour their loopholes & parapets down, De Seaforths very anxious for a searchlight.	
21-11-14	M	On the R. nothing to report. On the R. centre an officers' patrol under Lieut Wateridge was sent out to look at a new trench. I regret to say Lieut Wateridge & one man missing. We are almost certain that we can see Lieut Wateridge's body about 15 x from the enemy's trenches. Nothing to report on remainder of line. Work done :— Continuing underground saps towards enemy's lines, shall be ready by tonight for blowing up purposes. G.S. 14 - 550. Trenches 8 - 269. Killed 1 Wounded 1. Missing 1 Sick 6. Ammunition 4 30. Seaforths 7 - 255 (2 sick).	X.
	E	On R. Germans show no more diggings since last night & sappers put 4 shells into the new trench. During the day. On this flank we have suffered a great deal from shells today & I consider it of the greatest importance that we should be in a position to establish superiority in hand throwing over the Germans just the same as in rifle fire. This as you know we are not in a position to do owing to lack of means & material. R. centre farm enclosure was also heavily shelled and bombed today. On centre & left no movement reported, but usual sniping.	X.

WAR DIARY
INTELLIGENCE SUMMARY.
(Erase heading not required.)

Army Form C. 2118

Instructions regarding War Diaries and Intelligence Summaries are contained in F. S. Regs., Part II, and the Staff Manual respectively. Title pages will be prepared in manuscript.

Hour, Date, Place.	Summary of Events and Information.	Remarks and references to Appendices.
22-11-14 M.	Gen. R. & found continued sniping all night & volunteers were wanted for 2 hours. Rest of line nothing to report. Saps continued & wire entanglements repaired. Casualties: Killed 1, Wounded 9. F.S. Bn. 14 - 540, Trenches B - 257.	
E.	Go the R. a certain amount of howitzing. Remainder of front quiet except for sniping. On left enemy do not appear to be digging but a good many fires from their trenches & at our aeroplane. Our men brought yesterday missing men seen lying. Killed No. 5154 Pte. S. Worthington. It was not trying to get his body or that of Lieut. E.L. Watridge as enemy kept up a constant fire on the bodies all night. Casualties. 1 Wounded Reie. 1 Wounded, Sea forth. "A", "D" Coys, No.1 Gun & M. Gun, relieved by 1st Manchester Regt. left trenches by 8 p.m. & marched to Billets at LaCouture. "B" & "C" Coys & 1st line had moved to billets earlier in afternoon from billets at La Hamel.	
23-11-14	Orders to move at once to Bareilly Hd Qrs at Gorre. Orders to hold in readiness to move received at 3.32 pm 3.30 pm - Orders to hold in readiness to move received at 3.32 pm Duplicate of this record at 3.40 pm. Reached Gorre at 5.30 pm and ordered to proceed and report to Brig. Egerton Comdg Ferozepore Bde, centre sector (near Festubert). Eventually Major Gordon Comdg "B" & "C" Coys remained.	

WAR DIARY
INTELLIGENCE SUMMARY.
(Erase heading not required.)

Army Form C. 2118.

Hour, Date, Place.	Summary of Events and Information.	Remarks and references to Appendices.
24. 11. 14.	Report by Major H. GORDON on operations by "B" & "C" Coys on night of 23/4 November:— About 4 a.m. "B" & "C" Coys up the communicating trench to a point about 90* from the part of the fire Trench occupied by Germans, this fire trench was in prolongation of the trench held by 107th Pioneers. This Regt had been sent up to attack & recapture the part of the trench held by this enemy. This was the right of the German Trench. Unknown to us the 1/39 Garwhalis had been sent to attack the left & subsequently it appeared they entered the left part of the trench, at about 3 a.m. Brig. Genl. EGERTON ordered 1 Coy 2 LEIC: Regt to attack the trench in flank & 1 Coy 107th PIONEERS to extend to our left, while 1 Coy of 2nd Leic Regt was to be in reserve. I ordered "B" Coy to extend & put "C" Coy in support. "B" Coy got out in good order & gained their position by moving along a natural ditch parallel to & about 15* w/ rear of the fire trench. The Coy of PIONEERS who were to form in our left also got into position. When the advance began the PIONEERS for the most part instead of prolonging to our left closed on to "B" Coy & hampered their movement. Capt H.A. EGERTON his 2 Lieut BROWNE were killed Seton-Browne were killed & 2 Lieut M.W.	

Army Form C. 2118

WAR DIARY

INTELLIGENCE SUMMARY.

(Erase heading not required.)

Hour, Date, Place.	Summary of Events and Information.	Remarks and references to Appendices.
Cont. Oct. 11-14.	the enemy retired & we killed a number of them in their retirement. The Officer Comdg. the PIONEER Coy. came back & reported that his men were unable to advance on account of heavy losses. I went forward and separated our men from the Pioneers & brought them along to where the leading men of "D" Coy had established themselves in the Enemy's trench. I then reported the situation to the G.O.C. who ordered a retirement from the trench. This took place about 4 am. & by 4 am. I had got away all the wounded. Subsequently it transpired that the 1/39th GARWHALS actually passed by us at about 6.30 a.m. At 8.30 a.m. I left FESTUBERT with the 2 Coys. to proceed to billets at GORRE, when we came under shrapnel fire. En Ds. Remainder of Battn. (H. Qrs. "A", "B" Coys, M.Gun & 1st Line) returned to GORRE remaining in reserve under orders of Genl MACBEAN commanding BAREILLY Bde. Arrived at GORRE 1.45 a.m. 24th & eventually returned to billets at LA COUTURE during early afternoon.	

Army Form C. 2118

WAR DIARY
or
INTELLIGENCE SUMMARY.

(Erase heading not required.)

Instructions regarding War Diaries and Intelligence Summaries are contained in F. S. Regs., Part II, and the Staff Manual respectively. Title pages will be prepared in manuscript.

Hour, Date, Place.	Summary of Events and Information.	Remarks and references to Appendices.
25-11-14 27-11-14	Remained in Billets at LA COUTRE	
26-11-14	Batt'n left La Coutre at 12.45 p.m., marched to GORRE (N° 1 Co'y, Q.T. FEROZEPORE Bde) and received orders to relieve 2/39 GARHWALIS in trenches E. of FESTUBERT. C.O. taking over command of centre section (500 Leic: Regt, 300 55th Rifles, 230 9th Bhopals, 100 34th Pioneers) "A", "B", "D" 2 Platoons "C" in Firing Trenches, remainder "C" Co'y 2 M. Gun in support, frequent sniping by Germans. 1 man killed 2 wounded.	Z
29-11-14 E.	Day passed quietly except for bombing of "D" Co'y, whose reply with grenades & french mortar appeared effective. Situation unchanged. Much sniping & bombing in front of other Co'ys.	Z
30-11-14 M.	"D" Co'y. Quiet in front of other Co'ys. "A" Co'y made up to 100 by "D" Co'y. Indian Major R.N. KHATEHBULD.S.O L.t CHUDLEIGH. L.t HOWTHER, paraded for inspection by H.M. the King at LOCON. Having only returned from the trenches at midnight they were very dirty, a condition described by the King as "looking war-worn". H.M. spoke to the officers & several of the men, asking questions about work & conditions of life in the trenches. After his departure Lt-Col. J. BIRNEY. DC 2000 COCK'S addressing the men said "that he had been commanded by the King to express	Z

See Sheet 26
31-12-14

Army Form C. 2118

WAR DIARY

INTELLIGENCE SUMMARY.

(Erase heading not required.)

Instructions regarding War Diaries and Intelligence Summaries are contained in F. S. Regs., Part II, and the Staff Manual respectively. Title pages will be prepared in manuscript.

Hour, Date, Place.	Summary of Events and Information.	Remarks and references to Appendices.
1-12-14	His Majesty's Keen appreciation of the services rendered by the Battalion during the War and of the fine work which they have done. His Majesty hoped that at the conclusion of the War he would have an early opportunity of seeing the Regiment again "detached from Indian Regts were present, but there were no other British units.	to follow sheet 2.5 of same date (30-11-14).
30-11-14	Relieved by 1/39 Garhwalis in trenches by 8.30 p.m. & marched back to billets at LA COUTURE.	
1-12-14	At 1 a.m. received orders from Bde Major. gazumme Rde to send 100 men, preparation of officers M.C.0s to parade at 2 occn Fg. 9 a.m. for inspection by H.M. the King.	
2-12-14	Billets at LA COUTURE. C.O. met C.O. o'Manchesters at 15th Sikh Hdqrs in RUE DU BOIS as battalion relieves Manchesters in trenches tomorrow evening —	

3.12.1914
7.1.1915

WAR DIARY

OF THE

2ND BN LEICESTERSHIRE REGIMENT.

FROM 3RD DECEMBER 1914 TO 7TH JANUARY 1915.

Army Form C. 2118.

WAR DIARY
INTELLIGENCE SUMMARY.
(Erase heading not required.)

2nd Bn ~~LEICESTER R.S.M.~~ Re Regt. from 3-12-14 to 7-1-15.

Instructions regarding War Diaries and Intelligence Summaries are contained in F. S. Regs., Part II, and the Staff Manual respectively. Title pages will be prepared in manuscript.

Hour, Date, Place.	Summary of Events and Information.	Remarks and references to Appendices.
6pm 3-12-14	Batt'n relieved 1st Bn Manchester Regt in trenches previously occupied by the Batt'n	2.
4-12-14 M.	Situation normal. Work done :- Trenches loopholed, bomb proof shelters commenced, loopholes repaired & trenches generally improved	7.
5-12-14 M	Situation normal. Work done :- Improvement of loopholes, bomb proofs bags, new trenches & communications.	7.
E.	Situation normal, an unusually quiet day. 1 Officer & 194 N.C.O's & men joined Bn in trenches, being our 1st Reinforcements, men who were sick or wounded, official reserve, Section II.	7.
6-12-14 M.	Situation normal. Scouts on night 2 continued sniping on Touvenes owing to brightness of moon 2 advanced up natural ditch Touvenes left party of men advanced building a barricade in advance of the one at present held, but as sand bags were put up, it was shot away by the enemy. Our man wounded doing this. Work done :- Bomb proof shelters continued, sand bags & loopholes repaired where fallen in, communications improved & saps continued.	7.
E.	Situation- nothing unusual, though German iron jacket rifle grenades this evening. Snipers fired fairly heavily at our aeroplanes had this morning & this afternoon.	2.
7-12-14 M.	Situation as usually, Germans sent up a good many star shells last night more than usual and seemed to fire very brisk fire on the light 2 did so about 7 pm. Trenches improved, sand bags repaired, communications improved.	4.

No 3 Section
A. G's Office at Base
I. E. Force
Passed to _____ S. Sect'n
on 21/1/15

Army Form C 2118.

WAR DIARY
INTELLIGENCE SUMMARY.
(Erase heading not required.)

2nd Bn LEICESTERSHIRE Regt.

Instructions regarding War Diaries and Intelligence Summaries are contained in F. S. Regs., Part II, and the Staff Manual respectively. Title pages will be prepared in manuscript.

Hour, Date, Place.		Summary of Events and Information.	Remarks and references to Appendices.
8-12-14	M.	Nothing to report except that enemy trenches were all held last night and scouts were unable to discover anything. Saps continued, communication improved, parapets repaired. Owing to rain parapet is falling down everywhere, and a great many sandbags are urgently required for opening same.	?
	E.	Nothing to report.	?
9-12-14	M.	Nothing new to report. Scouts report sounds of digging and driving of stakes into the ground, also singing and talking going on in the trenches. Enemy appear to be very wide-awake as they fire at the slightest sound. Star-shells were thrown up in the night & rapid fire at once opened on the parapet. It appears to me that their procedure is different to what is used to be. They seem to sit in their trenches and fire at everything, opening rapid fire at the least provocation. Only over R.D. or a couple of men been reported as coming up to our wire. Their snipers are still excellent shots. – We are done! – Parapets & loopholes repaired. Communication improved. Saps continued, second line continued. Sand-bags are badly wanted.	Opposing [?] letter [?] [?] 7th [?]
	E.	When Emma were fired at this afternoon Emma pickel no Boman Knight & British helmets & army caps were waved at us but	

Army Form C. 2118.

WAR DIARY
or
INTELLIGENCE SUMMARY
2nd Bn: LEICESTERSHIRE REGT.
(Erase heading not required.)

Instructions regarding War Diaries and Intelligence Summaries are contained in F. S. Regs., Part II, and the Staff Manual respectively. Title pages will be prepared in manuscript.

Hour, Date, Place.	Summary of Events and Information.	Remarks and references to Appendices.
10-12-14 M.	Nothing new on the left. Scouts were in touch with enemy all night and the trenches were strongly held. Work done :- Rebuilding parapets & loopholes, improving bottom of trenches, continuing saps 2 repairing wire.	7.
9 pm 10-12-14 E	Battalion (less "C" Coy) relieved by 2/2 Gurkhas, and marched to billets at RICHEBOURG ST. VAAST.	7.
11-12-14	Remained in billets. "C" Company rejoined from trenches & relieved by 6th JATS.	7.
12th & 16th 12-14	In Billets	7.
17-12-14	Proceeded to trenches taking over from 2/3 Gurkha Rifles. A, B, D Coys in firing line. "C" Coy 2 H? Q?s in billets on RUE DES BERCEAUX.	7.
18-12-14	Mid-day, informed to Bn: 2/3 Gurkha Rifles to relieve us at once, as the Bn: was going to take part in capturing some of the enemy's trenches. The force consisted of the Bn:, ½ Bn 2/3 Gurkha Rifles, 1 Coy 107 4 Pioneers, party of Sappers & Miners. The Battn: in relief from trenches rendezvous at Battn: Head Quarters, and at 12.30 am 19-12-14 "C" Coy's Salient the plan was as follows :- C" Coy's Salient	7.

WAR DIARY
INTELLIGENCE SUMMARY.
(Erase heading not required.)

Army Form C. 2118.

Hour, Date, Place.	Summary of Events and Information.	Remarks and references to Appendices.
19-12-14	A bombing party proceeded to the ditch barricade up the ditch leading to the enemy and relieved the 6th JATS. One Coy was to deploy from the ditch out to the right outside the wire in front of our parapet & lie down. Another Coy was to do the same on the left. As soon as the advance commenced, the remaining two companies were to do the same (one on each side of the ditch) and advance in support. At 3.15 a.m. the deployment was completed in absolute silence and at 3.30 a.m. the advance commenced. The Companies had 3 platoons in the front line & one in support, the latter accompanied by a bombing party. As soon as the parties came up in line with the bombing party in the ditch, the latter jumped over barricade, cut the wire, advanced to enemys' barricade 2 hundred it. The left Company had barely gone 20 yards when a maxim opened on their right, 20 more yards and they were stopped by a hedge which barbed wire in the west. This caused a few moments delay. They got through and immediately a second maxim opened. The Company then entered the trench under the fire of the two maxims and captured it and the guns -	

Army Form C. 2118.

WAR DIARY

INTELLIGENCE SUMMARY.

(Erase heading not required.)

Instructions regarding War Diaries and Intelligence Summaries are contained in F. S. Regs., Part II, and the Staff Manual respectively. Title pages will be prepared in manuscript.

Hour, Date, Place.	Summary of Events and Information.	Remarks and references to Appendices.
(cont) 19-12-14	Only one German was found in it, the rest having escaped during the delay at the hedge & ditch. This trench was very deep and narrow, about 60 yards long. The Officer Comdg. the Company (Capt. Romilly) concluded that there must be another trench in rear. He accordingly got his men out of the trench and lined them up for a second advance. A maxim gun immediately opened on his right & another behind this one and to his left. He determined to go for the latter and advanced on it but got into the ditch in which it had been only to find it empty. The Company was now behind the maxim that had opened on their right, & Capt. Romilly reformed his Company to attack this. At this moment our batteries opened fire and shells commenced bursting over his company & the enemy's trenches; Capt. Romilly thinking he had gone too far decided to return to the 1st German trench he had taken. This he found occupied by the supporting Company. Dawn was now breaking, so this trench was put into a state of defence, and the natural ditch in front of it for a distance of some 200 yards	

WAR DIARY
INTELLIGENCE SUMMARY.
(Erase heading not required.)

Army Form C. 2118.

Instructions regarding War Diaries and Intelligence Summaries are contained in F. S. Regs., Part II, and the Staff Manual respectively. Title pages will be prepared in manuscript.

32/

Hour, Date, Place.	Summary of Events and Information.	Remarks and references to Appendices.
(cont.) 19-12-14	The company on the night in its advance missed the first German trench, as it were too much to the right. On passing this trench it was met by heavy machine & rifle fire, but they rushed forward & captured the trench about 100 yards in length. This trench lost none to the nights & they advanced along it until the howitzing party in front. This trench led into one of the enemy's main trenches & when within 20 yards of it, the whole of the howitzing party, 8 in number, crept one were put out of action. They also were met by a heavy enfilade rifle fire. The officer commanding decided to erect a barricade at once & this was accomplished under heavy rifle fire & hand bombing of the enemy. The trench was put into a state of defence. The company in support moved forward & reinforced this company & also 2 of a company of the 2/3 Gurkha Rifles was of the same purpose. I regret I have not been able to find out what happened to this company under Major ——— DUNDAS, but it evidently reinforced the 2 Pm 2/3rd in reserve at daylight, nor is it possible to say what happened to the supporting company	

WAR DIARY
INTELLIGENCE SUMMARY.
(Erase heading not required.)

Army Form C. 2118.

Hour, Date, Place.	Summary of Events and Information.	Remarks and references to Appendices.
(Cont.) 19-12-14	On the night as Major KRATCHBUHL was wounded, and Lieut TOOBY missing, but it eventually joined up with the leading Company. Stark was taken of the position as soon as it was light enough. The Pioneer Company immediately improved the communication trench, and as it could be seen that a main enemy trench flanked it, I ordered it to be made into a fire trench as well & to be traversed. This work was excellently done by the Company & they were of the greatest assistance. The captured trench on the right was also not only enfiladed by this trench but commanded by it. There were no traverses in it and being very narrow, was very hard to work in. It was not long before the enemy started on it with heavy bombs from mortars & bringing a machine up the trench bless the barricade closer. We were strenuously pushed back along it, until finally we only held 30 yards of it. Cap BAMBERGER, R.E. was killed while	

Army Form C. 2118.

WAR DIARY
or
INTELLIGENCE SUMMARY.

(Erase heading not required.)

Instructions regarding War Diaries and Intelligence Summaries are contained in F. S. Regs., Part II, and the Staff Manual respectively. Title pages will be prepared in manuscript.

Hour, Date, Place.	Summary of Events and Information.	Remarks and references to Appendices.
(cont'd) 19-12-14	gallantly directing the erection of the barricade. At the same time the two machine guns opened in front with object of enfilading the communication trench, & the parapet had to be built up again & again to prevent this. The enclosure were being fired on so that unless an attack was initiated in the night & the enemy's trench in that direction held, the position was untenable & I reported accordingly, with the result that we were carried out & without loss. Finally the net profits were 2 Maxim Guns, 4 Prisoners, & I personally saw 5 dead Germans left inside, but any officers report many more than this wounded & 9 consider were killed. One of the killed was an officer but it was impossible to get to him. Received orders went out at 6 p.m. to 2/3 Gurkha Rifles (Brigade Reserve) moving to position at LA QUINQUE RUE being somewhat unsettled.	Appendix "B" Letter from G.O.C. Meerut Divn.
20-12-14	Remained in same position.	
21-12-14		
22-12-14	Returned to billets at RICHEBOURG St. VAAST at 8 a.m	

Army Form C. 2118.

WAR DIARY
#
INTELLIGENCE SUMMARY.
(Erase heading not required.)

From 23-12-14 To:-7-1-15.

Instructions regarding War Diaries and Intelligence Summaries are contained in F. S. Regs., Part II, and the Staff Manual respectively. Title pages will be prepared in manuscript.

Hour, Date, Place.	Summary of Events and Information.	Remarks and references to Appendices.
23-12-14	Remained in Billets at RICHEBOURG ST. VAAST.	7.
24-12-14	Standing to in billets	7.
25-12-14	Standing to until 10 a.m.	7.
26-12-14	Remained in Billets	7.
27-12-14	Kept 1 a.m. Went out in reserve to 1/39 Garhwal Rifles Head Quarters, then to RUE DES BEREEAUX, eventually returned to Billets at RICHEBOURG ST. VAAST at 8.30 a.m.	7.
	Left RICHEBOURG ST VAAST at 3 p.m en route for LILLERS. Stayed at LESTEM for the night.	7.
28-12-14	Left LESTEM at 11 a.m arrived at ROBECQ at 2 p.m.	7.
29-12-14	Rested at ROUBECQ.	7.
30-12-14	Left ROUBECQ at 10 a.m. arrived at ECQUEDECQUES at 1.30 p.m	7.
31-12-14 to 3-1-15	Drill and War training carried out at ECQUEDECQUES daily.	7.
4-1-15	Inspection by Indian Army Corps Commander (Sir JAMES WILLCOCKS) who made the following speech to the Battⁿ. "2nd LEICESTERSHIRE REG^T:- I am very glad to meet you here today and I heartily congratulate you on your invariable good work throughout the campaign. Both in fighting and in discipline you have distinguished yourselves and no other Regiment has done better than you. The honours list which will shortly appear will contain the names of many of you	

35.

WAR DIARY
INTELLIGENCE SUMMARY.

Army Form C. 2118.

(Erase heading not required.)

Instructions regarding War Diaries and Intelligence Summaries are contained in F. S. Regs., Part II, and the Staff Manual respectively. Title pages will be prepared in manuscript.

Hour, Date, Place.	Summary of Events and Information.	Remarks and references to Appendices.
4-1-15	and a further list will shortly appear be Published later which deals with the battle after the 17th December. Your Commanding Officer, Colonel BLACKADER, has been given the command of a brigade and from that you know that the Regiment has done well in everything."	7.
5-1-15 & 6-1-15	Drill & War Training at ECAUEDEQUES.	8.
7-1-15	Inspection by the Commander-in-Chief (Field Marshal Sir JOHN FRENCH) who addressed the Battn and said:— "2nd LEICESTERSHIRE REGT — It gives me the greatest pleasure to inspect you here today & to see such a fine body of men. I have heard of your gallantry with great satisfaction and I have heard nothing but good reports of your work. You are a Regt with fine traditions. You have not only worthily maintained those traditions, but you have added great lustre to them. I wish personally to thank you for your good work and I am very grateful to you. I feel sure that I can depend upon you in the future as I have done in the past and I am certain you will still further gain still further honours with the campaign is completely finished."	7.

WAR DIARY
INTELLIGENCE SUMMARY
(Erase heading not required.)

Hour, Date, Place.	Summary of Events and Information.	Remarks and references to Appendices.
1-1-15	Major General Keary is taking leave of the Battalion on 1st January 1915 said:— "Officers, N.C.O's & men of the 2nd Leicestershire — I am very sorry to be saying Good-bye to you today. It has been a great pleasure as well as a great honour to have had you under my command and I cannot speak too highly of the work you have done. Personally I am very grateful to you as I feel it is in a great part owing to you great work that I have been placed in another and higher position in the Army Corps. I am very glad that your Commanding Officer has been appointed your Brigadier in my place and I feel certain that you will continue to do as well as you have done under me. Though I am no longer in command of you, I shall not be far off and I shall always take the greatest interest in your doing and in your welfare. I wish Good-bye to all of you."	

The following received from Corps Commander:-

"G.O.C. Meerut Div." I congratulate you in the good work done last night, which shows what can be done by enterprise & care. Please send my hearty congratulations to Maj-General Keary, the Leicesters, & the 2/3 Gurkhas for their gallant behaviour" ends.

It gives me much pleasure to forward this appreciative message of the Corps Commander both as regards the regiments mentioned. I feel sure that further information will show the other units engaged how well and ably supported the attack, the success of which is due to the gallantry of our officers & men and to the fact that the details of the attack were arranged after obtaining the valuable advice of yourself & the C.O.s of units entrusted with its execution."

(Sd) C.A. Anderson Lt. General
Commanding Meerut Division

To
The G.O.C
Garwhal Bde.

G. 165/14.

19-12-14

Appendix B

7.1.1915
3.3.195

Serial No. 184

WAR DIARY

2nd Bn. Leicestershire Regiment.
4th January 1915 – 3rd March 1915

Army Form C. 2118.

WAR DIARY
or
INTELLIGENCE SUMMARY.

Leicestershire Regt

(Erase heading not required.)

Instructions regarding War Diaries and Intelligence Summaries are contained in F. S. Regs., Part II, and the Staff Manual respectively. Title pages will be prepared in manuscript.

Hour, Date, Place.	Summary of Events and Information.	Remarks and references to Appendices.
23-1-15	against the reserve Coy when fit men before going to posts were well vaselined on whole oils could not be obtained	F.
24-1-15. M.	No change. German flares every half hour on right. Communication with Bns. E. R. & L.	F.
E.	No change. Officers post R. Coy shot German.	F.
25-1-15. 7 a.m	No change.	F.
7.30 a.m	German shelling RUE DU BOIS on advanced trenches	F.
9.45 a.m	Heavy firing to the left, some firing on my front, "C" Coy in Rouges 'A' & 'D' Coys in the trenches	F.
10.7 a.m	all former firing on my left reported to be enemy's fire.	F.
10.25 a.m	Received information from Brigade prisoner reports attack contemplated against this part British Front.	F.
11.20 a.m	BETHUNE shelled this morning. At present all quiet. Communication with Left Bn. (Sherwood Foresters) broken down. Used orderly who returns. I.O.P - 4 informed that Germans have been pouring a pice fine shells/bombs in their R. Section this activity has never occurred before. Germans did not show themselves.	F.
1.26 p.m	firing seen my left has ceased.	F.
5.15 p.m	Orderly again returns from left Battn who report all quiet. Telephone communication again established.	F. 24

2nd Bn. LEICESTERSHIRE REGT.

WAR DIARY
INTELLIGENCE SUMMARY.

(Erase heading not required.)

Army Form C. 2118.

Instructions regarding War Diaries and Intelligence Summaries are contained in F. S. Regs., Part II, and the Staff Manual respectively. Title pages will be prepared in manuscript.

From 7-1-15 To 3-3-15

Hour, Date, Place.	Summary of Events and Information.	Remarks and references to Appendices.
ECQUEDECQUES 7.1.15 to 20.1.15	War Training.	
21-1-15	Left Billets at 10.30 a.m. Marched to CALONNE-SUR-LA-LYS arriving there at 3.0 p.m.	
CALONNE 22-1-15	Left Billets at 12 noon. Marched to LA COUTURE arriving there at 3.0 p.m.	
LA COUTURE 23-1-15	Left Billets at 4.30 p.m. marched to trenches RUE DU BOIS, frontage junction RUE DU BOIS with ROUGE-CROIX LA BASSEE ROAD along RUE DU BOIS S.W. up to and inclusive of FACTORY. From right to left D.A.C. and in reserve "B" Coy Head Quarters. Machine Gun Detachment under Brigade orders. 1st Line — LA COUTURE ROAD at N.W. entrance to RICHEBOURG ST. VAAST. Front Coys. billetted in houses — trenches a redoubt all parallel to Line of Resistance — 70× to 150× S. of road. Advanced posts 2 of which were Officers' Posts in advance ranging from 70× to 200× from German trenches. There advanced posts we succeeded in draining of water where the men actually stood, but to get them men have to get wet up to their waists in some cases. Men in advanced posts relieved twice a day 5a.m. & 6p.m. when men relieved proceeded to Batt-House at once and eventually	

Army Form C. 2118.

WAR DIARY
or
INTELLIGENCE SUMMARY.
(Erase heading not required.)

Instructions regarding War Diaries and Intelligence Summaries are contained in F. S. Regs., Part II, and the Staff Manual respectively. Title pages will be prepared in manuscript.

Hour, Date, Place.	Summary of Events and Information.	Remarks and references to Appendices.
25-1-15 10.0 P.m	All quiet. continue to improve barricade on left and build breastwork also continue loopholing houses, &	
26-1-15.	No change, all quiet. Usual sniping. At 5.15 p.m. Bde wire information points to hostility. Still quiet. Relieved by 2/3rd GURKHAS & proceed to billets along RUE DES BERCEAUX. (in reserve. At 8 p.m German shelling 100x S. of Bn. H.Q. H.rs	
27-1-15.	½ Batt'n working fcg day at defences RUE DES BERCEAUX. ½ Batt'n working night RUE DU BOIS at barricade & breastwork.	
28-1-15	Same as 27st. ½ Batt'n change.	
29-1-15.	Left RUE DES BERCEAUX at 2 p.m. arrived at LA COUTURE 3 p.m. Relieved by 1/9th Gurkha Rifles (DEHRA DUN Bde) Standing by ready to support the DEHRA DUN Bde. Standing by until 3 p.m	
30-1-15		
31-1-15.	Batt'n found digging parties at various places.	
1-2-15	Batt'n outlying Batt'n from 3 p.m.	
2 & 3-2-15	Remained in billets at La Couture	

Army Form C. 2118.

WAR DIARY
or
INTELLIGENCE SUMMARY.
(Erase heading not required.)

Instructions regarding War Diaries and Intelligence Summaries are contained in F. S. Regs., Part II, and the Staff Manual respectively. Title pages will be prepared in manuscript.

Hour, Date, Place.	Summary of Events and Information.	Remarks and references to Appendices.
4-2-15	Left La Couture for front line. B & D Coys in front line + advanced posts. A & C Coys in support, billet in the RUE DES BERCEAUX. Relieved 1/9th Gurkha Rifles	F.
5-2-15	Situation unchanged. Telephone connection renewed with East Rancs. Regt. on the left. Advanced posts thick mud.	F.
6-2-15	No change. Enemy quiet. Patrols went out but discovered no movement of enemy. Water & food being stored in the orchard.	F.
7-2-15	No change. Patrol reports yells & shouts from German Machine Gun section when a shell burst on them. The Machine Gun did not fire again. Bombing Parties continued. B & D Coys changed positions with A & C Coys at 10 p.m.	F.
8-2-15	Enemy shelled my section.	F.
9-2-15	Patrols went out further 20× from German wire entanglements and reported no movement.	F.
10-2-15 M.	No change. The artillery did good work against a German working party	F.
E.	No change. The front line reports considerable sniping	F.

Army Form C. 2118.

WAR DIARY

or

INTELLIGENCE SUMMARY.

(Erase heading not required.)

Instructions regarding War Diaries and Intelligence Summaries are contained in F. S. Regs., Part II, and the Staff Manual respectively. Title pages will be prepared in manuscript.

Hour, Date, Place.	Summary of Events and Information.	Remarks and references to Appendices.
11-2-15	Batt'n relieved by 1st Manchester Reg't 'B' & 'D' Coys (billeted in houses in the RUE DES BERCEAUX) were relieved at 2 P.M. 'A' & 'C' Coy (in the front line & advanced posts) were relieved at 9.30 P.M.	77.
12-2-15 to 20-2-15 at 2.1"	From 5th to 11th being both inclusive, continued work of improvements. Marched to billets at LA COUTURE. Batt'n in reserve at LA COUTURE. With 'B' Company 1/3rd Gondon Reg't relieved 1/15th Surkha Rifles in Left Sub-Section of Indian Army Corps Right Section. Reliefs were completed by 8.30 P.M. 'B' & 'D' Coys 2 Pls: Reg't & 'B' Coy 1/3rd London Reg't in firing line & Supports. 'A' & 'C' Coys in billets at RUE DU BOIS in Sub-section Reserve. W.O.R. done — all parapets repaired and strengthened,	77. 77. 77.
22-2-15.	trenches were cleaned and sanitation work carried out. Stopped Germans from digging by firing and bombing. Situation unchanged. Patrol report no digging by enemy. W.O.R. was carried. A & C Coys	77.
23-2-15	Sub- section Reserve relieved B & D Coy in the firing line & supports. Reliefs completed by 8 P.M. Pw Fr.	

Army Form C. 2118.

WAR DIARY
-of-
INTELLIGENCE SUMMARY.
(Erase heading not required.)

Hour, Date, Place.	Summary of Events and Information.	Remarks and references to Appendices.
24.2.15.	No change. Flares very frequent during night.	Fr.
25.2.15.	No change. Relieved by 2/3rd Gurkha Rifles and went into Section Reserve on Rue Du Bois.	Fr.
26.2.15.	Remained in Section Reserve on Rue Du Bois. Received reinforcement of 25 rank & file and 2 machine guns.	Fr.
27.2.15.	Remained in Section Reserve on Rue Du Bois	Fr.
28.2.15.	Relieved by 1st Bn Coldstream Guards at 2 p.m. Marched to La Tomoe Willot arriving there at 5.30 p.m. Received reinforcement of 25 rank & file.	Fr.
1.3.15	War training &c. carried out at La Tomoe Willot	Fr.
3.3.15.	Same as 1st & 2nd. Received reinforcement of 34 rank & files, & horses & 2 limbers &c. for Machine Guns	Fr.

4.3.1915
31.3.1915

121/5114

WAR DIARY

4. Leicestershire Regiment.
~~Doncaster Staffs~~

From 4th March 1915 to 31st March 1915

HW
37 sheets

Army Form C. 2118.

WAR DIARY
INTELLIGENCE SUMMARY.
(Erase heading not required.)

2nd Bn. LEICESTERSHIRE REGIMENT.

FROM:- 4-3-15. TO:-

Hour, Date, Place.	Summary of Events and Information.	Remarks and references to Appendices.
4-3-15. to 7-3-15	War having carried out at LA TOMBE WILLOT.	"
8-3-15	Regt billets at LA TOMBE WILLOT at 7.50 p.m. and arrived close billet at RICHEBOURG ST VAAST at 10.30 p.m.	"
9-3-15	Remained in billets and marched off at 11 p.m. via Queen Mary's Road - RUE des BERCEAUX - EDWARD ROADS Communication trench parallel to RUE DU BOIS and thence to forward Breastwork of ROOMES communication trench just west of PORT ARTHUR. 'B' + 'A' then proceeded to front line trenches just west of Port Arthur and 'B'+'C' lined northern side of Parados of ROOMES trench extending from Breastwork to entrance to PORT ARTHUR, whilst 'D' found up an Eastern side of Parapet of Breastwork. All in position by 5.a.m. 10th March. At 7.30 a.m. the artillery bombardment commenced and at 7.45 a.m. 'C' Coy followed by 'D' Coy. moved up by communication trench to the Northern portion of Eastern face of PORT ARTHUR. At 8.5 a.m. 'B' & 'C' Coys advanced each Company having two platoons in front line closely supported by the other two platoons in 2nd line	Appendix A. B. C. "

Army Form C. 2118.

45.

WAR DIARY
INTELLIGENCE SUMMARY.
(Erase heading not required.)

Hour, Date, Place.	Summary of Events and Information.	Remarks and references to Appendices.
10.3.15 (cont)	The advance was carried out at a steady double. The first line of enemy trenches was captured and the advance was continued over several other enemy trenches and communication trenches reaching the final objective (line P.O to road) at about 8.30 a.m. 'B' Coy occupying that position of German trench extending from P to the joining D-5 and 'C' Coy on their right extending through O to the road. Two platoons from each 'A' + 'D' Coys had supported B + C Coy in third line. The 'D' Coy platoons occupied the houses about 'D' and covered 'C' Coys rear and finally moved up on 'C' Coys right joining 'C' Coys to north D.M. Meanwhile owing to the 1/39th edging off to their right a gap of about 200x of the 4th German trench had been unaccounted for and this portion was still held by Germans who moved down trench opposite our right. Two parties endeavoured to dislodge them from trench to North of ruined house and from ruined houses opposite our right. One platoon of Reserve under Capt Rowley succeeded in working their way back down trench eventually up to	

Army Form C. 2118.

WAR DIARY
or
INTELLIGENCE SUMMARY.
(Erase heading not required.)

Hour, Date, Place.	Summary of Events and Information.	Remarks and references to Appendices.
10-3-15 (cont')	within 20x of ruined house, here a barricade was built and with two reserve platoons of 'A' Coy was held until the Seaforth Highlanders advancing from our left took the line. at (The Companies in front line at once commenced improving the German trench & reversed the parapet) At about 5 p.m., the enemy endeavoured to retire N.Eastwards but with the 1/Seaforths attacking from the west, the 3rd Gurkhas from the S.W. and the fire of 'A' Coy enfilading them they raised the white flag and surrendered. About 80 prisoners were taken. About 3.40pm orders were received that the left of our advanced line was to swing round to P to connect with 2/3 Gurkhas this had already been done. At 3.45 information received that the DEHRA DUN Bde was going to pass through its attack the BOIS DE BIETZ and that GARHWAL Bde would remain on line T.P.O and consolidate position. At 5.15 P.M. front line of I.A. left to right 2/39th - 2/3rd 2/Leic: 1/Seaforths - 3/Londons - 1/39th - up to this hour the	

47.

Army Form C. 2118.

WAR DIARY
INTELLIGENCE SUMMARY.
(Erase heading not required.)

Hour, Date, Place.	Summary of Events and Information.	Remarks and references to Appendices.
10-3-15 (cont)	right flank of ground line but was not had been in the	"
	am. About midnight 10/11th the 2/39th were withdrawn and attached to the DEHRA DUN Bde.	
11-3-15	The DEHRA DUN Bde. advanced as far as the BOIS DE BIEZ but before dawn with orders and dug themselves in, the 2/2nd Gurkhas digging a trench 100x in front of the 2/3rd Gurkha trench & the 2/39th coming into that [portion] portion of our own line held by "C" & ½ "D" Coys. The trench dug by the 2/2nd made 60x of trench on my left, which was occupied by "B" Coy and faced North, of no account as this portion of the trench flanked the line held by the 2/3rd Gurkhas. The ½ of "A" Coy. in front line was drawn to "D" at dusk. During the night 4/12th the 2/2 m Gurkhas were withdrawn and the trench was left unoccupied.	"
12-3-15.	The enemy artillery shelled PORT ARTHUR. On the 12th at 5.15 a.m. the Germans counter-attacked and "A" Coy at "D" was called up but this counter attack more —	Appendix "D"
	[illegible] the night at 100x from our Trenches and On the left they occupied the trench vacated by the	

Army Form C. 2118.

WAR DIARY
INTELLIGENCE SUMMARY.
(Erase heading not required.)

Hour, Date, Place.	Summary of Events and Information.	Remarks and references to Appendices.
12-3-15.	2/2nd Gurkhas and advanced from there direct on the 2/3rd Gurkhas. They were received with a frontal fire from the Gurkhas and enfiladed by "B" Coy and M. Gun under Capt. McIntyre and Sen. returned to their trench. At 9 a.m a white flag was seen in this trench and at 9.30 a.m a company of the 1/4th Gurk advanced and as there was no further movement by the enemy a party under 2 Lieut McIntyre under fire from enemy behind white flags rushed to the trench & assisted the Gurkhas in clearing it of the enemy, many of whom were killed or wounded, the remainder surrendering to the 1/H.L.I. further North. Information received at 11 a.m the Sirhind Bde supported by Jullundur Bde was going to attack in easterly direction, but no attack took place although troops were formed up behind front line; owing to open nature of ground a lack of cover they suffered somewhat heavily. At 3.37 P.m. received information that Garhwal Bde would remain in possession of line Garhwal Bde. At 6 P.m Ferozepore Bde came up but by 11 P.m it was	

Army Form C. 2118.

WAR DIARY
INTELLIGENCE SUMMARY.
(Erase heading not required.)

Instructions regarding War Diaries and Intelligence Summaries are contained in F.S. Regs., Part II, and the Staff Manual respectively. Title pages will be prepared in manuscript.

Hour, Date, Place.	Summary of Events and Information.	Remarks and references to Appendices.
10-3-15 (cont)	right flank of forward line by was had been in the air - About midnight 10/11th the 2/39th were withdrawn and attached to the DEHRA DUN Bde.	"
11-3-15	The DEHRA DUN Bde. advanced as far as the BOIS DE BIEZ but before dawn withdrew and dug themselves in - the 2/2nd Gurkhas digging a trench 100x in front of the 2/3rd Gurkhas trench & the 2/39th coming into that portion of our line held by "C" + ½ "D" Coys. The trench dug by the 2/2nd made 60x of trench on my left, which was occupied by 'B' Coy and faced North, of no account as this portion of the trench flank Red the line held by the 2/3rd Gurkhas. The ½ of "A" Coy. in front line was drawn to 'D' at dusk. During the night 11/12th the 2/2nd Gurkhas were withdrawn and the trench was left unoccupied.	"
12-3-15.	The enemy artillery shelled PORT ARTHUR. On the 12th at 5.15 a.m. the Germans counter-attacked and 'A' ½ Coy at 'D' was called up but this counter attack more fizzled out. the night at 100x from our Trenches On the left they occupied the trench vacated by the	Appendix 'D'.

Army Form C. 2118.

WAR DIARY
~~INTELLIGENCE SUMMARY.~~
(Erase heading not required.)

Hour, Date, Place.	Summary of Events and Information.	Remarks and references to Appendices.
12-3-15.	2/2nd Gurkhas and advanced from there direct on the 2/3rd Gurkhas. They were received with a frontal fire from the Gurkhas and enfiladed by 'B' Coy and one M. Gun under Capt. McIntyre and fast returned to their trench. At 9 a.m. a white flag was seen in this trench and at 9.30 a.m. a Company of the 1/4th Gurk. was advanced and as there was no further movement by the enemy a party under 2 Lieut McIntyre under fire from enemy behind white flags rushed to the trench & assisted the Gurkhas in clearing it of the enemy, many of whom were killed or wounded, the remainder surrendering to the 1/H.L.I. further North. Information received at 11 a.m. the SIRHIND Bde supported by JULLUNDER Bde was going to attack in easterly direction, but no attack took place although troops were formed up behind front line; owing to open nature of ground & lack of cover they suffered somewhat heavily. At 3.37 P.M. received information that GARHWAL Bde would remain in possession of line At 6 P.M. FEROZEPORE Bde came up but by 11 P.M. it was	

WAR DIARY
or
INTELLIGENCE SUMMARY.

(Erase heading not required.)

Hour, Date, Place.	Summary of Events and Information.	Remarks and references to Appendices.
12-3-15. (cont.)	received that attack would not take place. — Heavy Artillery shelled PORT ARTHUR from 1 p.m. to 2.15 p.m. Bn. H'Qrs + ½ "D" Coy moved to "D" at 3 p.m. JULLUNDUR and FEROZEPORE Bdes. withdrawn about 11.30 p.m.	
13-3-15.	Heavy shelling in neighbourhood of "D" - NEUVE CHAPELLE during the morning — Snipers very active. At 12.30 p.m. it was reported by a Gunner observing officer that the enemy were collecting on the line of LAYES River S.5.b. to M.36.c. Orders were issued by Bde at 5.15 p.m. for relief of line by SIRHIND Bde (Appendix E) Operation Orders issued at 6.30 p.m. (Appendix F) At 5.30 p.m. information was received that appearances were in favour of the enemy attacking. Relief completed at midnight 13/14th all quiet and Battⁿ marched to L'EPINETTE via F. (Bde H'Q^{rs}) - RUE DES BERCEAUX - QUEEN MARY ROAD - LA COUTURE - ZELOBES - LOEON Road. arriving at billets at 6. am 14 March	Appendix 'E' Appendix 'F' Appendix 'G' Map - Appendix H

Army Form C. 2118.

WAR DIARY
or
INTELLIGENCE SUMMARY.
(Erase heading not required.)

Instructions regarding War Diaries and Intelligence Summaries are contained in F. S. Regs., Part II, and the Staff Manual respectively. Title pages will be prepared in manuscript.

50.

Hour, Date, Place.	Summary of Events and Information.	Remarks and references to Appendices.
15-3-15	Stretcher Bearers worked continuously from 8 a.m. 10th to midnight 11/12th. Scouts + Pioneers carried rations, ammunition + stores to Coy Trenches nightly.	"
16-3-15	In billets.	"
17-3-15	Inspection by Divisional Commander.	" appendix "J".
18-3-15	Inspection by Indian Army Corps Commander.	" appendix "J" "K".
19-3-15		
20-3-15		
21-3-15	War Training carried out at L'EPINETTE.	"
22-3-15		
23-3-15		
24-3-15	Left L'Epinette 10-45 p.m. arrived at new billets E of VIEILLE CHAPELLE 3-15 a.m.	" appendix "M" " appendix "N"
25-3-15		
26-3-15	Brigade in Divisional Reserve. War training	"
27-3-15		
28-3-15		

Army Form C. 2118.

WAR DIARY

INTELLIGENCE SUMMARY.

(Erase heading not required.)

Hour, Date, Place.	Summary of Events and Information.	Remarks and references to Appendices.
29. 3. 15	Marched from billets E. of VIEILLE CHAPELLE at 11-15 a.m. arriving at new billets N. of CALONNE (MCORNET MALO) at 2-45 p.m.	Appendix "O"
30. 3. 15	In billets - War training	"
31. 3. 15		

SECRET   A

~~Draft~~ OPERATION ORDER. No 25   Copy No. 1
by

Brigadier General C.G. Blackader. D.S.O.
Commanding GARHWAL BRIGADE

Reference 1/40,000 BETHUNE SHEET   Garhwal Brigade
          1/5000   Sketch Map No 589ᵇ   March 9th 1915.

INFORMATION 1. (a) No further information has been
received regarding the Enemy.

(b) The INDIAN and 4th Corps are to
cooperate in an attack on NEUVE CHAPELLE
on the 10th March. The 8th Division is to
attack from the 4th Corps front and
the Meerut Division from that of the
INDIAN Corps. The artillery of the two
Corps will bombard the area to be
attacked for 35 minutes before the
assault. This bombardment will
commence at 7:30am and cease at
8.5 am, artillery fire continuing with
increased fuse and range.

Copy No 1

INTENTION. 2. THE GARHWAL BRIGADE (simultaneously with the 8th Division attack) will assault the enemy's trenches East of the ESTAIRES-LA BASSÉE road at 8·5 a.m. as follows, assembling beforehand as detailed in table A.

3. DISTRIBUTION OF ATTACKING TROOPS.

UNIT.	Objective	Limits of zone of attack	Line to be occupied and immediately consolidated.	Special points to be made good and occupied
1/39. GARHWALIS	C	Left. Line from N.E. exit of RUE DU BOIS from Port Arthur to road D-N where it crosses R-des LAYES	S.E. corner of Port Arthur through C to road D·N. at crossing of R des LAYES.	Junction of enemy trenches at B.
2nd LEICESTERS	Group of houses around cross roads at D.	Right. As left for 1/39 G. Left. Natural ditch running towards enemy's lines from ESTAIRES-LA BASSÉE road 300* from P.A.* cross roads. *Port Arthur	Road D·N. at crossing of R des LAYES to O. and thence to road (inclusive) 100* N.E. of cross roads at D.	

Copy No 1

DISTRIBUTION OF ATTACKING TROOPS (continued.)

Unit.	Objective.	Limits of zone of attack	Lines to be occupied and immediately consolidated	Special points to be made good and occupied.
2/3. G.R.	Group of houses at road junction at F.	Right. As for left of Leicesters. Left. Road a 4 b 3 2 b (NEUVE CHAPELLE) (inclusive)	From road (inclusive) 100ˣ N.E. of cross roads at D through G to road (inclusive)	200ˣ from G.N. Enemy trench which runs parallel to road to NEUVE CHAPELL.
2/39. (GARHWALIS)	Line G-H	Right. As for left of 2/3 G.R., but road exclusive.	From left of 2/3 (road inclusive) to H.	To join hands with 8th Division

On the objectives (column 2 above) being attained, all trenches leading towards the enemy will be double blocked beyond bombing distance, and then cleared beyond the barricades made.

BRIGADE RESERVE. 4. 1/3 London Regiment - in the more westerly breastwork parallel to and 200ˣ ~~300ˣ~~ from ESTAIRES - LA BASSÉE Road - to move forward to the breastworks 100ˣ East when it is cleared after the bombardment.

Copy No 1

MACHINE GUNS 5. Each assaulting battalion will have two machine guns. The remaining machine guns will be disposed under orders of the Brigade Machine Gun Officer to support and guard the left flank of the attack.

RIGHT FLANK PROTECTION 6. Bomb guns will be disposed to support and guard in cooperation with artillery, and with rifle and machine gun fire of the BAREILLY BRIGADE, the right flank of the attack.

AMMUNITION etc to be carried 7. Each man will carry 150 rounds of S.A. Ammunition, two sandbags, emergency rations and unexpended portion of the days rations - each assaulting unit will carry 192 bombs.

RESERVES of Ammunition and bombs 8. Magazines of reserve S.A.A. and bombs with 100 boxes S.A.A. and 192 bombs in each of the following points:—
Southern portion of Port Arthur.
Northern portion of Port Arthur.
Southern portion of Advanced post at S.4.b.3.2. and Northern portion of Advanced post at S.4.b.3.2.

Copy No 1

RESERVE of Ammunition and bombs (Continued)	Twenty boxes S.A.A. is also stored for Brigade Machine Guns at S.4.a.8.7. The Brigade Ammunition Reserve (with some additional bombs) will be at Brigade H.Q. Company ammunition mules with ammunition will be at Brigade ammunition reserve. Battalion ammunition carts will be with first line transport, animals ready to hook in.

9. In order to indicate to artillery and to units supporting the attack by fire the locality reached by attacking troops, coloured flags (pink for flank battalions, light and dark blue for centre battalions) will be placed by leading bodies of troops on our side of enemy trenches or buildings captured.

First line of Transport	11. First line transport (less ammunition mules and medical equipment) at LACOUTURE

COMMUNICATION	10. Telephonic and visual signalling communication will be maintained between Bde H.Q. & H.Q's of units.

Copy No 1

DRESSING   12.   ~~A.E.~~ At existing aid posts in Rue
STATION   des Berceaux (S.8.b. and S.3.c)

REPORTS.   13. Reports to Farm at S.3.a.5%, where
                 Brigade Headquarters have been
                                      established.

                        Lieutenant Major
                          Bde Major
                          Garhwal Bde

Issued through Signal Section Company at 6.30 p.m.
 Copy No 1. 2/Leicesters
  "   No 2 1/3 Lens
  "   No 3 2/3 G.R.
  "   No 4 1/39 G
  "   No 5 2/39 G
  "   No 6 Meerut Divn.
  "   No 7 Bareilly Bde.
  "   No 8 Dehra Dun Bde.
  "   No 9 War Diary
  "   No 10. Staff -

Copy no 1

TABLE A.
{ with O.O. No.   d }

Unit.	Place of assembly.	Route	Time to pass starting point Road Junction at S.2.C.2.2.
Leicesters.	Trenches from Port Arthur road junction to 300° N.N.W. along La Bassée Road - Southern half of front breastwork parallel to and 100° west of the Estaires-La Bassée Road.	Edward Road. Rue du Bois. Roume's Trench.	11.30 a.m. Night 9/10"
2/3 G.R.	Trenches on line of Estaires-La Bassée Rd. from left of Leicesters to road junction S.4.b.3.2. and Northern half of front breastworks parallel to and 100 yds west of the Estaires La Bassée Road.	S.3.C.4.2. Rue du Berceaux to S.4.a.0.4 thence across country	12.30 a.m.

Copy No 1

TABLE A. (continued)

UNIT.	Place of assembly.	Route.	Time to pass starting point Road Junction at S.2.C.2.2.
1/39 G.	Part of Port Arthur S. of Rue du Bois and in Roome's trench	As for Leicesters	1. a. m.
2/39 G.	In trenches on line of ESTAIRES-LA BASSÉE Road N.N.W. of road junction S.4.b.3.2.	As for 2/39 to S.4.a.0.4. thence continues along Rue de BERCEAUX to destination	1.30. a. m.
Leicesters	Second breast-work parallel to and 200ˣ from the ESTAIRES LA BASSÉE Road. Leaving 60ˣ at Southern end clear for Pioneers	EDWARD ROAD and thence across country	1. 15 a. m
BRIGADE M.G's	Trenches at S.4.a.8.9.	as for 2/39	Time verbally communicated to Brigade Machine Gun Officer

SECRET
                    Copy No 1
        Addition to Operation Order No 25
            by
        Brig Genl C.C. Blackader D.S.O
            Commanding Garhwal Bde.

Information 1.
                    The General object of
the attack is to enable the Fourth
and Indian Corps to establish
themselves on a more forward line
to the East, the eventual objective
being the high ground from AUBERS
to LIGNY LE GRAND.
        The Dividing line between the
Fourth and Indian Corps is point
where the dividing line between
Squares M & S cuts NEUVE-
CHAPELLE-Cross Roads in S 6 a 6.9 -
Cross roads at LA CLIQUETERIE Fe.
        The 1st Corps is assaulting the
enemy's line N.E of GIVENCHY.
        The ~~final~~ subsequent objective
to the line each, Which the Bde is
to assault will be,
    (a) The best available line on the
East side of the PORT ARTHUR — NEUVE
CHAPELLE road,
    (b). The Eastern edge of the BOIS
        de BIEZ and
    (c) line through LE HUE and LIGNY
LE GRAND to LA CLIQUETERIE Fe (exclusive)

During these several advances all Commanders must bear in mind the necessity for being prepared to specially protect the right flank of the movement.

The 8th Division assault on the village of NEUVE CHAPELLE will commence at 8.35 a.m.

The DEHRA DUN Brigade will be in close support of the Garhwal Brigade. The BAREILLY Brigade will continue to hold the present line of trenches. Parties of Sappers and Miners and Pioneers have been ordered to put localities in a state of defence.

Assembly 2. Both Battalions will be in position for assault by 4.30 a.m.

Prisoners 3. Any prisoners taken will be sent back in parties, (under escorts to be specially detailed, and not by individuals on their own initiative) to the Front line of the Bareilly Bde. to whom the prisoners will be handed over, escorts returning to their units immediately.

J.H.K. Stewart, Maj.
O.D.

"A" Form. Army Form C. 2121.

MESSAGES AND SIGNALS.   No. of Message _____

| Prefix _____ Code _____ m. | Words. | Charge. | This message is on a/c of: | Recd. at _____ m. |
| Office of Origin and Service Instructions. | Sent At _____ m. To _____ By _____ | | _____ Service. (Signature of "Franking Officer.") | Date _____ From _____ By _____ |

TO {

| Sender's Number. | Day of Month | In reply to Number | A A A |

From _____
Place _____
Time _____

The above may be forwarded as now corrected.   (Z)

Censor.   Signature of Addressor or person authorised to telegraph in his name

* This line should be erased if not required.
(24473). M.R.Co.,Ltd. Wt.W4843/511. 50,000. 9/14. Forms C2121/10.

Copy No 1

Issued through Signal Office
at ~~8.40~~ 9.10. p.m.

Copy No 1.   2/ Leicesters
 "   " 2   1/3 Londons
 "   " 3   2/3 O.R
 "   " 4   1/39
 "   " 5   2/39
 "   " 6 – Meerut Division
 "   " 7 – War Diary
 "   " 8 = Staff
        9 – Sirhind Bde.

B　　　Operation Orders　Copy No 7
by
Lieut Colonel H Gordon D.S.O.
Comdg Leicestershire Regt

　　　　　　　　　　　　　　March 9-1915

Ref 1/m,000 BETHUNE map
　　1/5,000 SKETCH map No 589 B

Information　1. a No further information about enemy
b Indian & 4th Corps to co-operate in an attack
on NEUVE CHAPELLE, 10th March, the Artillery
will bombard for 35 minutes before the assault.
This bombardment will begin at 7-30 am and
cease at 8.5 am Artillery fire continuing
with lengthened fuse and range.

Intention　2. The GARHWAL Bde will assault the enemy
trenches at 8 5 am as pointed out to O.C.
Coys in following order from right to left
1/39, Leic, 2/3, 2/39.

Distribution　3 a OBJECTIVE Group of houses round cross-
for Bn　　　roads at D.
b Limits of Zone of Attack
RIGHT Lane from N.E. exit of PORT ARTHUR
to road DN where it crosses R de: LAYES -
LEFT Natural ditch running towards enemy
300x N from PORT ARTHUR cross-roads-
c. LINE to be occupied and immediately
consolidated - as pointed out to O.s Comd Coys
On the objective being attained, all trenches
leading towards enemy are to be double
blocked beyond bombing distance.
"C" Company supported by "D" Coy on
the RIGHT.
"B" Company supported by "A" Coy on the
LEFT - as already pointed out to O.s Comd.
Coys -

Dress & 4. 150 rounds, 60 sandbags, Emergency
Ammunition   rations and unexpended portion per man.
             Two bomb boxes - tools as already detailed
             per Coy.
             Dress as already detailed.
             Reserve of Ammunition and Bombs as
             already pointed out to O. Comdg. Coys.

Aid Post 5. Cross roads - RUE DES BERCEAUX and
             EDWARD Road.

Reports 6. Reports to Hd Qrs at Northern point where
            RUE DU BOIS cuts PORT ARTHUR.

Order for March 7. Fall in ready to march off at 11 p.m.
                   Head of Column - Clear of D. Coy billets
                   Order - B.A. C.D. Scouts, Pioneers, Signallers, M.G.
                   Stretcher Bearers.
                   Route and place of assembly as already
                   detailed.

Kits 8. Packs, dixies, bicycles & will be stored
        by 10 p.m. in place already allotted.
        Officers Yakdans required to be left
        behind will be at H.Q. by 10. p.m.

        Copy No 1 A Coy
        "   No 2 B Coy
        "   No 3 C Coy   Latham   Captain
        "   No 4 ~~Military~~
        Copy No 5 - D Coy Adjt 2nd Lieutenant R?
        "   No 6 - M.G.
        "   No 7 - War Diary
        "   No 8

Special Order.

To the 1st Army.

We are about to engage the enemy under very favourable conditions. Until now in the present campaign, the British Army has, by its pluck and determination, gained victories against an enemy greatly superior both in men and guns. Reinforcements have made us stronger than the enemy in our front. Our guns are now both more numerous than the enemy's are, and also larger than any hitherto used by any army in the field. Our Flying Corps has driven the Germans from the air.

On the Eastern Front, and to South of us, our Allies have made marked progress and caused enormous losses to the Germans, who are, moreover, harassed by internal troubles and shortage of supplies, so that there is little prospect at present of big reinforcements being sent against us here.

In front of us we have only one German Corps, spread out on a front as large as that occupied by the whole of our Army (the First).

We are now about to attack with about 48 battalions a locality in that front which is held by some three German battalions. It seems probable, also, that for the first day of the operations the Germans will not have more than four battalions available as reinforcements for the counter attack. Quickness of movement is therefore of first importance to enable us to forestall the enemy and thereby gain success without severe loss.

At no time in this war has there been a more favourable moment for us, and I feel confident of success. The extent of that success must depend on the rapidity and determination with which we advance.

Although fighting in France, let us remember that we are fighting to preserve the British Empire and to protect our homes against the organized savagery of the German Army. To ensure success, each one of us must play his part, and fight like men for the Honour of Old England.

(Sd) D. HAIG, General,
Commanding 1st Army.

9th March, 1915.

1st Printing Co., R.E. G.H.Q. 673.

MESSAGES AND SIGNALS.

No. of Message 47

Army Form C. 2121

Date 11/3/15

TO Leicesters Londons
Leicesters
HQ 139 / 39

Sender's Number: SC 964
Day of Month: 11
AAA

Following from Genl Haig begins Field Marshal commanding in chief wishes his heartiest congratulations to be conveyed to corps commanders and all ranks of First Army for the splendid success they have gained today aaa would you also kindly express my gratitude for the magnificent determination which you and all ranks have displayed in executing my orders for todays battle aaa The enemy has been completely surprised and I trust that tomorrow the effect of todays fighting will result in still greater success ends

From: Brigade
Place: 5.0 a.m.
Time: 2.5 p.m.

E   OPERATION ORDER No. 26   Copy No. 1

by

Brig. Genl. C.G. Blackadder A.D.C
Commanding Garhwal Bde

Refcs. 1/40000   Bde. H.Q.
Bethune Sheet.   13th March 1915
_____

1. The Garhwal Bde including 1st Seaforths will be relieved in the trenches tonight by the Sirhind Bde.

2. One hundred rounds per man S.A.A. will be taken out, the remainder being handed over to relieving units.
   All tools will also be handed over & receipts taken.
   Very pistol ammunition and bombs will also be handed over.

3. Companies on being relieved will march to road junction immediately North of O in COUR ST VAAST where battalions will assemble, using the following routes:—
   2/3 G.R.
   3/Londn Regt (less Companies in trenches)
   2 Leicesters

Route – via F (1/5000 sketch map)
Work A1, RUE DES BERCEAUX
RICHEBOURG ST VAAST.

1 Seaforths
3 Londons (companies in trenches if any)
1/39 G.

Route – Communication trench, PORT ARTHUR, RUE DU BOIS, FACTORY, S8C, RICHEBOURG ST VAAST.

4. When each battalion is assembled it will march complete (except in the case of 3 Londons whose two parties may march separately) as follows.

1 Seaforths to VIEILLE CHAPELLE to rejoin DEHRA DUN Bde
Remainder to a billeting area and by a route to be detailed later.

5. Machine guns will leave the trenches (except those of PIONEERS and cavalry) with the units in whose trenches they are, and

3/

proceed to the road at ~~the~~ their G in RICHEBOURG-ST-VAAST, where their transport will be assembled to meet them.

The Seaforths machine guns will then join their battalion at its place of assembly.

The remainder will march under the Bde M.G.O. to billets and by a route to be detailed later.

The machine guns of Pioneers and Cavalry lent to the Brigade will be handed over to the Sirhind Bde which will man them; the present detachments being withdrawn under orders of the D.M.G.O.

6. Reports, till reliefs are complete, to Farm opposite work A1.

Subsequent H.Q. will be notified later.

J.H. Stewart, Major
B.M. Garhwal Bde.

Issued thro' Signal Section at 5.15 pm
Copy No 1 Leicesters
           Seaforths
Copy No 4 2/3
        5 1/39
        6 Sirhind Bde

F

Operation Orders
by
Lieut H. Gordon Offg.
Cmmd, Leicestershire Regt.

ref. BETHUNE.   D
& 1/5000 Sketch Map.   13-3-15

1. The Bn will be relieved by the 1/4th G.R this evening.

2. One hundred rounds Amtn will be carried on the man. VERY pistols, bomb-boxes (brigade pattern only), periscopes will be taken out. Remainder of Amtn, flares cartridges, all bombs, Tools & other stores will be handed over, and a receipt obtained by each O.C. Coy for tools only.

3. B & A Coys will be relieved first and on completion of this relief C & D will be relieved.
Machine Guns in our Battalion trenches will be relieved after the companies under orders of

Captain McIntyre –

1. Companies will march independently to road junction immediately North of Q in COUR ST VAAST where the Btn will assemble.

4. Route – (1/5000 Sketch map) F. Work A1 (i.e. Bde Hd Qrs) RUE DES BERCEAUX, RICHEBOURG ST VAAST.

5. M. Guns will proceed to the road at the G in RICHEBOURG ST VAAST where their transport will be assembled to meet them – & there will come under orders of Bde M.G.O.

6. Captain LEWIS will arrange details with O.C 1/4th E.R. as soon as possible – and time of relief will be notified later.

7. O.C. Coys will report on passing Hd Qrs at D.

by orderly to
Capt Lewis   6-30pm
to infantry coys

"Special Order of the Day"   War Diary
by
Brigadier General C. G. Blackader D.S.O.
Commanding Garhwal Brigade

G.   14th March 1915

216 " The following has been received by the Brigadier General Commanding Garhwal Brigade, from Lieut. General Sir James Willcocks. K.C.B., K.C.S.I., K.C.M.G., D.S.O., Commanding Indian Army Corps, and is to be communicated to all ranks of the Garhwal Brigade —

"Begins" "Please convey to all ranks of your gallant Brigade my hearty thanks and congratulations on their splendid work at NEUVE CHAPELLE — I am indeed fortunate and proud to have such fine soldiers in my Command. I feel sure notwithstanding their great efforts, they are prepared for still greater in the immediate future" ends

           " " " " " " " "

In more than endorsing the above, the Brigadier General, wishes to congratulate every Unit in the Brigade, on the splendid example they have shown of gallantry, dash, endurance & discipline in the operations of the last few days. He feels sure that every member of the Brigade, is not only proud of the success they have achieved, but also of having added fresh honor to the past traditions of their Units.

                               C.G. Blackader "Brigadier General"
                                 Commanding Garhwal Brigade

Appendix I

Speech by Genl Anderson on 16-3-15

"Colonel Gordon, Officers NCOs & men of the Leicestershire Regt.

"First, I hope you all realize how deeply we all feel about all the good fellows you have lost. Some of them have gone back wounded, we hope to see again, as good fellows as ever they were. The others who are gone, died in a fight that is a credit even to the Leicestershire Regt.

I know the Leicestershire Regt. I knew them six and thirty years ago in Afghanistan. They were a magnificent regiment then. You, their successors are a magnificent regiment now.

I can't say more than that I am proud to command troops that contain such a corps as the Leicestershire Regt.

Wherever the Leicestershire Regt is I know that that part of the line is safe and more than safe. Whatever they have to do I know that they will do all that is asked of them, and more than could be hoped for.

Colonel Gordon will I am sure have very many recommendations to make of those who have specially distinguished themselves, and I am sure that your old Colonel, General Blackader, will take jolly good care that they are sent in to me and I can tell you that I will take jolly good care that they go into the Corps. Colonel Gordon, I congratulate you on your command of so fine a Regiment."

Colonel Gordon "Leicestershire Regt Three cheers for Genl Anderson

Speech by Sir James Willcocks on 14-3-15

"Leicestershire Regt. You don't want a lot of talk. I have spoken to you before.

I congratulate you and thank you most heartily for what you have done.

You have fought now for five months and fought well.

I am proud and thankful to have such a battalion in my corps, and bigger people than I think the same. I have had congratulatory messages from the Viceroy, from Sir John French, and from others at home.

I thank you."

As the General rode off parade he remarked in loud tones to General Blackader "By Jove! that Regiment fights well! Young fellows just coming out to join them ought to feel pretty proud of themselves"

Appendix K

Appendix M.

Copy No 5

N Operation Order
by
Lieut Col. ~~H~~ Gordon D.S.O
Comdg Leicestershire Regt

Ref: 1/40000 CETHUNE map — 24.3.15

Outlying Bns 1. Two Bns will be detailed daily
ready to fall in on their alarm
posts within 15 minutes. All other
Bns will be ready to fall in
within one hour.

Alarm 2. If Bn is one of the Outlying Bns
Post to Bde then Bn less C Coy will
fall in in the following order
~~D A B~~ Scouts Sigs. D A B. Pioneers
1st Line Transport (less water
with its head and Cook Carts) C. Coy will
by D. Coys
Eastern Billet move along road to S.E. and
halt with its head at road
junction M.20.c.1.c. where
it will await orders. If the Bde
will concentrate then Bn will
form up on road with head of
column facing S.E 10 yards

128

from road junction in
M.20.c.1.3. in the following
order Scouts, sig rs, B.A.P.C.
Pioneers, First Line Transport
(less water & cook's cart).

J Hallam
Adjt of Leic Regt Capt

Issued at 6 p.m. by orderly.
Copy No 1 A Coy
" No 2. B. Coy
" No 3 C Coy
" No 4 D. Coy
" No 5 War Diary
" No 6 Qr. Mr.
" No 7. M. O.
" No 8. H. Q.

O

Operation Order Copy N° 5
by
Lieut Colonel A Gordon DSO
Comdg ½ Leicestershire Regt

Ref 1/40,000 BETHUNE Sheet   29-3-15.

Intention 1. Garhwal Bde will march to
            CALONNE today.
Order of 2. R.E., A.D.C. Pioneers, 1st Line Transport,
march.   Horse Train, Scouts, Signallers.
             Bn will be fallen in by 11 a.m.
             with head of column on road 50
             yards W. of 'B' Coy billet.
Breakfast 3. Breakfast 7-30 a.m. Cooks cart
             will collect dixies etc in following
             order C.D.A.H.Q.B commencing
             with 'C' Coy at 8-15 a.m. Cooks
             will accompany cart which
             will leave for new billets
             as soon as cart is loaded.

Baggage	4.	Baggage waggons to be loaded by 9-30 a.m. The
Mess Yakdans	5.	Coy Officers Mess Yakdans will be ready by 9-30 a.m. D. A. & B Coys Yakdans will be brought to H.Qrs by 10 a.m.
Billeting Party	6.	Lieut Morgan and C.S.M. Sq 75 with bicycles will meet the Qr. Mr. at 9 a.m.
Cleanliness	7.	O.C. Coys etc will ensure that all billets are left thoroughly clean.
Certificates	8.	Lieut Morgan will obtain "No-demand" certificates. Lieut Pickin will obtain "Certificates of cleanliness" from incoming units.

Copy No 1 A Coy
  " No 2 B Coy
  " No 3 C Coy
  " No 4 D Coy
  " No 5 Wardrm
  " No 6 Qr. Mr.
  " No 7 M.O
  " No 8 H.Q

Adjt Xxx Regt
Captain

1.4.1915
30.4.1915

121/5504

Bound No 187.

WAR DIARY
of
Leicestershire Regiment.

From 4th April 1915 To 30th April 1915
1/5

5.W.
4 sheets

Army Form C. 2118.

WAR DIARY

Lieut-Colonel Reg.?

INTELLIGENCE SUMMARY.

(Erase heading not required.)

Instructions regarding War Diaries and Intelligence Summaries are contained in F. S. Regs., Part II, and the Staff Manual respectively. Title pages will be prepared in manuscript.

Hour, Date, Place.	Summary of Events and Information.	Remarks and references to Appendices.
4 to 9. 4. 15	In billets. War training	Fr.
10. 4. 15	Left billets at 9.10 a.m. and marched to new billets at LES LOBES arrived 12.30 p.m.	Fr.
11. 4. 15	In Billets. War training	Fr.
12. 4. 15	Battalion (less 2 Coys) left billets 9.45 a.m. marched to new billets at LA COUTURE arrived 11 a.m. and went into Divisional Reserve. A+C Coys moved into Brigade Reserve at Redoubt A.1. marching from LES LOBES at 6 p.m.	Appendix "N" shows front line & supports, period 12th 15 28th Garwhal Bde.
13 to 18. 4. 15	2 Coys in Brigade Reserve at Redoubt A.1, 2 Coys in Divisional Reserve in Billets. War training.	Fr.
19. 4. 15	2 Coys in Brigade Reserve A.1. relieved by 5th D Coys. B Coy to front trenches B Coy to Brigade Reserve at A.1. A+C Coys arrived at billets 9.30 p.m. went into Divisional Reserve.	Fr. (pages 5+6)
20. 4. 15	1 Coy in Trenches. 1 Coy Brigade Reserve at A.1. 2 Coys Divisional Reserve in billets. War training.	Fr.
21. 4. 15	D Coy from Redoubt A.1. relieved Coy of 1/3 London Regt. in trenches front of orchard. Relief completed at 8.30 p.m. B Coy in Reserve. 2 Coys in billets. War training	Fr.
22. 4. 15	Two Coys in front trenches. Two Coys in billets. War training	Fr.
23. 4. 15	Bn. (less two Coys in trenches) left billets at 12 noon and marched to new billets N of CALONNE (N LE CORNET MALO) arriving at 3—4.45 p.m.	Fr.

WAR DIARY
INTELLIGENCE SUMMARY.
(Erase heading not required.)

Army Form C. 2118.

Instructions regarding War Diaries and Intelligence Summaries are contained in F. S. Regs., Part II, and the Staff Manual respectively. Title pages will be prepared in manuscript.

Hour, Date, Place.	Summary of Events and Information.	Remarks and references to Appendices.
24.4.15	Bn. (less two coys in trenches) left billets at 10 a.m. and returned to old billets at LA COUTURE arriving at 1-30 p.m.	?.
25.4.15	D Coy. in trenches. Two coys in billets. War Training. B Coy. moved out of trenches to Redoubt A.I. (S.R.Q.2.2. BELGIUM & FRANCE)	?.
26.4.15	D Coy in trenches. Two Coys in billets. War Training. B Coy at Redoubt A.I.	?. "A" unknown also as "LANSDOWNE POST"
27.4.15	D Coy in trenches. Two coys in billets. War Training. B Coy relieved from Redoubt A.I. and took over billets vacated by A Coy. A Coy took over billets vacated by The GARHWAL RIFLES at VIEILLE CHAPELLE.	?.
28.4.15	A & C Coys left billets at 5.55 p.m. and marched to new billets in RUE du PUITS at CROIX BARBEE. D Coy returned from trenches at about 11 p.m. and took over billets vacated by C Coy. moving their on return to DEHRA DUN Brigade.	?.
29.4.15	Bn (less 2 Coys) left billets at 7-45 p.m. and marched to CROIX BARBEE where A & C Coys rejoined Bn. Bn proceeded to relieve 1/Seaforth Highrs. in trenches between LA BASSEE Road and road to its East (S106 to S.6.C. BELGIUM & FRANCE) A & C Coys front line. D Coy in support in PORT ARTHUR. B Coy in reserve at junction of RUE MASBERCEAUX and LA BASSEE Road. 10th Gurkhas at LES 8 MAISONS. Relief completed at 11.25 p.m. Right Coy two Two Advanced Posts each of 2 N.C.Os. and 14 men	?. "A" Coy on Left. "C" Coy on Right.
30.4.15	Orders are that Support Coy during the day moves out of PORT ARTHUR leaving 1 Platoon in Redoubt, 1 Platoon behind left Coy. and 2 Platoons behind Right Coy. This order is in force because PORT ARTHUR so obtains agility. Supporting Platoon and also our PORT ARTHUR Left Supporting Platoon had 13 casualties from shell fire.	?.

13th Bde 28 April 1915. APPENDIX 'N'

1.5.1915
31.5.1915

Serial No. 784.

121/5799

6 W.
42 sheets

WAR DIARY
with Appendices.
of
2nd Leicesters

From 1st May 1915 To 31st May 1915.

WAR DIARY
or
INTELLIGENCE SUMMARY.

(Erase heading not required.)

Army Form C. 2118.

Instructions regarding War Diaries and Intelligence Summaries are contained in F.S. Regs., Part II and the Staff Manual respectively. Title pages will be prepared in manuscript.

Hour, Date, Place.	Summary of Events and Information.	Remarks and references to Appendices.
1-5-15	4.30 a.m. Enemy commenced heavy Artillery bombardment to which our Artillery commenced to reply at about 4.50 a.m. All fire was landed on "D" Coys parapets which was heated up to pieces, also in communication trench on the left of "A" Coy. 2 dugouts being demolished "D" Coy and their parapets suffered no damage, only one shell landing just in front of the parapet. On the right also landed chiefly between the front line and the salient, only one shell landed in the salient which demolished a dugout and also about supporting trench connecting PORT ARTHUR and SNIPERS House. This trench was unoccupied. On the right shells landed in rear of front line and also about parapet of supporting trench from SNIPERS House and dugout which was above unexpected. In the centre many shells landed round SNIPERS House, one landing in the long communication trench. About 5 a.m. the enemy apparently lengthened their fuzes and shell appeared to be better northwards, along the ESTAIRES Road. No shells landed in the work where the Reserve Coy lay. No aircraft, though one fell short of it. Enemy's bombardment exceeded 5.30 a.m. One airplane and one monoplane of the enemy were above our lines from 5.30 to 9.60 a.m. Our Battery treated enemy's Parapet in 8 places. Our casualties were 1 Lieut Mc Dooley and 2 men killed, and 18 N.C.Os and men wounded. Enemy at no time showed themselves. Replied by 11 a.m. Our Snipers accounted for 2 German Snipers. Note :- All Regiments in Reserve were ordered to fall S during the early morning and that 1 Platoon 1/4 Suff.R was on right	Appendix "P"

72.

Army Form C. 2118.

WAR DIARY
or
INTELLIGENCE SUMMARY.
(Erase heading not required.)

Instructions regarding War Diaries and Intelligence Summaries are contained in F. S. Regs., Part II. and the Staff Manual respectively. Title pages will be prepared in manuscript.

Hour, Date, Place.	Summary of Events and Information.	Remarks and references to Appendices.
2. 5. 15	Enemy shelled position at intervals during the day. Very little damage was done to defensive works. Our casualties were 8 wounded.	
3. 5. 15	Shelling at intervals during the day. No damage. B. Coy commenced to relieve A. Coy at 9 p.m. C. Coy relieved B. Wilcox A. — D & B in fire trench, C. in support and A in Reserve. Reliefs completed at 12.45 a.m.	7.
4. 5. 15	Enemy quiet during greater part of the day. Shelled position for about 20 minutes at 3 p.m.	7.
5. 5. 15	Same as previous day shelling rather more frequent. Relief by 4/Suffolks commenced about 12 midnight. Companies marched to billets at CROIX BARBEE independently as they were relieved.	7.
6. 5. 15	Relief completed at 2.30 a.m. Billeted at CROIX BARBEE during day.	7.
7. 5. 15	Billeted at CROIX BARBEE. Capt M K WARDLE to Brigade as Assistant Staff Captain CROIX BARBEE	7.
8. 5. 15	Billeted at CROIX BARBEE Attack by DEHRADUN Bde ordered for tonight, postponed for 1 day	7.

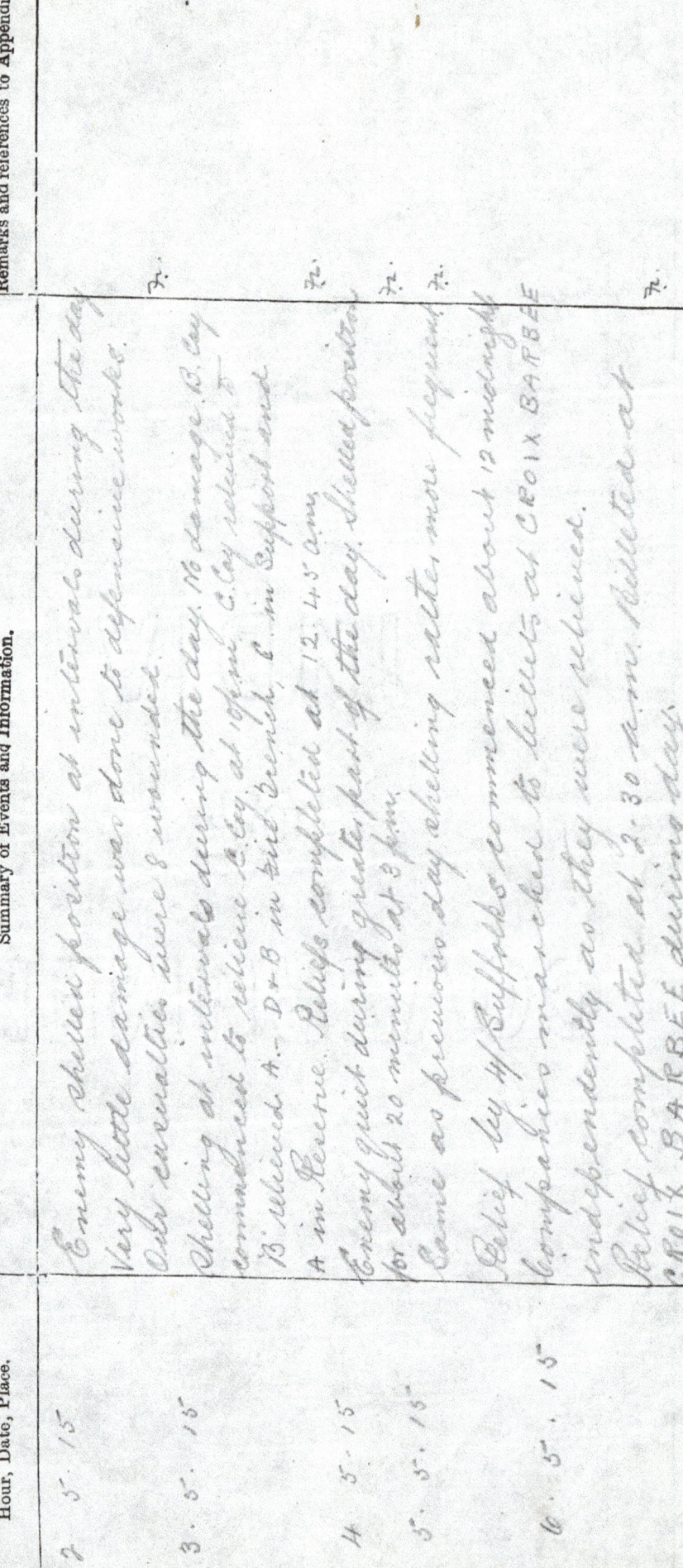

WAR DIARY
or
INTELLIGENCE SUMMARY.

(Erase heading not required.)

Army Form C. 2118.

Instructions regarding War Diaries and Intelligence Summaries are contained in F. S. Regs., Part II, and the Staff Manual respectively. Title pages will be prepared in manuscript.

Hour, Date, Place.	Summary of Events and Information.	Remarks and references to Appendices.
9 · 5 - 15	On the 6th, 7th and 8th the whole ground between CROIX BARBEE and LANSDOWNE POST was reconnoitred and alternate routes laid out. Bridges placed over the many ditches and streams which cut up the country. For the operations which commenced on the 9th the DEHRA DUN Brigade were to be the attacking troops on DD1 DD2 and DD3 trenches, the attack to take place from the ORCHARD Trench and trench to its immediate East. BAREILLY Brigade were in support in Breastwork Breastworks East of the RUE DU BOIS and just West of the ESTAIRES - PORT ARTHUR Road. (DD4 B1 B2 B3 G1 Breastworks - GARHWAL Brigade (less 2 Battalions) in Reserve at Breastworks South of CROIX BARBEE. 39 of Garhwal Rifles and 2/3 Gurkhas under Lieut Colonel Brook Cookburn in G2 Breastworks near BAREILLY Brigade Headquarters. These operations commenced on this front until 2'st May onwards. The Bn paraded at 1-30 a.m. and had moved into trenches 300 x East of CROIX BARBEE by 3 a.m. The DEHRA DUN attack was not successful. At 1-45 the Bn left the trenches and advanced to breastworks RUE DES BERSEAUX on a front of 1 Coy in 8 small Columns on file at 150 x distance. Coy A Coy in front followed by O.C. and B Coy and H.Q. This advance was made under heavy fire which became heavy as they approached LANSDOWNE POST. It was accomplished with a loss of only 2 or 8 casualties. A platoon moving their way across the field. The evening at Breastwork RUE DES BERSEAUX boys closed in their left and advanced up West 2 R 34 1/2. Communication trench.	Appendix P.2. — " — P.3 — " — P.4

Gulab Singh & Sons, Calcutta—No. 22 Army C.—5-8-14—1,07,000.

WAR DIARY
or
INTELLIGENCE SUMMARY.

(Erase heading not required.)

Army Form C. 2118.

Instructions regarding War Diaries and Intelligence Summaries are contained in F. S. Regs., Part II, and the Staff Manual respectively. Title pages will be prepared in manuscript.

57

Hour, Date, Place.	Summary of Events and Information.	Remarks and references to Appendices.
9. 5.15	This Trench was badly blocked owing to wounded and detached bodies of troops (which no British Officer) in command, owing down it, eventually B. reached the head of the trench by B3 Northern Breastwork at 3 p.m. Soon after arrival there Captain A.W.S. Buck was hit in the arm by shrapnel and Captain M.K. Wardle was also wounded while hanging a message from the G.O.C. to the O.C. 4th 49th BAREILLY Rifle attached. This attack was also unsuccessful. Shortly after 4 p.m. Lieut de Butts, the Brigade Signalling Officer, delivered a message "do not move in" B3 until 2/3 Gurkhas are clear. About 6 p.m. Captain Murray 13th Pioneers brought a message that the C.O. wished to see the O.C. Lieut de Butts asked as guide, followed by the C.O. and Captain Luscombe (as they were passing along behind B1 Southern Breastwork Lieut de Butts was hit by shrapnel. On arrival at the S & S orders were received that the Bn. should move into Breastwork as between CRESCENT communication Trench and the main Train. At 8 pm received orders to stand fast and at 11 p.m. received orders to take over DD2 Trenches. A Coy. and S3 to front line 2/3 B Coy in Redford (CRESCENT) and 5 Coy. v H.A. in Reserve. Relief completed 10.30 a.m. 10 May.	7.
10. 5.15	Intermitted German shelling, little sniping. Received order to move into Breastwork No 3. vicinity RUE DU BOIS as soon as 2/3 Gurkhas relieved. Commenced moving out of trenches at 8 p.m. and Bn settled down behind breastwork by 10 pm.	7.
11. 5.15	Shelled by German heavies at 6 a.m. and again by shrapnel and shrapnel from 9 a.m - 11.30 a.m. and by shrapnel only from 2.30 to 4.30 pm.	7.
12. 5.15	Intermittent shelling during day.	7.
13. 6.15	We ... of shelling. All medical Officers replied fairly warm from 4 to 5 and 6 to 6.45 pm. Intermittent shelling of all weights after the Bn. left Breastwork 3 at 9-10 pm and moved	7. APPENDIX "P5"

Gulab Singh & Sons, Calcutta—No. 22 Army C.—5-8-14—1,07,000.

Army Form C. 2118.

WAR DIARY
INTELLIGENCE SUMMARY.
(Erase heading not required.)

Instructions regarding War Diaries and Intelligence Summaries are contained in F. S. Regs., Part II, and the Staff Manual respectively. Title pages will be prepared in manuscript.

Hour, Date, Place.		Summary of Events and Information.	Remarks and references to Appendices.
13.	5.15	As follows:— D Platoon C Coy to trench line W. of Orchard front trench. 1 Platoon C Coy and B Coy in Orchard Trench. D Coy and Head Quarters in Breastwork just N. of RUE DU BOIS. A Coy in Breastwork 60x N. of above Breastwork	
14.	5.15	Intermittent shelling by enemy all M of A60, during day. Men ordered to reconstruct LANSDOWNE POST during evening. Advanced by 10 p.m.	7.
15.	5.15	In reserve during day in LANSDOWNE POST. Houses off at P 2 of our own front line from which the assault was to be made and by 9-30 p.m. Coys were in position. Telephonic communication established with left and right and commenced to place bridges on left and 2nd Division on my right. Seven bridges were placed over the stream which also handed to position and about 20x to 30x in front of it, there with the bursting in bridges made a total of 16 on the Bn front. It was not possible to place more bridges in position as the stream had been widened at many points by high shell holes and the trucks and branches of fallen trees also blocked any other places where bridges might have been put. This opening of the bridges into position was an operation of great difficulty on account of the constant flares and bursts of fire from the enemy's parapet. It was carefully and quickly done with only 2 or 3 casualties. At 10.45 p.m. Platoons were sorted over to the far side of the stream. Four men platoons were formed up ready in the trenches to go forward and support the leading platoons. The remaining two Coys were formed up lying down behind the parapets in close columns of platoons ready to advance. Thus the whole Bn was got into its final position in order to attack and as close up as possible.	7. APPENDIX "G" — — Q.1. — — Q.2. — — Q.3.

Army Form C. 2118.

WAR DIARY
— or —
INTELLIGENCE SUMMARY.
(Erase heading not required.)

Instructions regarding War Diaries and Intelligence Summaries are contained in F. S. Regs., Part II, and the Staff Manual respectively. Title pages will be prepared in manuscript.

Hour, Date, Place.	Summary of Events and Information.	Remarks and references to Appendices.
15. 3. 15.	This final formation was complete by 11-20 p.m. and thanks to the able leading of Company Commanders the movement was carried out in perfect order and with no noise. At 11-30 p.m. the leading platoons went forward to the assault slowly supported by the 2nd line. The time in rear went forward to take up the position vacated by the leading line. At the same time, as if anything some seconds before 11-30 p.m. the enemy opened a very heavy fire with rifles and machine guns. A few minutes afterwards he also mortars and Shrapnel started the village and the ground on both sides of it. The enemy threw from their trenches some kind of fire grenade which burnt into fire in contact with the ground, and these with continuous flares of all colours, literally turned night into day. The leading men pushed on, but only a few were able to reach near the enemy's parapet. Each succeeding line came under a very heavy fire the bridges got so blocked and the obstacles caused by fallen trees and elsewhere so impeded movement that effective support could not be given. Thus the impetus of the assault was broken before it really got a proper start. The enemy being fully manned and the accuracy	

Army Form C. 2118.

WAR DIARY
or
INTELLIGENCE SUMMARY.

(Erase heading not required.)

Instructions regarding War Diaries and Intelligence Summaries are contained in F. S. Regs., Part II, and the Staff Manual respectively. Title pages will be prepared in manuscript.

Hour, Date, Place.	Summary of Events and Information.	Remarks and references to Appendices.
15. 5.15	and intensity may be understood from the fact that 8 officers Platoon Commanders were killed or wounded. About 12 a.m. reports were received from the front that our attack could not reach the German line. Orders were then given to withdraw to our own trenches.	"
16. 5.15	At 9 a.m. Bn came back to Euerts Trench and Eueine Trench N of the RUE DU BOIS. 3 a.m. where Bn were entrenched. 5pm N of RUE DU BOIS. 8.30 pm. moved to CROIX BARBEE.	"
17 & 18-5-15	At CROIX BARBEE.	"
19. 5.15	At 4.30 pm Bn moved to take up front line from Cinder Track on to COPSE Communication Trench or relieving 2/8 Gurkhas. A Coy and B Coy (less Platoon) in firing line, D Coy and 1 platoon of B Coy in Support. C Coy rendezvous at CROIX BARBEE. Relief completed at 10.30pm.	Appendix 'R' " R 2 " R 3
20. 5.15	At 10 am shelling of V2 commenced aided by trench mortars. Bomb Guns and Machine Guns. Enemy bombarding our lines from 6.30 to 4.30 pm. and from 10 to 11.20 pm.	"
21. 5.15	A quiet day, except for a little shelling during afternoon. At 9.45 pm B coy moved out along front line to V.1. to co-operate with the attack of the SIRHIND Brigade by making a bomb-attack against the German Trenches between V.1 and V.2. One platoon D Coy to front line to	"

Gulab Singh & Sons, Calcutta—No. 22 Army C.—5-8-14—1,07,000.

Army Form C. 2118.

WAR DIARY
INTELLIGENCE SUMMARY.
(Erase heading not required.)

Instructions regarding War Diaries and Intelligence Summaries are contained in F. S. Regs., Part II, and the Staff Manual respectively. Title pages will be prepared in manuscript.

Hour, Date, Place.	Summary of Events and Information.	Remarks and references to Appendices.
21.5.15	Replace B Coy. A Coy to leave work N of factory. No further orders received from SIRHIND Brigade only a slip of instructions from the Brigadier. Operation Orders issued for B Coy. SIRHIND attack failed.	"
22.5.15	B Coy withdrew from V1 having left a Bombing Party and a platoon to support it to hold this flank. Rey 11-25 am they repaired the few in front line. A Coy moved from Stalburgh N of factory to the trenches occupied by our supports. From 5.30 to 7.30 am enemy put in about 10 large shells about Head Quarters and support trenches. During the night all bridges over the ditch in our immediate front were withdrawn. The platoon of B Coy at V1 was withdrawn to our support trenches after relief by H.L.I.	"
23.5.15	Bombing party relieved by 1st H.L.I. and during afternoon B Coy moved back to billets at CROIX BARBEE. A Coy relieving them in the front line. A Coy remaining as supports.	"
24.5.15	German Machine Gun Emplacement located about 200x N.E. of V3. This was shelled by 29 Battery. More shelling.	"
25.5.15	At 12.15 am. Lifeguards and scouts were thrown over no German battery located behind clumps of trees	

Army Form C. 2118.

WAR DIARY

or

INTELLIGENCE SUMMARY.

(Erase heading not required.)

Instructions regarding War Diaries and Intelligence Summaries are contained in F. S. Regs., Part II, and the Staff Manual respectively. Title pages will be prepared in manuscript.

Hour, Date, Place.			Summary of Events and Information.	Remarks and references to Appendices.
25.	5.	15.	N.E. of LA BASSEE Church and another behind Distillery S.E. of LA TOURELLE. M.G. fired from V3 and V6 apparently strongly held as much fire from there at our aircraft. Put wire entanglement and chevaux de frise in front of our line. Bn relieved by Garhwal Rifles, leaving A Coy in Reserve to Garhwal Rifles.	7.
26.	5.	15.		
27.	5.	15.	In Billets at Croix Barbee. War Training. A Coy in Reserve to Garhwal Rifles.	7.
28.	6.	15.		
29.	5.	15.		
30.	5.	15.		
31.	5.	15.	Bn left CROIX BARBEE at 2.45 p.m. and marched to new billets at PARADIS arriving 6 p.m.	

P.2

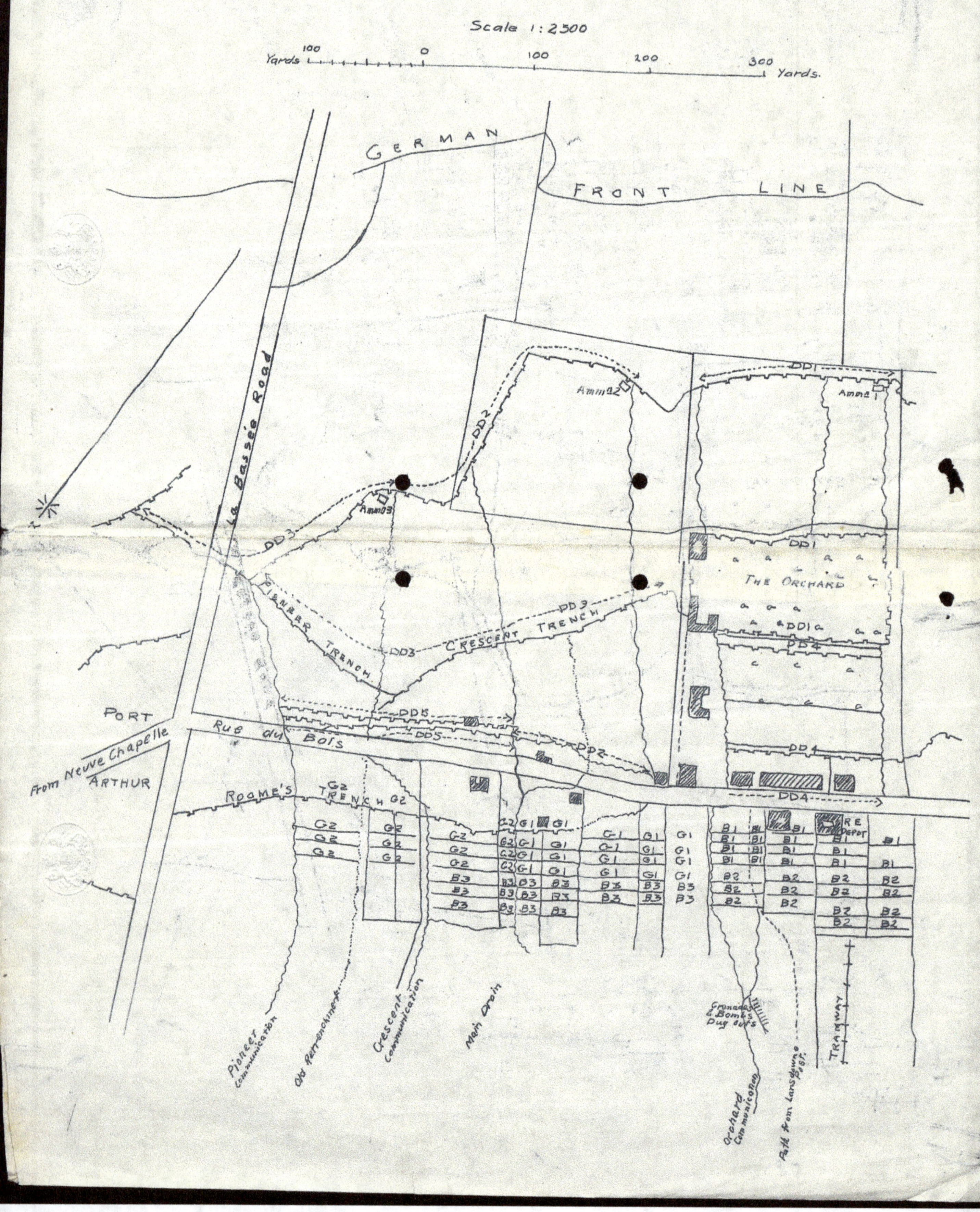

Scale 1:2500
Yards 100 0 100 200 300 Yards.
GERMAN FRONT LINE
La Bassée Road
Amm 1
Amm 2
Amm 3
DD1
DD2
DD3
DD4
DD5
THE ORCHARD
PIONEER TRENCH
CRESCENT TRENCH
PORT ARTHUR
From Neuve Chapelle
Rue du Bois
Roame's TRENCH
RE Depot
Pioneer communication
Old Retrenchment
Crescent communication
Main Drain
Grenades & Bombs Dug outs
Orchard Communication
Path from Lansdowne Post
TRAMWAY

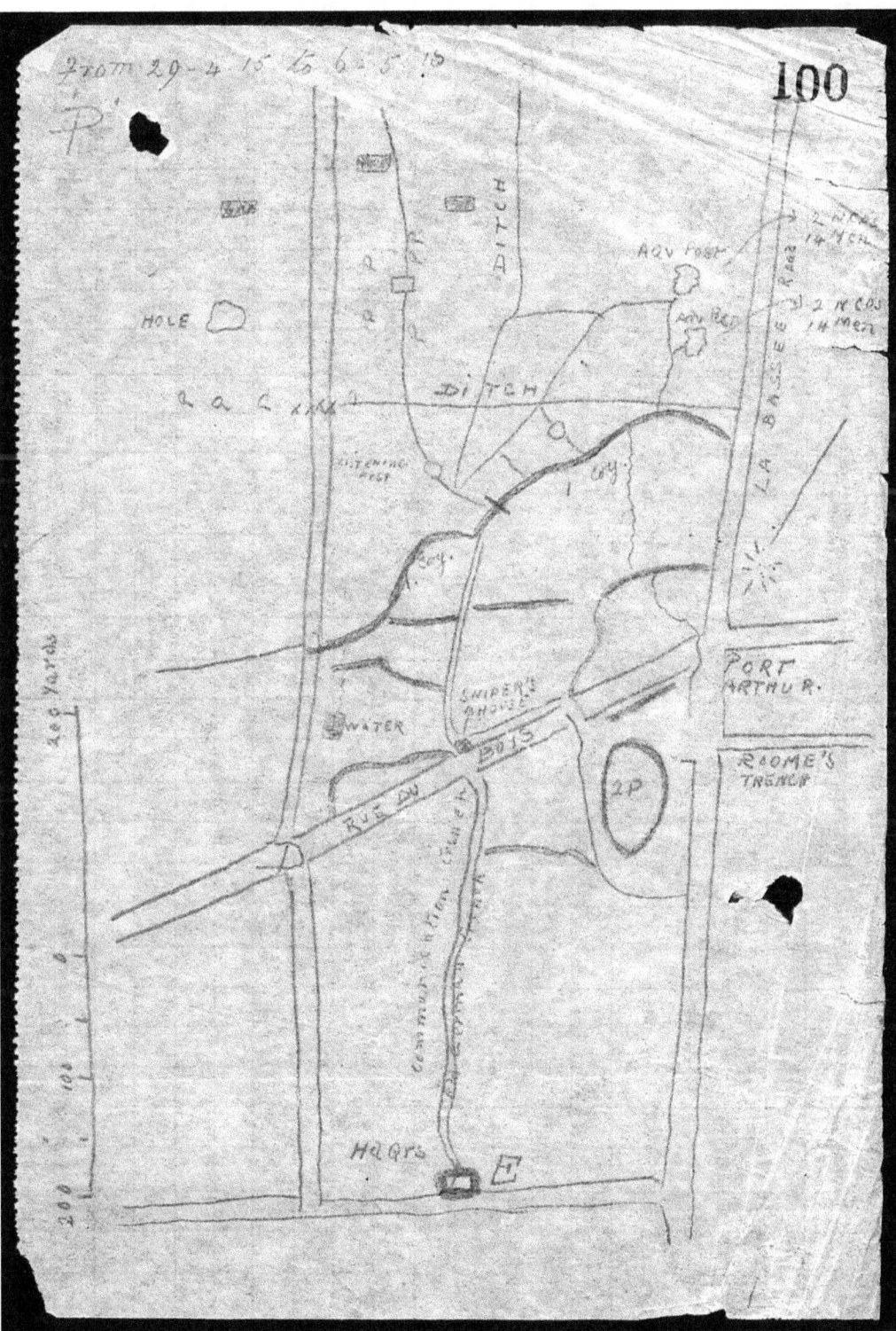

110 P3

Operation Orders Copy No. 6
by
Lieut Colonel H Gordon D.S.O.
Comdg Leicestershire Regt.

Reference maps   7-5-15
Trench map 1/10,000
FRANCE-BELGIUM No 36 1/40,000
BETHUNE sheet 1/40,000

1. The 1st Army is attacking on the
    8th May with a object of breaking
    through the enemy's line and
    gaining the LA BASSEE-LILLE
    Road between LA BASSE and
    FOURNES and then advancing
    to the line BAUVIN-DON.
    The 1st Corps, retaining it
    right at GIVENCHY advance
    on the RUE DU MARAIS,
    LORGIES and ILLIES.
    The Indian Corps will
    operated to cover the left

of the 1st Corps, capture the FERME DU BIEZ, and subsequently advance to the line LIGNY LE GRAND – LA CLIQUETERIE FERME.

The 4th Corps operate through AUBERS with a view to effecting a junction with the Indian Corps at LA CLIQUETERIE FERME

LAHORE Division holds the front except that portion from which the attack is to be delivered.

MEERUT Division is to deliver the attack. The DEHRA DUN Brigade is to assault the enemy's front line trenches from the point V6 to the vicinity of the point 56 and push on against further objectives, leaving garrisons at SOUTHERN end of LA TOURELLE, DISTILLERY, Road junction S.11.a, (points 52 and 53), houses near point 50 and the FERME DU BIEZ.

BAREILLY Brigade (less 1 Bn) in trenches North of RUE DU BOIS.

and in and East of LANSDOWNE POST is to occupy the assembly positions of BARA DON Brigade as they are vacated and to support that Brigade.

1 Bn BAREILLY Brigade (less two Coys with S.M.) will remain in LANSDOWNE POST and follow the GARHWAL Brigade into the assembly trenches just NORTH of the RUE DU BOIS.

2. GARHWAL Brigade (less two Bns) will be Divisional Reserve.

3. GARHWAL Rifles, 2/8 G.R., their M.G. and 2 trench guns under Lt. Col. DRAKE-BROCKMAN will be formed up in the two EASTERN Blocks of assembly trenches NORTH of the RUE DU BOIS by 1 a.m. the Bn will be formed up in quarter column facing SOUTH on ground by the track leading from CROIX BARBÉE to RICHEBOURG ST VAAST by 1-30 a.m. in following order. H. A. A.D. C.B.

The Bn will occupy trenches 300 ys.
SOUTH of the CROIX BARBEE - LA
COUTURE - RICHBOURG Road. Coys
moving to positions allotted to them
on receiving orders to do so. Position
of trench to be occupied has been
pointed out to O.C. Coys.
When the Bn is ordered to reinforce
it will move in the following order
A.D.C.B. Coy Commanders will direct
Coys by routes already pointed out
and in the manner previously
intimated.

4. 200 rounds ammn per man will be
carried.
S.A.A. Depôts have been established at
R.E. Depôt, RUE DU BOIS, and dugouts
in rear of front trench, as shown
on sketch of RUE DU BOIS in vicinity
of PORT ARTHUR which has been
sent to O.C. Coys.

Advanced R.E. Depots will be as RUE DU BOIS and FARM at M.33.d.7.7.

6. An advance base for bombs (trench guns) and hand grenades has been established 100 yards in rear of the Right of the assembly position of the BAREILLY Brigade.

7. The unexpended portion of the days ration and the emergency ration will be carried by each man.

8. A collecting station will be established between LANSDOWNE POST and where the Tramway Line crosses the RUE DES BERCEAUX. The route for wounded returning from the front will be by the Orchard Communication Trench, which runs from the RUE DU BOIS to the RUE DES BERCEAUX along the N.E. side of the Tramway Line and some 100 yards from it.

This trench will be reserved for the return of the wounded only after fighting has commenced.

9. Every man will carry 2 sandbags.

10. All respirators will be kept in readiness and soaked in soda solution.

11. All ranks should know the distinguishing flags for marking the position of advanced troops of the various divisions.

12. Prisoners will be handed over to the LAHORE Division at DEHRA DUN report centre in the RUE DU BOIS.

13. Official time will be given to O.C. Coy at their respective billets about 9.15 pm

14. 1st line transport is parked at R.35.d. 2.2. and from 10 a.m. tomorrow will be ready to move at ½ hours notice

Latham
Capt
Adjt 2nd Regt

Copy No 1 A Coy
" " 2 B Coy
" " 3 C Coy
" " 4 D Coy
" " 5 Q. Mr
" " 6 War Diary
" " 7 M.O. & H.Q.

Copy No 3

Operation Orders
Lt Col H. Gordon DSO.
Comdg Lancashire Regt.
Maps. BETHUNE 1/40,000   15th May 1915.
Trench Map 1/10,000.

Information 1. The 1st Corps & Indian Corps are to attack &
establish a line FESTUBERT — QUINQUE RUE — LA
TOURELLE Xroads — PORT ARTHUR, and are thento
push on to VIOLAINES and BEAURAINS.
    2nd Division & 7th Division are to attack on
MEERUT Division right, SIRHIND Bde support
GARHWAL Bde, BAREILLY Bde divisional Reserve,
DEHRA DUN in corps reserve.

Artillery 2. Artillery bombardment will cease at 11.25 p.m.
bombardment will continue on points 59 & 60
& on points EAST of the line 59 & V1E – V5E

Action 2. CORPS wd Bde attack enemy's line between
the two ditches indicated. Lancashires with
six Machine Guns will assault with
right on the ditch which runs through V5,
having as objective trenches already painted
out on the tracing maps.

joining up with the 2nd Devons on the right and the Garhwalis on the left — clearing and double blocking any trenches leading to the front. (The objective of the Garhwal Rifles is the Redoubt S.E. of V.B. making a defensive flank to the left.)

Time of Assault 3. The Assault will be delivered from the enemy's side of the ditch at 11.30 p.m. tonight.

Supporting Bns 4. Two Coys 2/3 G. Rifles will support the Battalion & will be in the Guards Trench, the 3rd Londons support the Garhwal Rifles.

Consolidation 5. The objectives given will be consolidated before daylight.

Bombing &c 6. Bombing, blocking, sandbag & tool parties will be organized in companies and are to use the flags issued.

Rations 7. Tomorrow's rations will be carried on the man in addition to the Iron Ration

Depots 8. Ammunition, bombs & sandbags, very
pistol ammunition will be kept in
depots in our front line. Bombs are
not in boxes so boxes must be sent back
when more bombs are required.

Masks 9. Masks will be got ready and soaked
and will be worn during the assault.

Wounded 10. Wounded will return by the trench
50 yards east of orchard to the Rue du
Bois dressing station.

OutPost
11. 96 Piccadilly, & dug-out close to.

Collecting 12. Collecting station just WEST of
Stn LANSDOWNE POST.

Distinguishing   2nd Divn wearing white ribs, at night
Marks 13.   showing to front & rear.
Distinguishing marks of bombing parties:—
2nd Divn marked by yellow screens in the
case of battalions & yellow flags for companies

1st Divn Red flags with white perpendicular stripe.

London Division sandbag discs with Black cross in centre.

LAHORE Divn Yellow flags 16" square.

Cont. 14. As soon as possible we will open the ditch that marks our right as communication to captured position, the ditch on left of GARHWAL rifles will also be opened.

Watchword 15. GARHWAL.

Reports 16. Reports to extreme right or left of present front line i.e. O.C. on left and 2nd in command on the Right.

Orders 17. Companies will be ready to move off at
March. 7.30 p.m. in following order. A.D.B.C. on arrival at front line companies will form up as personally explained to O.C. Coys. As soon as in position A & D Coys will put out bridges.

7-15 p

2/Lt SUTHERLAND will march from here with "A" Coy & assist with bridges.
Companies will begin to move into final position at 10.45 p.m.; as one platoon moves forward its place will be taken by another.
In the assault there will not be more than 20 yards between platoons.

Maintenance of The leading platoon of B & C Coys Communication will leave a party with bombs etc. of
   1 B, 1 NCO and 7 men at the right and left respectively of the first captured trench so as to ensure joining up with the units on either flank and preventing enemy gaining ingress to that trench. They fix the posts.

Messages 19. As soon as any trench is captured a message is to be sent to H.Q.

Time 20. Time will be given to O.C. Coys.

Lamps 21. The signalling lamps issued to A & D Coys will be taken up with the rear platoons of these companies and should as far as possible be carried on the inner flanks.

22. After beginning of operations the Western Communication Trench will be used only for FORWARD traffic and the Eastern one for REARWARD traffic. (except for wounded vide order No 10.)

Copy No 1.   A.
Copy No 2.   B.   F Latham Capt
- - - 3.   C.   adj Leic Regt.
- - - 4.   D.
- - - 5.   War Diary.
x + + x

7 - 15 p

Lt Sutherland will march from here
with "A" Coy & assist with Bridges.
Companies will begin to move into
position at 10.45 p.m.; as one
platoon moves forward its place
will be taken by another.
In the assault there will not be more
than 20 yards between platoons.

Maintenance of Communication — The leading platoon of B & C Coys
will leave a party with bombs etc. of
18. 1 NCO and 7 men at the right and
left respectively of the first captured
trench so as to ensure joining up
with the units on either flank and
preventing enemy going anywhere to
that trench.

Messages 19. As soon as any trench is captured a
message is to be sent to H.Q.

Time 20. This will be given to O.C. Coys.

Lamps 21. The signalling lamps issued to A & D Coys will be taken up with the rear platoons of these companies and should as far as possible be carried on the inner flanks.

22. After beginning of operations the Western communication trench will be used only for FORWARD traffic and the Eastern one for REARWARD traffic. (except for wounded vide order No 10.)

Copy No 1.   A.
Copy No 2   B.   F Latham Capt
---- 3.   C.   Adj Leic: Regt.
---- 4.   D.
---- 5.   W/A Diary
x x x 6.

P.4

OPERATION ORDER No. 40
by
Brigadier General C.G.Blackader, D.S.O.
Commanding GARHWAL BRIGADE.

COPY No. 1.

Reference Maps.   7th May, 1915.
Trench map, 1/10/ 1/10,000.
Map of France & Belgium, Sheet 36 (3rd edition) 1/40,000
Map of France, Bethune sheet, 1/40,000

Information. 1. The 1st Army is attacking on the 8th May with the object of breaking through the enemy's line and gaining the LA BASSEE-LILLE road between LABASSEE and FOURNES and then advancing on DON. *to the line BAUVIN — DON.*

The 1st Corps, retaining its right at GIVENCHY advances on the RUE DU MARAIS, LORGIES and ILLIES.

The Indian Corps will operate to cover the right of the 1st Corps, capture the FERME DU BIEZ, and subsequently advance to the line LIGNY LE GRAND,- LA CLIQUETERIE FERME.

The 4th Corps operate through AUBERS with a view to effecting a junction with the Indian Corps at LA CLIQUETERIE FERME.

LAHORE Division holds the line front except that portion from which the attack is to be delivered.

MEERUT Division is to deliver the attack.

ARTILLERY of the MEERUT Division, reinforced by that of LAHORE Division, one section HOTCHKISS motor battery, one section mountain artillery and some heavy batteries will prepare and support the attack.

The DEHRA DUN Brigade is to assault the enemy's front line trenches from the point V6 to the vicinity of the point 56 and push on against further objectives, leaving garrisons at SOUTHERN end of LA TOURELLE, DISTILLERY, road junction S.11.Xa, (points 52 & 53.), houses near point 50 and the FERME DU BIEZ.

BAREILLY Brigade (less one battalion) in trenches north of RUE DU BOIS, and in and east of LANSDOWNE Post is to occupy the assembly positions of DEHRA DUN Brigade as they are vacated and to support that brigade.

One battalion BAREILLY Brigade (less two companies with S & M) will remain in LANSDOWNE Post and follow the Garhwal Brigade into the assembly trenches just north of the RUE DU BOIS.

Intention. 2. Garhwal Brigade (less two battalions) will be Divisional reserve.

Detachment. 3 Lt.-Col. Drake-Brockman   will pass road junction M.
                commanding.   27. d. at 10 p.m., and march
            Capt. Etherton, staff offr.   via PONT LOGY and the area
            GARHWAL Rifles.   between the main drain on the
            2/8th GURKHA Rifles.   west and the ESTAIRES- LA
            Machine guns of above.   BASSEE road on the east to
            Two trench guns.   the two eastern blocks of
                                                assembly trenches north of
                                                the RUE DU BOIS, to be in
position by 1 a.m., reporting arrival to G.O's.C DEHRA DUN and GARHWAL Brigades.

Infantry 4. The Garhwal Brigade (less two Battalions, machine
movements.   gun sections and trench gun battery) will occupy trenches
              pointed out to O's. C., moving as under:-

Copy No. 1.

	Unit.	Position of assembly.	To march off at.
	2/3 Gurkhas.	North and clear of cross roads in CROIX BARBEE.	2.30 a.m.
	2/Leicesters.	CROIX-BARBEE – RICHEBOURG ST VAAST track.	2.15 a.m.
	3/ Londons.	East and clear of cross roads in CROIX BARBEE.	2.15. a.m.

Main roads are not to be blocked; troops will form up off the roads for filing into their trenches.
All units will report by 3 a.m. that they are in their allotted positions.

Machine & trench guns.
5. The Brigade machine gun detachments (less 6 guns) and the brigade trench gun battery (less 2 guns) will march at 2 a.m., via RUE des PUITS and ESTAIRES-LA BASSEE road to trenches at S.4.a.8.7., and will report when in position.

S.A.Ammn. 6. Two hundred rounds per man will be carried.
S.A.A. depots have been established at R.E. depot, RUE du BOIS, and dug outs in rear of front trench, as shown on sketch of RUE DU BOIS in vicinity of PORT ARTHUR, which have been sent to O'S. battalions.
The 3/ Londons, when ordered to advance, will carry up one box of S.A.Ammn. per two men from breastwork east of LANSDOWNE Post to the front line trenches and on from thence.

R.E.Depots, 7. Advanced R.E. depots will be at RUE DU BOIS and FARM at M.32.d.7.7.

Hand grenades and Bombs.
8. Each battalion has been provided with approximately 150 hand grenades in carrying boxes. An advanced base for bombs (trench gun) and hand grenades has been established 100 yards in rear of the right of the assembly position of the BAREILLY brigade.

Rations. 9. One day's cooked or tinned rations in addition to The unexpended portion of the day's ration will be and the emergency ration will be carried by each man.

Medical. 10. A collecting station will be established between LANSDOWNE Post and where the tramway line crosses the RUE des BERCEAUX. The route for wounded returning from the front will be by the "orchard" communication trench, which runs from the RUE du BOIS to the RUE des BERCEAUX along the north east side of the tramway line and some 100 yards from it. This trench will be reserved for the return of the wounded only, after fighting has commenced.

Sandbags. 11. Every man will carry two sandbags.

Masks. 12. All masks will be kept in readiness and soaked in soda solution.

Flags. 13. All ranks should know the distinguishing flags for marking the positions of advanced troops of the various divisions.

Prisoners. 14. Prisoners will be handed over to the LAHORE Division at DEHRA DUN report centre in the RUE du BOIS.

Time.

Time. 15. An officer from brigade head quarters will give the official time to all units about 8 p.m.

First line 16. First line transport will march via WELLINGTON Road in
accordance with orders issued separately, and will be parked
at R.35.b.2,3. It will be ready to move at half an hour's
notice from from 10 a.m. tomorrow onwards.

Report 17. Brigade head quarters will be at LANSDOWNE Post from 9
Centre. p.m. tonight.

                                            J.H.E.Stewart   Major,

                          Brigade Major, GARHWAL Brigade.

Issued through signal section at   p.m.

Copy No, 1 ....2/ Leicesters.
        2 ....2/ Londons.
        3. ,,,,,,,,,2/3 G.R.
        4. ....Garhwal Rifles.
        5. ....2/8th G.R.
        6. ,,,,,,,,,Bde. M.G.O.
        7. ....Bde. TRENCH GUN Offr.
        8. ......MEERUT Division.
        9. ....DEHRA DUN Bde.
       10. ....BAREILLY Bde.
       11. ....Col Drake-Brockman.
       12. ....War Diary.
       13 to15....Staff.

"P5"

Operation Order No. _____ copy no. ___
by
Brigadier General C.G. Blackader D.S.O.
Commanding, Garhwal Brigade

13rd May 1915.

1. The following reliefs will take place tonight.
At 8.30 p.m. the 2nd Leicesters will relieve the 2/8th Gurkhas in front line and support and reserve trenches, moving by the front of the assembly trenches N of the Rue du Bois.

2. At the same time the companies of the 2/8th Gurkhas at present in support and reserve will be moved past the rear of the assembly trenches and will relieve the 1/8th Gurkhas in the left subsection taking over at the same time from the 1/3rd London Regt. the front trench in front of the Orchard up to but excluding the centre communication trench

3. After the 2nd Leicesters have filed past the block of B1 Assembly trenches the Garhwal Rifles will relieve the 1/3rd London Regt. in the front trench from the centre Orchard Communication trench (inclusive) to the West and in the Orchard.

4. The 1/3rd London Regt on relief will move into that part of the B1 and B2 Blocks of assembly trenches north of the RUE DU BOIS, which lie East of the track passing Brigade Headquarters.

5. The 2/3rd Gurkhas on relief will move into the assembly trenches now occupied and about to be vacated by the 2nd Leicesters.

6. Officers commanding will arrange details mutually.

J.M. Stewart Major
B.M. ~~commanding~~ Garhwal Brigade

Issued through Signal Section 4 p.m.

Copy No 1 1/3 Londons
         2 2nd Leicesters ✓
         3 2/3rd Gurkhas
         4 Garhwal Rifles
         5 2/8th Gurkhas
         6 War Diary
         7 Staff

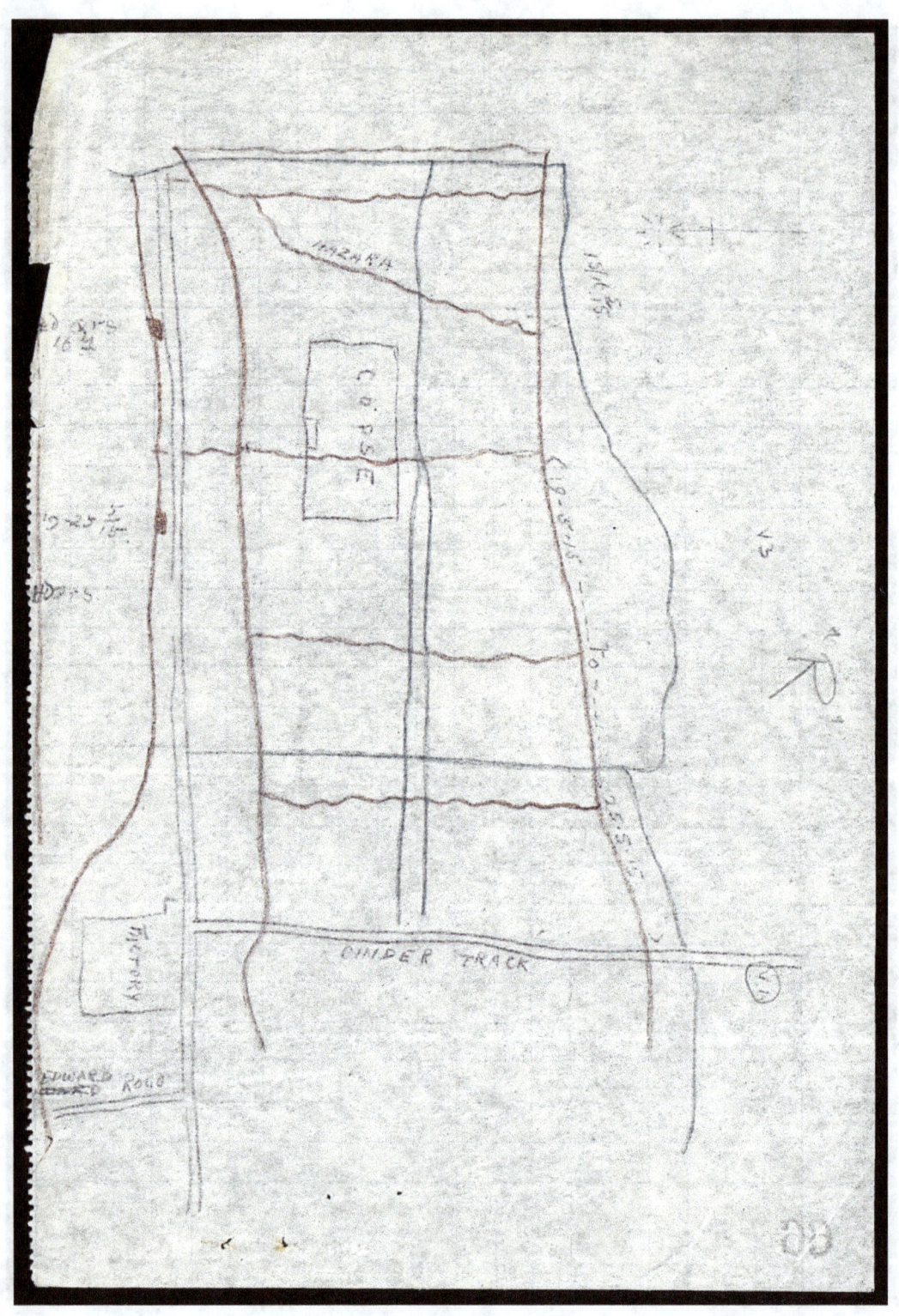

OPERATION ORDER No. 43   Copy No.

by,

Brigadier General C.G. Blackader, D.S.O.

Commanding Garhwal Brigade.

Reference Map   18th May 1915.
1/40000 Sheet No. 36.

Intention   1.   The following reliefs by the Garhwal Brigade
                      will take place to night of troops in a portion of
                      the front line held by the Bareilly Brigade.

                      2nd Leicesters will relieve 2/8 G.R. commencing
                      at 8-30 p.m.

                      2/3 G.R. will relieve 58th Rifles commencing
                      at 10 p.m.

                      1/3rd Londons will relieve 4th Black Watch in
                      the ORCHARD Redoubt and line in front of the
                      Orchard commencing at 8-30 p.m.

Routes   2.   The Leicesters will move by the EDWAED Road,
                      the 3rd Londons and the 2/3 G.R. west of the
                      Tramway Line.

Brigade Reserve 3.   The 2/8 G.R. will occupy billets vacated by the
                      Leicesters and will be in Brigade Reserve.

Divl. Reserve   4.   The Garhwal Rifles will be in Divisional Reserve
                      in their present location.

Brigade H.Q.   5.   Will remain at CROIX BARBEE.

                                                        Stewart
                                                                Major.
                              Brigade Major, Garhwal Brigade.

Issued through Signal Section at 5-30 p.m.

Copy No. 1 to 2nd Leicrs.
         2 to 1/3rd Londons
         3 to 2/3rd Gurkhas
         4 to The Garhwal Rifles
         5 to 2/8th Gurkhas
         6 to Bde. M.G.O.
         7 to Bde. B.G.O.
         8 to Bareilly Brigade
         9 to Meerut Division
        10 to War Diary
        11   Record
        12 to Staff Captain

OPERATION ORDER No. 44   Copy No. 1
by,
Brigadier General C.G. Blackader, D.S.O.
Commanding Garhwal Brigade.

Reference Map,
1/40000 Sheet No.36.   24th May 1915.

Reliefs   1. The following reliefs will take place:-
                 (a) The 2/3rd G.R. will relieve the 1/3rd Londons
                     in the line in front of the ORCHARD on the
                     night of the 24th/25th May.

                 (b) The Garhwal Rifles will relieve the 2nd Leicr.
                     Regiment in Subsection "A" on the night of the
                     25th/26th May.

                 Details of reliefs will be arranged mutually by
                 C.Os concerned.

Reserves, etc.   2. The Leicesters will leave one company as reserve
                 to the Garhwal Rifles.
                 The 1/3rd Londons will leave one company as
                 permanent garrison of the ORCHARD Redoubt.

Routes   3. The Garhwal Rifles will move by the track which
                 runs from the RUE des BERCEAUX approximately 300
                 yards east of WINDY CORNER to the Headquarters of
                 the Leicesters.

                 The 2nd Leicesters less one company on relief will
                 move by the same route and proceed to CROIX BARBEE.

                 The 1/3rd Londons on relief will march across
                 country west of the Tram Line and will move to
                 CROIX BARBEE.

Head Quarters   4. Brigade Head Quarters in RUE DU PUITS, M 26.d7.7.
                 from 6-30 p.m. to-day.

                                                    Major.
                             Brigade Major, Garhwal Brigade.

        Issued through Signal Section at 4-30 p.m.

Copy No. 1 to 2nd Leicesters   Copy No. 9 War Diary
         2   1/3rd Londons   10 Record
         3   2/3rd G.R.   11 Staff.
         4   Garhwal Rifles
         5   2/8th G.R.
         6   Bde. M.G.O.
         7   Bde. B.G.O.
         8   Meerut Division

A.M 27 10th May 1915

Report on Operations from 10th to 16th May 1915

The following report on the operations up to the 16th May is submitted in continuation of that on the action of the 9th.

2. After the line had been taken over from the Bareilly Brigade on the night of the 9th May, the battalions not actually holding the front line were kept in the assembly trenches near the RUE DU BOIS in preparation for operations which were ordered from time to time but were subsequently cancelled.

There was not only no available space for the occupation of these battalions further in rear, but it would also have seemed inadvisable to move back battalions who might almost immediately be required to be brought up again, owing to the uncertainty as to when operations would definitely take place. The movements to the rear and forward again would also have had to be carried out through communication trenches exposed to shrapnel and shell fire, and the amount of rest that would have been obtained would not in my opinion have compensated for the extra fatigue involved in the movement.

3. On the 14th May definite orders were received for the assault to take place during the night of the 15/16 May. The trenches at and near LANSDOWNE POST being vacant, the two battalions destined to make the attack were moved back there so that they might get some rest from the continuous shell fire to which they had been exposed since the 9th.

4. On the 15th May the positions of the battalions of the brigade were as follows:—

2/8th Gurkha Rifles, holding the line from the ESTAIRES–LABASSÉE road, to but excluding the centre communication trench from the ORCHARD redoubt to the front line.

4 (cont'd)

The 3rd Bn London Regt, holding the rest of the Orchard front.

The 2/3rd Gurkha Rifles holding the front recently taken over from the 2nd Bn.

The 2/Leicestershire Regiment and the Garhwal Rifles in trenches at and about LANSDOWNE POST.

5. At 8 p.m. on the 15th, the 2/Leicestershire Regiment and the Garhwal Rifles moved up into the trenches and took over those held by the 2/3rd Gurkhas and the 3/ London Regt respectively, and prepared for the assault ordered to take place at 11.30 p.m.

6. The work of placing bridges over the ditch in front was taken in hand at once, but periodical heavy firing in the direction of NEUVE CHAPELLE caused the Germans to throw up numerous flares and open fire, rendering the placing in position of the bridges a task even more difficult than it would otherwise have been. The number of bridges that could be placed over the ditch was limited, owing to the number of shell holes in the banks and the debris in the ditch itself. Beyond the ditch in many places there was an abattis of fallen tree trunks and branches. Even when the bridges had been placed in position, the obstacle remained formidable enough to break up any attack whether delivered by day or by night.

7. The fronts allotted to the Assaulting battalions were:—

2/Leicestershire Regt, right on ditch running from near V.5 towards our line; left on a line continuing that of the ditch bounding the western side of the ORCHARD.

Garhwal Rifles, right in contact with the Leicestershire Regiments left, left on ditch which runs from the vicinity of V.6 towards our line.

8. The objectives given were:—

Garhwal Rifles, the redoubt to the S.E. of V.6

2/Leicestershire Regt, enemy's trench running from the western corner of the above redoubt across the front allotted to the battalion.

9. Each assaulting battalion had 6 machine guns in close proximity to the front line, ready to move

9 (cont)

up immediately after any successful assault. The remainder of the machine guns of the Brigade and those of the BAREILLY Bde, were placed along the front of the edge of that part from which the attack was to issue, and in houses in rear, to support the attack by fire on the enemy's line beyond the left flank of the Garhwal Rifles.

The Trench guns of the 3 brigades, and No 4 trench mortar battery, were placed behind the front line in positions to enable them to bomb the enemy's front trench east of V 6.

10. As soon as bridges were in position, the 2/ Leicestershire Regiment and the Garhwal Rifles began to get their companies in position for assaulting. Each battalion sent forward the platoons who were to assault to the enemy's side of the ditch.

By 11.25 pm both battalions were in position as follows :—

2/ Leicestershire Regt.

  2 platoons lying on the enemy's side of the ditch
  2 platoons lying on our side of the ditch
  4 platoons in the front line trench ready to go
    forward and support the assaulting platoons
  2 Companies lying behind the parados
    of the front line trench.

The Garhwal Rifles.

  1 Company lying on the enemy's side of the ditch
  2 platoons lying on our side of the ditch
  2 platoons in our front line trench
  2 platoons in rear of the parados.
  Remainder of the battalion in rear of the
    above

11.

Two companies 2/3 Gurkha Rifles in close support of the 2 Leicestershire regiment, and the 3 London Regt in close support of the Garhwal Rifles, closed up to the front, occupying the trenches vacated by the leading battalions.

The remainder of the 2/3 Gurkhas was in Brigade reserve in the assembly trenches north of the Rue du Bois.

12. During the evening the Germans were heard to call out, "Come on, we are ready for you", and it appears to be more than a coincidence, that, though there was little loss while bridges were being put out, and advanced platoons were moving out to the front, at 11.30pm, as the assaulting platoons rose to advance, if not slightly before, the German machine gun and rifle fire broke out, sweeping the front on which the assault was to be delivered, and not that to the East of it.

In spite of efforts to reach the German trenches the advance of both battalions was brought to a standstill, and each successive line as it advanced met the same fate. The whole front was lit up by German flares and light bombs which, thrown over the parapet, burst, on impact on the ground, into flame.

13. About midnight it was evident that there was no prospect of success even if the attack were pressed. Officers commanding the Leicestershire Regt and the Garhwal Rifles were therefore ordered to withdraw their battalions, and the 2/3rd Gurkhas and 2/London were directed to take up the rôles of the battalions which they had respectively been supporting.

14. At 2.45 a.m. the bombardment of the enemy's trenches was begun, and at 3 a.m. the battalions detailed for the second assault were in position with their leading platoons in our front line trenches. It was not possible, owing to light, to launch the assault in this case from the enemy's side of the ditch, as men could not have reached that position unseen.

15. At 3.15 a.m. the assault was launched. As soon as the first line surmounted the parapet the enemy opened a heavy rifle, machine gun and artillery fire, and the assaulting troops were unable to reach the enemy's trenches, the majority being shot down as they crossed our own parapet.

16. In these bold attacks a few officers and men arrived within a few yards of the German wire, before they were shot down, but none were able to get any further.

17. In these circumstances it appeared to me that, in the face of the intense rifle, machine gun and artillery fire, directed against our parapets and on the ground immediately in front of it, any attempt to renew the assault could not meet with success, and would only lead to a great and useless loss of life. I therefore directed the 3rd London Regt & 2/3 Gurkhas to hold the line and reorganise in case they should be required to make another attempt.

18. The 2 Leicestershire Regiment and the Garhwal Rifles were brought back to the assembly trenches north of the Rue Du Bois, and the whole brigade kept in readiness to take advantage of any opportunity, opened up by the success of the 2nd Division, to attack once more to break the enemy's line in my front.

19. In the evening of the 16th the Garhwal Bde was relieved by the Bareilly Brigade in the trenches and marched to CROIX BARBEE leaving the 2/8th Gurkha Rifles at LANSDOWNE POST

20. The following gives the approximate numbers of casualties during the period 9th to 16th May both dates inclusive —

2nd Batn Leicestershire Regt   Killed 5 officers   22 ORs
                               Wounded 6   192
                               Missing   5 "
3rd Batn London Regt   Killed   10
                               Wounded 3   26
                               Missing   5
2/3 Gurkha Rifles   Killed 2   1 CO   13 ORs
                               Wounded 1   1   111
                               Missing   3
Garhwal Rifles   Killed 3   15
                               Wounded 4   10   274
1/39 Gurkha Rifles   Missing
                               Killed 1   7
                               Wounded 4   5   249
                               Missing
Bde H.Q.   Killed   1
                               Wounded 1   2   4

20 (cont.)

The total casualties of the brigade amounted to approximately

	Killed	Wounded	Missing
British Officers	1	19	
Other ranks British	33	280	59
Indian Officers	1	16	
Other ranks Indian	35	638	48
Totals	75	953	107

Total casualties 1138.

21. I have lists of recommendations for rewards to submit, these will follow as soon as possible.

C.P. Blackader
Brigadier General
Commanding Garhwal Bde

Garhwal Brigade

War Diary

Appendices:—

Tactical Progress Reports
20th to 31st May 1915

B.M. 1330.

Tactical Progress Report
Garhwal Brigade.
up to 6 p.m. 20-5-1915.

1. (a) <u>Action by our own troops</u>.

Relieved Bareilly Brigade in trenches from Orchard inclusive to left of Sirhind Brigade.
Patrols went close up to German lines last night but heard little movement.
Trench mortars, Bomb Guns and maxims were concentrated to fire on V.2, on which artillery also were firing.

(b) <u>Action by enemy's troops</u>.

Enemy has been inactive and quiet during the night and day. They shelled the Leicesters front line intermittently all day. Many shells were blind.
There were few flares last night and in front of Leicesters these were reported to have been thrown up from the 2nd line.

2. <u>Information</u>.

A German biplane passed over our lines about 1.30 p.m. but was turned back by our guns.
A machine gun fired from V.3 last night.
State of ground and trenches much improved.

3. <u>Work done</u>.

Strengthening and repair of parapets and parados and of communication trenches.
Cleaning up of trenches.

C.P. Blackader Brigadier General
Commanding Garhwal Brigade.

Tactical Progress Report
Garhwal Brigade
up to 6 pm. 21st May 1915

B.M. 1335.

1. (a) <u>Action by our Own troops</u>.
Short bursts of rifle and machine gun fire on enemy's trenches during the night.

(b) <u>Action by Enemy's troops</u>.
Enemy not aggressive during the last 24 hours except for shelling at 6-30 p.m. and 10-30 p.m. yesterday and occasionally during the day on RUE DU BOIS and communication trenches.

2. <u>Information</u>.
Enemy have done some work in repairing parapets in the night, new sandbags showing in places.

3. <u>Work Done</u>.
Improving parapets and parados.
Cleaning and bricking communication trenches.

CPBlackader   Brig. General
~~Major~~
~~for~~ G.O.C. Garhwal Brigade.

Tactical Progress Report
Garhwal Brigade.
up to 6 p.m. 22nd May 1915.

B.M. 1354

1 (a) <u>Action by our own troops</u>
Fired with maxims on enemy's parapets where work might be in progress.

(b) <u>Action by Enemy's troops.</u>
Enemy machine guns fired during the night.
Enemy shelled at 7 p.m, 11-30 p.m, and 2.30 a.m.
A considerable number of heavy shells on the Assembly trenches and Reserve trenches north of the RUE DU BOIS, about 1 p.m. and 5 p.m. today

2. <u>Information.</u>
Enemy's front line appeared to be strongly held last night.
Machine gun fired from V.6.
German biplane passed over our lines at 7-30 a.m.
Patrols report enemy not seen working on parapets or wire last night.

3. <u>Work Done.</u>
Improvement of front and reserve trenches.
Continuation of parados, shelters, firing platforms and communication trenches.

C.P. Blackader
Brigr General.
Commanding Garhwal Brigade.

Tactical Progress Report
Garhwal Brigade.
up to 6 p.m. 23-5-15.

1 (a) <u>Action by our own troops</u>.
Snipers and Machine Guns fired on enemy's loopholes and working parties.

(b) <u>Action by enemy's troops</u>.
Enemy shelled RUE du BOIS and vicinity with heavy shells between 6 p.m. and 7 p.m. last evening. RUE du BOIS from CRESCENT to west of COPSE, ORCHARD HAZARA and COPSE Communication trenches shelled at intervals during the day.

2. <u>Information</u>.
Enemy did not display much activity during the night no wire mended but some parapets repaired.
Scout of Leirs got up to enemy's parapet and discovered Germans removing ammunition from front to 2nd line. It is also reported enemy's front trench said to be about 7 feet deep with firing platform. Scout also saw two bomb guns and some bomb gun ammunition.
Two aeroplanes seen during the day one at 9 a.m. and the other at 1.30 p.m.
A new Machine Gun emplacement located 500ˣ N.E. of V.3.

3. <u>Work Done</u>.
Bridges taken in and wire obstacles begun.
Repairs and improvements to parapets, parados and trenches continued.

C/Blackader Brigr. General.
Commanding Garhwal Brigade.

Tactical Progress Report
Garhwal Brigade.
up to 6 p.m. 24. 5. 1915.

1 (a) <u>Action by our own troops.</u>
Machine Guns fired at intervals during the night.
Machine Gun and rifle fire employed against
German machine Guns located 200/NE of V-3.

(b) <u>Action by Enemy's troops.</u>
Enemy threw up flares throughout the night especially
in direction of R.C.V.1. where 6 or 7 were thrown up
together continuously.
Enemy opened heavy rifle fire on "A" subsection trenches
from 12-45 a.m. to 12-55 a.m. accompanied by a burst of
shelling from 77 m.m. guns.
Heavy rifle and artillery fire again opened at
1-40 a.m.
Enemy shelled RUE du BOIS with heavy shells at
11-15 a.m. and the ORCHARD and vicinity with 77 m.m.
guns at 5 p.m.

2. <u>Information.</u>
Enemy repaired some parapets but no wire during
the night.
Patrol of Leicestershire Regiment located a field
Battery in a clump of trees near Q.19 or the FERME de
TOULOTTE. This position was pointed out to Artillery
observing officer.
German aircraft seen during the day:-
Biplane at 6-30 a.m. and another at 11 a.m. both
driven back by anti aircraft gun.

3. <u>Work Done</u>
Bridges brought in.
New chevaux de frise and wire entanglement
put out.
Repairs and improvements to parapets, parados,
fire and communication trenches.

C.P. Blackader Brigr. General.
Commanding Garhwal Brigade.

Tactical Progress Report
Garhwal Brigade
up to 6 p.m. 25.5.15.

1 (b) Action by the Enemy's troops.
Enemy opened a heavy fire of machine guns and Rifles from V.1 and vicinity of FERME du BOIS between 11.50 p.m. and 12.30 a.m. and again at 12.50 am. and 1.30 a.m. Also field artillery shelled our trenches and RUE du BOIS during the night.
Enemy machine gun fired from V.3 during the day.
Enemy's shelling much less to-day.

2. Information.
Enemy seemed nervous last night, throwing up a greater number of flares than usual.
An enemy battery appears to be behind a clump of trees North of LA BASSEE Church and another behind the Distillery S.E. of LA TOURELLE.
Patrols report noise of wood being cut and shovelling of earth inside enemy's trenches.
Enemy's front line is said to be apparently empty during the day.
Aircraft seen - One aeroplane about 8 a.m. and another at 11 a.m.

3. Work Done.
New wire entanglement put out.
Front line, Reserve and communication trenches repaired and strengthened.

C P Blackader
Brigadier General.
Commanding Garhwal Brigade.

B.M. 1440.

Tactical Progress Report
Garhwal Brigade
up to 6 p.m. 26-5-15.

1. (a) <u>Action by our own troops</u>.
Garhwal Rifles relieved Leicesters in right subsection.

(b) <u>Action by Enemy's troops</u>.
Enemy shelled RUE DU BOIS with heavy howitzers for two hours during the middle of the day. Very little rifle fire.

2. <u>Information</u>.
Patrols reported sounds of enemy driving stakes and shovelling earth in front of ORCHARD. Maxims opened on them.
Hostile aeroplanes seen at 4-30, 7 and 8-30 a.m. They turned back upon being fired at.

3. <u>Work Done</u>.
Repairing and improving parapets and communication trenches.
A new communication trench begun between HAZARA and COPSE Communication trenches.

CG Blackader   Brigadier General
Commanding Garhwal Brigade.

B.M. 1462.

Tactical Progress Report
Garhwal Brigade
up to 6 pm 27-5-15.

1 (a) **Action by our own troops.**
Maxims fired on portions of enemy's parapets on which it was suspected that work might be done.

(b) **Action by Enemy's troops.**
Enemy shelled front line and RUE DU BOIS at intervals during the day also between WINDY CORNER and LANSDOWNE POST. Sniping a little heavier than usual.

2. **Information.**
Some black sandbags have been recently placed in broken portions of the enemy's front line, but his wire appears not to have been repaired at all.
A German Aeroplane was seen last evening at about 7 p.m.

3. **Work Done.**
Wiring of front line completed.
Strengthening and repairs of parapets and parados continued.
Communication trenches repaired and new one continued.

C P Blackader Brigadier General.
Commanding Garhwal Brigade.

B.M. 1480

Tactical Progress Report.
Garhwal Brigade
up to 6 p.m. 28-5-15.

1 (b) Action by the Enemy's Troops.
Very little sniping during the last 24 hours.
Enemy shelled front trench this afternoon doing little damage.
A few howitzer shells near the Factory.

2. Information.
No alteration in Enemy's parapet or wire.
Patrols report that they got within 30 yards of the enemy's wire and heard them talking and working behind the parapet, there were no workers out in front.
German aeroplane moving South Westward passed over line very high at 6.20 p.m.

3. Work Done.
Work continued in front line trenches and communications.

CG Blackader Brigadier General
Commanding Garhwal Brigade.

B M

Tactical Progress Report
Garhwal Brigade
up to 6 pm 29.5.15

1. (a) <u>Action by our own troops</u>

Enemy working parties were fired on and dispersed.

(b) <u>Action by enemy's troops</u>

Very little sniping by the enemy.

Enemy shelled area behind fire trench on right of right subsection, also area round factory and N of Rue-du-Bois near right subsection HQ.

Some howitzer shells were thrown into area N of Rue-du-Puits evidently in search of a battery.

77 m.m. shells along the Rue-du-Puits.

2. <u>Information</u>

Enemy appears to have made some repairs to his parapet.

Scouts heard work going on inside his trenches.

One aeroplane seen at 4.40 pm which returned on being fired at, but came back at intervals later, turning back each time when fired on.

3. <u>Work Done</u>

Work continued on repairing and strengthening parapet of fire trench and in improvement and tracking of communication trenches.

C.P. Blackader, Brigadier General,
Commanding Garhwal Brigade.

BM. 1511

Tactical Progress Report.
Garhwal Brigade.
up to 6 p.m. 30.5.15.

1. (a) *Action by our own troops.*
   Scouts patrolled front as usual.

   (b) *Action by enemy's troops.*
   A greater amount of sniping than usual last night.
   Two machine guns in front of right subsection active during the night.
   Enemy shelled Guards trench and new portions of communication trench in centre of right subsection near RUE DU BOIS.

2. *Information.*
   Enemy have been strengthening their parapets especially in the vicinity of V2, where they appear to be digging other trenches in rear.
   An unusual amount of singing and noise in German trenches last night, perhaps indicating a change of troops.

3. *Work Done.*
   Guards trench converted into a fire trench in left subsection where shelters had been made behind the parapet.
   Eastern communication trench from Orchard to front line cleared, improved, and completed.
   Traverses and parados in front line improved.
   COPSE and centre communication trench of right subsection improved and repaired.
   Strengthening and repairing front line parapet continued.
   Repair of Guards trench on right of right subsection commenced.

   C/Blackader Brigadier General.
   Commanding Garhwal Brigade.

B.M. 1525.

Tactical Progress Report.
Garhwal Brigade
up to 6 p.m. 31.5.15.

1 (a) <u>Action by our own troops</u>.

Orchard front handed over last night to Jullundur Brigade. (30th/31st)
A working party dispersed by maxim gun fire.

(b) <u>Action by Enemy's troops</u>.

Enemy shelled right of Right Subsection at 12-30 a.m. and 2-30 a.m., and also the communication trench in rear.
Snipers appeared more active.

2. <u>Information</u>.

Some flares used by Germans last night appeared to have a longer range than usual. One nearly reaching the Guards' trench.
Enemy has been continuing work behind V-2 and this portion appears to be becoming strong.
Aeroplanes seen at 3-30 and 6. a.m. which returned on being fired at.

3. <u>Work Done</u>.

Trenches and communications improved.

H R B Reed Captain.
for Brigadier General.
Commanding Garhwal Brigade.

Garhwal Brigade

War Diary.

Appendices

Operation Orders.

OPERATION ORDER No. 39.   Copy No. 10
by,
Brigadier General C.G.Blackader, D.S.O.
Commanding Garhwal Brigade.

Reference Map
1/40000 Sheet 36.   4th May 1915.

Information.   1. The Garhwal Brigade will be relieved by the
                      Jullundur Brigade on the night 5th/6th May.

Reliefs.   2. Relieving units will arrive at PONT LOGY road
                      junction at the following times:-
                      "A" Subsection- Suffolks- ~~8.15 p.m.~~ 10 pm
                      Southern half "C" Subsection-58th Rifles- ~~8.15 pm~~ 10.15 pm
                      "B" Subsection- (40th Pathans) ~~8.00 pm~~ 8.30 pm
                                      (47th Sikhs   )
                      Northern half "C" Subsection)- ~~8.15 pm~~ 8.45 pm.
                      "D" Subsection   )
                      Units now occupying each Subsection will send
                      guides to meet relieving units at PONT LOGY
                      accordingly.

Assembly of Units 3. On relief units will assemble by companies at
                      points which will be notified later, where they
                      will be met by Quartermasters and led to their
                      bivouacs. *Troops from A & B Subsections will move by the RUE DES*
                      BERCEAUX and those from C and D by the tramway line and the
                      LORETTO Road.

Ammunition.   4. Two hundred rounds of ammunition will be carried
                      by each man.

Rifle Grenades,5.   The following will be handed over to relieving
etc.   units:-
                      S.A.Ammunition other than that carried on the man.
                      Very Pistol ammunition (but not Very Pistols)
                      Rifle Grenades.
                      Any bombs in trenches other than those in boxes
                      which units took in with them. These latter
                      will be brought out and retained by units.
                      C,Os will hand over to relieving units lists
                      showing the numbers of the above articles which
                      are being handed over.

Machine Guns.   6. Machine guns will be relieved and withdrawn at
                      the same time as the units in whose Subsection
                      they are located.

Reports.   7. The G.O.C. Garhwal Brigade will remain in
                      command of the line till reliefs are completed
                      after which Headquarters will be at M.27.a.1.1.

                                                        Major.
                              Brigade Major, Garhwal Brigade.

Issued through Signal Section at 6 a.m. 5.4.15

Copy No. 1 to 2nd Leics   *Copy No. 9 to Meerut Div*
"   "   2 to 1/3 Londons   *"   " 10 War Diary*
"   "   3 to 2/3 G.R.   *"   " 11 Staff.*
"   "   4 to Garhwal Rifles
"   "   5 to 2/8 G.R.
"   "   6 to Bde M.G.O.
"   "   7 to Bde B.G.O.
"   "   8 to Jullundur Bde

OPERATION ORDER No. 43   Copy No. 10

by,

Brigadier General C.G.Blackader, D.S.O.

Commanding Garhwal Brigade.

Reference Map   18th May 1915.
1/40000 Sheet No. 36.

Intention   1. The following reliefs by the Garhwal Brigade
                    will take place to night of troops in a portion of
                    the front line held by the Bareilly Brigade,

                    2nd Leicesters will relieve 2/8 G.R. commencing
                        at 8-30 p.m.

                    2/3 G.R. will relieve 58th Rifles commencing
                        at 10 p.m.

                    1/3rd Londons will relieve 4th Black Watch in
                        the ORCHARD Redoubt and line in front of the
                        Orchard commencing at 8-30 p.m.

Routes   2. The Leicesters will move by the EDWAED Road,
                    the 3rd Londons and the 2/3 G.R. west of the
                    Tramway Line.

Brigade Reserve 3. The 2/8 G.R. will occupy billets vacated by the
                    Leicesters and will be in Brigade Reserve.

Divl. Reserve   4. The Garhwal Rifles will be in Divisional Reserve
                    in their present location.

Brigade H.Q.   5. Will remain at CROIX BARBEE.

                                           Major.
                        Brigade Major, Garhwal Brigade.

Issued through Signal Section at 5-30 p.m.

Copy No. 1 to 2nd Leicrs.
         2 to 1/3rd Londons
         3 to 2/3 rd Gurkhas
         4 to The Garhwal Rifles
         5 to 2/8th Gurkhas
         6 to Bde. M.G.O.
         7 to Bde. B.G.O.
         8 to Bareilly Brigade
         9 to Meerut Division
        10 to War Diary
        11   Record
        12 to Staff Captain

OPERATION ORDER No. 44   Copy No. 9
by,
Brigadier General C.G.Blackader, D.S.O.
Commanding Garhwal Brigade.

Reference Map,
1/40000 Sheet No.36.   24th May 1915.

Reliefs
1. The following reliefs will take place:-
   (a) The 2/3rd G.R. will relieve the 1/3rd Londons in the line in front of the ORCHARD on the night of the 24th/25th May.

   (b) The Garhwal Rifles will relieve the 2nd Leicr. Regiment in Subsection "A" on the night of the 25th/26th May.

   Details of reliefs will be arranged mutually by C.Os concerned.

Reserves, etc.
2. The Leicesters will leave one company as reserve to the Garhwal Rifles.
The 1/3rd Londons will leave one company as permanent garrison of the ORCHARD Redoubt.

Routes
3. The Garhwal Rifles will move by the track which runs from the RUE des BERCEAUX approximately 300 yards east of WINDY CORNER to the Headquarters of the Leicesters.

The 2nd Leicesters less one company on relief will move by the same route and proceed to CROIX BARBEE.

The 1/3rd Londons on relief will march across country west of the Tram Line and will move to CROIX BARBEE.

Head Quarters
4. Brigade Head Quarters in RUE DU PUITS, M 36.d7.7. from 6-30 p.m. to-day.

Major.
Brigade Major, Garhwal Brigade.

Issued through Signal Section at 4-30 p.m.

Copy No. 1 to 2nd Leicesters   Copy No. 9 War Diary
        2   1/3rd Londons   10 Record
        3   2/3rd G.R.   11 Staff.
        4   Garhwal Rifles
        5   2/8th G.R.
        6   Bde. M.G.O.
        7   Bde. B.G.O.
        8   Meerut Division

OPERATION ORDER No. 45   Copy No. 9
by
Brigadier General C.G. Blackader, D.S.O.

Reference Map
1/40000 Sheet 36.   26th May 1915.

Inlying Battalion 1. While the Brigade is at CROIX BARBEE one battalion will be detailed daily as Inlying Battalion to be ready to move in 15 minutes.

The remaining battalions will be ready to move in 30 minutes.

Concentration 2. On the word "MEET" the units in Brigade Reserve will concentrate as follows:-

Battalion in trenches south of CROIX BARBEE- Head of column facing south 20 yards north of junction of LORETTO and OXFORD Roads.

Brigade M.G. Section in rear of above Battalion.

Battalion at CROIX BARBEE Cross Roads-in rear of M.Gs,- column along OXFORD Road, tail clear of the cross roads.

Battalion to west of Cross Roads-head of column facing east 20 yards clear of cross roads.

Reports 3. An officer from each unit to report to Brigade H.Q. at the head of the column as soon as it is in position.

                                        J.M.R.Stewart,
                                                Major.
                    Brigade Major, Garhwal Brigade.

Issued through Signal Section at 11 a.m.

Copy No. 1 to 2nd Leicesters
     2   1/3 Londons
     3   2/3 G.R.
     4   Garhwal Rifles
     5   2/8th G.R.
     6   Bde M.G.O.
     7   Bde. B.G.O.
     8   Meerut Division
     9   War Diary
    10   Record
    11   Staff

OPERATION ORDER No. 46   Copy No. 9
by,
Brigadier General C.G.Blackader, D.S.O.
Commanding Garhwal Brigade.

Reference Map
1/40000 Sheet No. 36   26th May 1915.

Reliefs   1. On the night of the 27th/28th May the 2/8th G.R. will relieve the 2/3rd G.R. in the front line commencing at 8-30 p.m.

           Route for relieving and relieved troops to be via WINDY CORNER, RUE DES BERCEAUX and across country west of the tramway line.

           Details will be arranged mutually by C.Os concerned.

           The 2/3rd G.R. on relief will proceed to billets vacated by the 2/8th G.R.

                                                  Major.
                      Brigade Major, Garhwal Brigade.

    Issued through Signal Section at 5-30 p.m.

    Copy No. 1 to 2nd Leicesters
            2   1/3rd Londons
            3   2/3rd G.R.
            4   Garhwal Rifles
            5   2/8th G.R.   1-30/pm
            6   Bde. M.G.O.
            7   Bde. B.G.O.
            8   Meerut Division
            9   War Diary
           10   Record
           11   Staff

OPERATION ORDER No.47   Copy No. 10
by,
Brigadier General C.G.Blackader, D.S.O.
Commanding Garhwal Brigade.

Reference Maps:-
1/40000 BETHUNE SHEET,
36 SHEET, and 1/5000   31st May 1915.
Trench Map.

Information	1. The Indian Corps has been reorganised with effect from to-day and now includes the 8th, 42th, LAHORE and MEERUT Divisions and is to hold the front from near TOUQUET ~~the~~ QUINQUE RUE (exclusive). The Meerut Division is to hold the line from a point midway between V.1 and R.6 to but excluding the the QUINQUE RUE.
Intention	2. The Garhwal Brigade will be relieved on the night of the 31st May/1st June by the FEROZEPORE Brigade, and will move into billets.
Orders for Units	3. The 2/3rd Gurkhas will march at 9-0 p.m. to-day to X.3.d. and X.4.a. via M.35.d. and LA COUTURE. The 2nd Leicesters (less 1 company) and 1/3rd Londons will march at 3-10p.m.and 3-0p.m.respectively to PARADIS via M.20.c., R.28.d., FOSSE, R.20.c., Q.24.1. The Garhwal Rifles will, on relief, march by companies to R.34.b., via WINDY CORNER, RICHEBOURG-ST VAAST, R.35.d. and R.34.d. The 2/8th Gurkha Rifles, on relief, will march by companies to R.34.c. via WINDY CORNER, RICHEBOURG-ST VAAST, R.35.d. and LA COUTURE. One company 2nd Leicesters, on relief from Reserve trenches, will march to bivouac near LES LOBES. For Machine Gun Section and Bomb Gun Section instructions will be issued later.
Baggage Wagons	4. Baggage wagons will not be ordered up to-day.
Ammunition	5. Two hundred rounds per man will be carried out, all other ammunition loose or in boxes will be handed over to relieving units.
Very Pistol Ammunition.	6. Very Pistol Ammunition (but not Very Pistols) will be handed over.
Hand Grenades	7. Each unit will carry with them their full complement of hand grenades in boxes.
Brigade H.Q.	8. At its present position until reliefs are completed. Subsequent location will be notified later.

Major.
Brigade Major, Garhwal Brigade.

Issued through Signal Section at 12 noon

Copy No.1	to 2nd Leicesters		Copy No. 7	to Bde. B.G.C.
2	1/3rd Londons		8	Ferozepore Bde.
3	2/3rd Gurkhas		9	Meerut Division
4	Garhwal Rifles		10	War Diary ✓
5	2/8th Gurkhas		11	Record
6	Bde. M.G.C.		12	Staff

Garhwal Brigade.

War Diary

Appendices

Operation Orders (others)

Copy No. ...5..

OPERATION ORDER NO. 29.

By

Lieutenant-General Sir. C. A. ANDERSON, K.C.B.,

Commanding MEERUT Division.

Reference - Map of FRANCE 1/40000.   4th May 1915.

1. Under orders of the Indian Corps, the LAHORE Division will take over the Northern Section of the Indian Corps' front on the night 5th/6th May 1915.

   The LAHORE Divisional Artillery will move into the line on the nights 5th/6th and 6th/7th May 1915.

2. The MEERUT Divisional Area is modified, its northern boundary running through PORT ARTHUR - ROUGE CROIX - Road junction R.29.b. 7.0 inclusive - road junction R.27.c. 1.0, exclusive, road junction Q.24.d. 5.1., inclusive, through PARADIS (road inclusive) to road junction in Q.12.c., and thence due west to CLARENCE River.

3. The GARHWAL Brigade and the Machine Guns of the 107th Pioneers, will be relieved by the JULLUNDUR Brigade under arrangements to be made by Brigade Commanders in consultation with one another. The Battalions holding Sub-Sections (a) and (c) will not be relieved until the reliefs of those holding Sub-Sections (b) and (d) are completed.

4. On being relieved the G.O.C. GARHWAL Brigade will billet and bivouac his troops in the vicinity of the RUE DU PUITS, and in such orchards affording him cover as he can occupy, using LORETTO Road, and the RUE DES BERCEAUX when moving out of the trenches.

5. The present depôts of the Sapper Companies of the MEERUT Division and the billets of the 107th Pioneers, will be retained for the meanwhile. (The 34th Pioneers will re-occupy their billets in "les 8 Maisons", the G.O.C., DEHRA DUN Brigade making arrangements to vacate these by 8.30 p.m. on the 6th May).

C Nore Colonel,

General Staff, MEERUT Division.

Issued to Signal Company for despatch at 10.30 p.m.

Copy No. 1 to Indian Corps.   Copy No. 12 to Meerut Signals.
         2   Eighth Division   13   Divl. Train
         3   LAHORE Division   14   A.A. & Q.M.G.
         4   DEHRA DUN Bde.   15   D.A.A.G.
         5   GARHWAL Bde.   16   D.A.A.& Q.M.G.
         6   BAREILLY Bde.   17 ⎫
         7   C.R.A. MEERUT   18 ⎬
         8   C.R.E.   "   19 ⎬
         9   4th Ind. Cavalry   20 ⎭ Diary & Files.
        10   107th Pioneers   21
        11   A.D.M.S. MEERUT

38 T   5-5-15

Headquarters Jullundur Bde

URGENT OC 1st Manchesters 4th Suffolks
         59th Rifles 40th Pathans
Diary.   47th Sikhs No. 2 French Mortar Bty
         Bde Bomb Gun Officer No 3 Coy LDT
         The Garhwal Bde

Memo

Units marching up to the trenches tonight will march as follows:-

Route - FOSSE BRIDGE - LES 8 MAISONS - road junction R 29 b - road junction M 20 c 1·3 - RUE DU PUITS - ROUGE CROIX - PONT LOGY

2 No troops will pass East of road junction R 29 b before 7.40 pm

3 Units will march independently and will pass FOSSE BRIDGE at following times:-
   Suffolk Regt   8.45 pm
   59th Rifles   9.0 pm
   40th Pathans   7.15 pm
   47th Sikhs
   Manchester Regt   7.30 —

4 Machine Gun vehicles or animals carrying machine guns will follow units as far as ROUGE CROIX and return to depots at LES 8 MAISONS via PONT DU HEN and road junction R 18 c 5·1

The carrying parties for the machine guns are to march to ROUGE CROIX with the transport carrying the guns and no time is to be lost on arrival at ROUGE CROIX in getting under weigh, manhandling the guns.

All other 1st Line T will move to and remain at LES 8 MAISONS.

5 Separate orders will be issued to OC No 2 TMB and O/c Bde Reserve SAA regarding time they are to move.

6 Owing to no troops marching East of Road junction R29b before 7.40 pm units will probably be at PONT LOGY rather later tonight than the time given to them yesterday. Os C should remember this when arranging with Os C Units they relieve for guides &c

Bde Major Jullundur Bde

"A" Form.
MESSAGES AND SIGNALS.
Army Form C. 2121.

Prefix **M** Code **m.** Words **123** Charge
Office of Origin and Service Instructions.
J.G.R.
Priority

Sent At ___ m. To ___ By ___

This message is on a/c of:
95 Service.
(Signature of "Franking Officer")

No. of Message
Recd. at 7/10 pm
Date 17/3/15
From J.G.R.
By Musgrove

TO Advanced Garhwal Bde

Sender's Number	Day of Month	In reply to Number	
G.60	17th		A A A

SIRHIND Bde will take over from right of present front held by GOC BAREILLY Bde to right flank of Fifth Bde inclusive at least and as much more of the new British front as possible to the right aaa GOC Sirhind Bde will arrange in direct communication with GOC Second divn as to extent thus to be taken over* and will inform this office where his right flank will rest aaa First Corps will find artillery support for SIRHIND Bde aaa Sirhind Bde will communicate direct with artillery

From
Place
Time

(Extent x)

The above may be forwarded as now corrected. (Z)
Censor. Signature of Addressor or person authorised to telegraph in his name.

"A" Form.
MESSAGES AND SIGNALS.
Army Form C. 2121.

Prefix	Code	m.	Words	Charge	This message is on a/c of:	Recd. at	m.
Office of Origin and Service Instructions.			Sent		Service.	Date	
			At	m.		From	
			To			By	
			By		(Signature of "Franking Officer.")		

TO

Sender's Number.	Day of Month	In reply to Number	AAA

Commander supporting him aaa progress of relief to be reported addressed Bareilly Bde rept Second divn Bareilly Garhwal Bde's CRE Meerut and Meerut Divisions

From
Place O.C. Meerut Div
Time 6.55 pm

SECRET.   OPERATION ORDER NO 32   Copy No......6

by

LIEUTENANT-GENERAL SIR CHARLES ANDERSON, K.C.B.,

COMMANDING MEERUT DIVISION.

Reference Maps:- FRANCE (BETHUNE) Sheet 1:40000,   18th May 1915.
& Special map 1:10000.

-:-:-:-:-:-:-:-:-:-:-

INFORMATION. 1. Germans are holding FERME DU BOIS and trenches about and to East of it, also the COUR D'AVOINE.
The Indian Corps will attack the FERME DU BOIS at 4-30 P.M. today, in conjunction with an attack on COUR D'AVOINE by the Guards Brigade.
Meerut Division reinforced by Sirhind Brigade, is to carry out the attack.
Dehra Dun Brigade has again come under the orders of Meerut Division

INTENTION. 2. The intention is to obtain possession of the FERME DU BOIS and of the trench Q 16-Q13-Q14, up to the LA TOURELLE - QUINQUE RUE Road in conjunction with the progress of the attack on the COUR D'AVOINE by the Guards Brigade, with whom touch will be obtained at xxx.Q12.

ARTILLERY. 3. Artillery will co-operate as below:-
A slow and deliberate bombardment till 4-0.P.M. when fire will quicken up to 4-20.p.m.
An intensive bombardment from 4-20.P.M. to 4-30.P.M.
Objectives as below :-

9.2.Howitzers.   Two hour bombardment of FERME DU BOIS ending with a salvo, after which 9.2. will work along trench from Q16 to FERME DE TOULOTTE.

60 prs & 18 prs.   Shrapnel fire on trench Q17 - P19 -P20 -N25 -N22 and N23.

6" & 4.5 How.   FERME DU BOIS and trenches between there and ESTAIRES - LA BASSEE Road.

18 prs.   Trench Q17 -P19 -P20 -N25 -N22 and N23.
Trench B2 -R9; trench V3 -V4 -R10 -R11 to R9 and R13 and R12.
Trench V5E -R17E and also all other trenches between this trench and the ESTAIRES - LA BASSEE Road.

SIRHIND BDE. 4. Sirhind Brigade will make the attack on the FERME DU BOIS, and will capture it and points Q15 and Q16. It will push forward by bombing along the trenches from R5 to Q15, so as to establish a front whence the attack can be launched against the FERME DU BOIS from the East and South East, the position being kept under heavy fire from the front V1 - R5, and any opportunity for attack even across the open being seized.
The Brigade will establish itself at the FERME DU BOIS, and then push South West along the trench Q15 - Q11 -Q12, in conjunction with the progress of the attack on the COUR D'AVOINE by the Guards Brigade, with whom touch will be obtained at Q12. The trench Q15 -Q11 -Q12 will be turned into a fire trench, facing North East, and the line V1 -R7 -R8 -FERME DU BOIS -Q16 -Q15 -Q11 -Q12 thoroughly consolidated and held as a defensive flank, in connection with the left of the Guards Brigade.
Subsequently the trench Q16 -Q13 -Q14 is to be seized.
Bombing parties will also be organised to work North East from V1 towards V2 and V3 at the earliest possible moment prior to the main attack.

BAREILLY BDE.   Bareilly Brigade plus "2/8th Gurkha Rifles will hold

2/.

their present line of trenches from the ESTAIRES LA BASSEE Road to the point where the new communication trench from our old line near CINDER TRACK to the captured German trenches takes off. Full use to be made of fire to assist the attack of Sirhind Brigade.

Garhwal Bde 6. Garhwal Bde less 2/8th Gurkha Rifles will be in support of Bareilly Brigade and will remain in its present location.

Dehra Dun Bde 7. Dehra Dun Bde will be in Divisional Reserve, and will remain in its present location.

Distinguish-ing flags 8. Advanced portion of Sirhind Bombing parties will be marked by yellow flags.

Colonel
General Staff
Meerut Division.

Issued to Signal Coy
for distribution at 4.0 P.M.

1 & 2	to Indian Corps
3	Lahore Divn
4	2nd Division
5	Dehra Dun Bde
6	Garhwal Bde
7	Bareilly Bde
8	Sirhind Bde
9	Meerut Arty
10	Lahore Arty
11	Meerut Engrs
12	No. 1 Group H.A.R.
13	107th Pioneers
14	4th Cavalry
15	A.D.M.S. Meerut
16	A.A.& Q.M.G. Meerut
17	Meerut Signals

SECRET. BRIGADE OPERATION ORDER No. 30. Copy No. 6

by

BRIGADIER-GENERAL W.M. SOUTHEY C.M.G.,

COMMANDING BAREILLY BRIGADE.

REFERENCE MAP:-
FRANCE (BETHUNE) 1/40,000   19th May 1915.

INTENTION. 1. The following reliefs of Troops in Front Line will take place tonight:-

(A) E Subsection (2/8th GURKHA RIFLES) by 2nd LEICESTERS - commencing at 10 p.m.

(B) A Subsection (58th RIFLES) by 1/3rd GURKHA RIFLES commencing at 10 p.m.

(C) B Subsection - Garrison of ORCHARD Redoubt by 1/3rd LONDONS and remainder of Subsection by 4th BLACK WATCH (less 2 Coys) commencing at 8.30 p.m.

(D) C Subsection - 41st DOGRAS by 2 Coys 125th RIFLES commencing at 8.30 p.m.

(E) Machine Gun reliefs in A and B Subsections will be arranged by Brigade M. G. O.

(F) 4 inch Trench Gun Battery will come under orders of GARHWAL BRIGADE from 8.30 p.m. tonight.

ROUTES FOR RELIEFS. 2. 4th BLACK WATCH will move by routes EAST of Tram Line, 1/3rd LONDONS and 1/3rd GURKHA RIFLES West of Tram Line, and 2nd LEICESTERS by EDWARD Road route.

All other details of reliefs will be arranged by O's C. relieving Subsections.

LOCATION OF RELIEVED TROOPS. 3. On relief Units will move to following positions:-
2nd BLACK WATCH to LANSDOWNE POST and breastworks on North side road opposite - vacated by 4th BLACK WATCH (less 2 Coys).
58th RIFLES - to Trenches at CROIX BARBEE to be pointed out by Staff Captain.
41st DOGRAS - to former position in LANSDOWNE POST.
This cancels all previous orders on these arrangements.

DISTRIBUTION OF BRIGADE. 4. On completion of above Reliefs the Brigade will be disposed as follows:-
(A) BAREILLY SECTION OF DEFENCE:-
A Subsection, from EAST of ORCHARD Redoubt to and inclusive of CRESCENT Communication Trench.
Garrison - ½ Battalion.

B Subsection - from CRESCENT Communication Trench (exclusive) to and inclusive of LA BASSEE ROAD.
Garrison - 1 Battalion.
1½ Battalions in Brigade Reserve.

(B) Remainder of Brigade will be in Divisional Reserve.

RELIEFS. 5. On completion of reliefs G.O.C. GARHWAL BRIGADE will assume command of ORCHARD Redoubt and the Line WEST of it previously held by this Brigade.

REPORTS. 6. Reliefs will be carried out under the orders of G.O.C. BAREILLY BDE and completion of each relief should be reported to that Brigade Headquarters which will remain in present position.

Captain,
BRIGADE MAJOR.

ISSUED TO SIGNAL SECTION AT 2.50 P.M.
Copy No. 1. 2nd BLACK WATCH.   Copy No. 5. 41st Dogras.
"   " 2. 4th BLACK WATCH.   "   " 6. Garhwal Bde.
"   " 3. 125th RIFLES.   "   " 7. Meerut Divn.
"   " 4. 58th RIFLES.   "   " 8. War Diary
                                  "   " 9.
                                  "   " 10. file.

"A" Form.
Army Form C. 2121.

MESSAGES AND SIGNALS.

No. of Message _____

Prefix _____ Code _____ m.
Office of Origin and Service Instructions.

Words | Charge
Sent
At _____ m.
To _____
By _____

This message is on a/c of:
1563 Service.
(Signature of "Franking Officer")

Recd. at _____ m.
Date _____
From _____
By _____

Priority

TO { Garhwal Bde

Sender's Number	Day of Month	In reply to Number	
G-106	Nineteenth	-	AAA

OPERATION ORDER NO THIRTYTHREE AAA (1) GARHWAL Bde will relieve BAREILLY Bde on the Indian Corps front from CINDER TRACK exclusive to front of ORCHARD redoubt inclusive tonight AAA Bomb guns now in position on above front will be taken over by GARHWAL Bde and remain in position AAA Brigadiers will arrange between themselves details of relief and will report to ADVANCED MEERUT DIVISION when they are completed AAA Billets at CROIX BARBEE for two battalions are placed at disposal of GARHWAL Bde AAA At CROIX BARBEE redoubt for one battalion and at LANSDOWNE POST for two battalions at disposal of BAREILLY BDE AAA GARHWAL Bde Headquarters at CROIX BARBEE AAA BAREILLY Bde Headquarters LANSDOWNE POST Addressed Indian Corps Second and LAHORE Divns MEERUT and LAHORE Artillery DEHRA DUN GARHWAL BAREILLY and SIRHIND Bdes MEERUT Engineers 4th Indian Cavalry 107th Pioneers MEERUT Signals Number one group H A R A D M S and A A and Q M G MEERUT

From | ADVANCED MEERUT DIVISION 6 p m
Place |
Time | PRIORITY

The above may be forwarded as now corrected. (Z)

Col. G.S.

Censor. Signature of Addressor or person authorised to telegraph in his name

* This line should be erased if not required.

SECRET   Copy No. 8

OPERATION ORDER No. 34.
by
Lieutenant- General Sir Charles ANDERSON, K.C.B.,
Commanding MEERUT DIVISION.

21st May 1915.

Reference maps:-
  FRANCE-BETHUNE - 1:40,000
  & Special map 1:10,000.

Information.	1.	ALDERSON's Force will make an intensive bombardment on COUR D'AVOINE from 1.10 A.M. to 1.25 A.M., 22nd May. The bombardment will include area inside points P.14 through Q.9, just east of Q.8, the FERME COUR D'AVOINE (D'AVOUE), north corner of moat Q.12 and trench Q.17 - Q.18.
Intention.	2.	The German position Q.15 - Q.16 and R.8 FERME DU BOIS is to be captured tonight.
SIRHIND Bde	3.	Sirhind Brigade will carry out the attack and consolidate the position. The assault will take place at 1.0 A.M., 22nd May.
Garhwal Bde	4.	The G.O.C. Garhwal Bde will detail an organised bombing party, supported by a platoon of infantry, to support the attack of Sirhind Bde by bombing along German trench from V.1 to V.2, with the object of establishing themselves there. This party will not start operations until ten minutes after the Sirhind attack starts, unless enemy opens fire on our attacking troops, in which case it will commence immediately enemy opens fire. G.O.C. Garhwal Bde will also detail a platoon to occupy part of the trench running from his right towards V.1 with the object of assisting the bombing party by their fire.
Artillery	5.	The following bombardment has been arranged by C.R.A. This programme commenced at 1.0 P.M. today, and will continue till five A.M. on 22nd May.-

    (a) 18 pdr shrapnel, with occasional H.E., on trenches V.2, R.7, R.8, round FERME DU BOIS up to South-west corner of FERME DU BOIS.

    (b) 4.5" howitzer: 90 rounds lyddite during today at V.2, and also along trenches as in (a); also on the trench which connects German first and second line a short way east of V.2.

    (c) 6" howitzer: commencing at 5.0 P.M. tonight will expend 60 rounds lyddite at V.2 and trenches round FERME DU BOIS from south-west corner round north-east corner to R.8 and on trench connecting German first and second lines east of V.2.

    (d) All above trenches will be shrapnelled to prevent repairs being carried out after the bombardment by lyddite.

    (e) Barrages will be formed along trenches:-
        i. Q.11, Q.12, Q.17 - P.19 and Q.13, Q.14, Q.18 - P.19 to N.23.
        At half an hour after the assault fire will be lifted and no fire will be directed north of line FERME DU TOULOTTE - Q.17 - or east of line Q.17 - M.18. Rate of fire to be quickened ten minutes after hour of assault, and maintained for twenty minutes, when it will again be slowed down.
        ii. R.13 to R.10.
        iii. V.5 to line of German second line trench north of V.5.
        iv. LA BASSEE Road from V.9.E to R.17.
        v. Q.12 to Q.20 till half an hour after our assault, then from LA TOURELLE cross roads along QUINQUE RUE towards R.13

2/.

Bomb-guns. 6. Except in case of getting a really good target, no bomb-gun will fire at vicinity V.2 till 6.0 P.M. to avoid interference with artillery observation.

From 6.0 P.M. to 8.30 P.M. a steady fire will be maintained on this vicinity.

From 8.30 P.M. to within fifteen minutes of hour of assault, an occasional round only will be fired.

From fifteen minutes to the hour of assault till ten minutes past that hour, no firing.

Ten minutes past the hour fixed for the assault, one salvo of all bomb-guns is to be fired at V.2 and vicinity, after which no bomb-gun fire will be directed nearer than 100 yards to the east and to the south of V.2.

Sappers & Pioneers. 7. C.R.E. will hold a working party of one company S. & M. and two companies 107th Pioneers, in readiness to proceed at short notice from R.E. Depot ST VAAST to assist in putting the captured position in a state of defence.

Crorie.
Colonel,
General Staff,
MEERUT DIVISION.

Issued to Signal Coy for
distribution at 4.0 P.M.:-
Copy Nos. 1 & 2 Indian Corps
           3 Alderson's Force
           4 Lahore Divn
           5 Highland Divn
           6 No. 1 Group H.A.R.
           7 Sirhind Bde
           8 Garhwal Bde
           9 Bareilly Bde
          10 Dehra Dun Bde
          11 C.R.A. Lahore
          12 C.R.A. Meerut
          13 C.R.E. Meerut
          14 107th Pioneers
          15 A.D.M.S. Meerut
          16 A.A. & Q.M.G.
          17 Signals - Meerut
      18 to 24 War Diaries and files.

"A" Form. Army Form C. 2121.
MESSAGES AND SIGNALS. No. of Message_____

Prefix____ Code____ m. Office of Origin and Service Instructions.	Words	Charge	This message is on a/c of:	Recd. at____ m.
SECRET	Sent At____ m. To____ By____		____Service. (Signature of "Franking Officer")	Date____ From____ By____

TO: GOC Sirhind CRA Lahore
    Garhwal — Meerut
    Bareilly CRE ———

Sender's Number	Day of Month	In reply to Number	AAA
G 131	21		

Reference Operation Order No 34 of todays date aaa Aldersons force is not attacking COUR D'AVOINE tonight aaa The bombardment of that locality is intended to confuse the Germans and lead them to expect an attack there aaa Aldersons force is actually attacking K5

From Place ____
Time 3.45 pm

Advd Meerut

(Z)
Censor.   D Davis Maj GS
Signature of Addressor or person authorised to telegraph in his name

* This line should be erased if not required.

"A" Form. Army Form C. 2121.

MESSAGES AND SIGNALS. No. of Message_____

Prefix___ Code___ m.	Words	Charge	This message is on a/c of:	Recd. at___ m.
Office of Origin and Service Instructions.	Sent			Date___
SECRET	At___ m.		___Service.	From___
	To___			
	By___		(Signature of "Franking Officer")	By___

TO { CRA Lahore   Sirhind Bde
     { CRA Meerut   Bareilly Bde
                      Garhwal Bde

| Sender's Number | Day of Month | In reply to Number | |
| G-737 | 21 | | AAA |

Indian Corps wires that Alderson's force is attacking K5 and M10 tonight aaa Infantry attack on K5 takes place at 8.30 pm tonight aaa Alderson's force is also arranging to throw forward and entrench a line from left of Canadian Divn on QUINQUE RUE through the two advanced posts east of P9 and Q7 and is to be ready to throw the left forward to conform with the right of the Indian Corps Ends

Lahore Divn has also arranged to open a heavy fire along its front from 10 to 10.30 pm tonight

From
Place
Time 7.30 pm

A. Wardrop (?)

The above may be forwarded as now corrected. (Z)

Censor.   Meerut Divn
Signature of Addressor or person authorised to telegraph in his name

* This line should be erased if not required.
C27642 P.G. Ltd. Wt. W14142/641—20,000 3/15. Forms C2121/10.

"A" Form.
Army Form C. 2121.
MESSAGES AND SIGNALS.

SECRET

TO 2 Leicesters

Sender's Number: M 415
Day of Month: 21
AAA

The following are the orders for the O/C Bomb gun detachments in supercession of those previously given to you. Except in case of getting a really good target no bomb gun will fire at vicinity V.3.d 6 pm to avoid interference with artillery observation. From 6 pm to 8.30 pm a steady fire will be maintained on this vicinity. From 8.30 pm to within 15 minutes of the hour of assault, an occasional round only will be fired. From 15 minutes to the hour of assault till 10 minutes past that hour, no fire. Ten minutes past the hour fixed for the assault, one salvo of all bomb guns is to be fired at V.3. and vicinity, after which no bomb gun fire will be directed nearer than 100 yards to the road and to the South

"A" Form.
MESSAGES AND SIGNALS.
Army Form C. 2121.

2. Please get into communication with O+C 2/2 QR + 3 Londons and inform them if there are any special precautions that you require regarding their fire.

3. The following information may be of use:— There is good ground for believing that the Germans hold the parados of their trench as front line, making or having made a new trench behind it.

new trench — → front
— original front parapet
original parados
original trench

From: Garhwal Bde
Time: 6.25 pm

G.143   Operation Order No. 35   22nd   AAA

1 AAA Dehra Dun Bde will relieve Sirhind Bde in the trenches tonight AAA

2 AAA Hour of relief and other details will be arranged mutually by G.O.s C, Brigades who will report hour at which reliefs completed AAA

3 AAA All trench howitzers and bomb-guns now in position will remain in position AAA The Divisional Bomb gun Offr will arrange for the manning of the trench howitzers relieving the R.A. teams and the G.O.C. Dehra Dun Bde will take over the bomb-guns AAA

4.AAA   Sirhind Bde will exchange headquarters with Dehra Dun Bde and will occupy the billets vacated by the Dehra Dun Bde AAA

Addressed Indian Corps - 51st Highland Divn - Lahore Divn
Number one Group - Sirhind Bde - Garhwal Bde - Dehra Dun
Bde - Bareilly Bde - Meerut Arty - Lahore Arty - Meerut
Engrs - A.D.M.S. Meerut - Meerut Divn - Meerut Sigs -
107th Pioneers - Divnl Bomb Gun Offr

ADV MEERUT DIVN

8.0 A.M.

Colonel,
General Staff,
Meerut Division

Advanced MEERUT Division.
22nd May 1915.

G-143-A   22nd   AAA   The relief ordered in Operation Order number thirtyfive will be carried out tomorrow night instead of tonight under otherwise same arrangements AAA Acknowledge AAA Addressed Indian Corps - LAHORE Divn - Number one Group - 51st Highland Divn - SIRHIND Bde - GARHWAL Bde - DEHRA DUN Bde - BAREILLY Bde - MEERUT ARTY - LAHORE Arty - MEERUT Engrs - A D M S MEERUT - MEERUT Divn - MEERUT Signals - 107th Pioneers - Divisional Bomb Gun Officer

ADVANCED MEERUT DIVISION 12.5 p m
PRIORITY

Major,
G. S.

OPERATION ORDER NO 36. Copy......7......

by

LIEUTENANT-GENERAL SIR CHARLES ANDERSON, K.C.B.,
COMMANDING MEERUT DIVISION.

Reference maps:-
    FRANCE (BETHUNE) 1:40000,
    & Special Map   1:10000.

23rd May 1915.

(OPERATION ORDER No 35 IS HEREBY CANCELLED).

INFORMATION. 1. (a) The Indian Corps has been allotted a front from where its present left rests in Sq. M.35.d. to the QUINQUE RUE exclusive.
The Divisions will occupy the above front, LAHORE Division on left, MEERUT Division in centre and HIGHLAND Division on right.
(b) The MEERUT Division will hold from the ORCHARD inclusive on the left to a point West of FERME DU BOIS on the right, where it meets the left of the HIGHLAND Division. This point will be more definitely settled later. The above front will be divided into two sections at V.1. (inclusive to right section).

RELIEFS. 2. The DEHRA DUN Brigade will relieve the SIRHIND Brigade on the night 23rd/24th May, and will hold the right section.
The BAREILLY Brigade will be relieved by the FEROZEPORE Brigade on the night 24th/25th May, and will move into the area vacated by the DEHRA DUN Brigade.
Details to be arranged by the Brigade Commanders concerned. Reports to be made to Divisional Headquarters as soon as reliefs completed.

MOVEMENTS. 3. DEHRA DUN Brigade will move up to the trenches by the North road from LACOUTURE to RICHEBOURG ST VAAST, (Queen Mary Road), and area East of it including OXFORD Road.
SIRHIND Brigade will move out by ALBERT Road, KING GEORGES Road, HUMP-BACK Bridge and ZELOBES to LESTREM billetting area where the Brigade will come under the orders of G.O.C. LAHORE Division. The LOCON-LESTREM Road to be cleared by 7-30.a.m. on 24th May.

BOMB GUNS. 4. Brigades will take their Brigade bomb guns out with them. Trench howitzers will remain in position. The Divisional Bomb Gun Officer will arrange for manning trench howitzers, relieving the R.A. teams as necessary.

ARTILLERY. 5. The Artillery will arrange for the support of each infantry section by a Brigade of R.F.A. in close liaison. Orders for artillery reliefs are being issued separately.

                                        Colonel.
                                   General Staff.
Issued to Signal Company for despatch   MEERUT DIVISION.
at 11-30.a.m.

Copy No 1 and 2 to Indian Corps.   7 Garhwal Bde.   16. A.D.M.S.
"   3   Lahore Divn.   8 Bareilly Brigade.   17 A.A.&Q.M.G
          4   Highland Divn.   9 Sirhind Brigade.   18 D.A.A.G.
          5   No 1 Group H.A.R.   10. Lahore Divnl.Arty.   19 War diary
          6.   Dehra Dun Brigade   11. Meerut Divnl. Arty.   25 & files.
         12   Meerut Engineers.   13. 107th Pioneers.   26 Bomb gun Off
         14   4th Indian Cav.   15. Meerut Signals.

"A" Form.
Army Form C. 2121

MESSAGES AND SIGNALS.

No. of Message 85

Prefix: A3 Code: AH
Office of Origin and Service Instructions.
Words: 42
JGR
Priority

Recd. at 1.54 p.m.
Date 23/5/15
From JGR
By Longpra

TO — Garhwal Bde

Sender's Number: G155
Day of Month: 23rd
AAA

That portion of MEERUT DIVN operation order number thirty-six of date which refers to relief of Bareilly Bde by Ferozepore Bde is postponed for twenty-four hours aaa acknowledge aaa addressed all concerned

From
Place: ADS Meerut Divn
Time: 1.30 pm

"A" Form.   Army Form C.2121

MESSAGES AND SIGNALS.   No. of Message 91

| Prefix SB Code BFP m. | Words 68 | Charge | This message is on a/c of: | Recd. at 2.50 m. |
| Office of Origin and Service Instructions. YGR priority | Sent At ___ m. To ___ By ___ | | ___ Service. (Signature of "Franking Officer") | Date 23/3/15 From YGR By Shelton |

TO Garhwal Bde

| Sender's Number 6158 | Day of Month 23rd | In reply to Number | AAA |

Reference Meerut divn operation orders para three aaa orders have been received that DEHRIND bde will now bivouac at RIEZ BAILLEUL and BOUT DEVILLE aaa derha dunn bde will consequently move into trenches by RICHEBOURG ST VAAST - RUE DE BERCEAUX S-8B S-15 a aaa Serhind Brigade will move at by S 9 Central OXFORD ROAD aaa addressed all concerned

From   Adv Meerut Divn
Place
Time   2.30 PM

The above may be forwarded as now corrected.   (Z)

Censor.   Signature of Addressor or person authorised to telegraph in his name

* This line should be erased if not required.

"A" Form.   Army Form C. 2121.

MESSAGES AND SIGNALS.

No. of Message 177

Prefix SB Code m.
Office of Origin and Service Instructions.

SB 1050
6R
Priority

Words 33 Charge
Sent
At _____ m.
To _____
By _____

This message is on a/c of:
_____ Service.
(Signature of "Franking Officer")

Recd. at 9.24 p.m.
Date 23/I
From 6R
By Mansell

TO { Garhwal Bde

Sender's Number	Day of Month	In reply to Number	
*NoG/63	23RD		AAA

in Meerut division Operation Order No 36 of date Para two RELIEFS aaa for FEROZEPORE Brigade Read SIRHIND Brigade and addressed all concerned

From Place: Advanced Meerut division
Time: 9.20 PM

The above may be forwarded as now corrected.   (Z)

Censor.   Signature of Addressor or person authorised to telegraph in his name

* This line should be erased if not required

Secret

Copy No 4

Ferozepore Brigade Order No 31

31st May 1915

Ref: FRANCE (BETHUNE) Map 1/40000
and Special numbered Map 1/10000 (ILLIES, VIOLAINES, FESTIBERT)

1. Ferozepore Brigade will relieve troops of the Meerut Division (Dehra Dun and Garhwal Brigades) on the front from Point R6 — ORCHARD Redoubt exclusive on the night 31st May/1st June.

2. The above Section will be divided into Right, Centre and Left Subsection as follows:-

   The dividing line between the Right and Centre Subsections is the line where the SEAFORTH HIGHLANDERS and GARHWAL RIFLES meet, and that between the Centre and Left Subsections is the line where the GARHWAL RIFLES and 2/3 GURKHA RIFLES meet.

3. The Section will be occupied as follows:-

   Right Subsection - Connaught Rangers - HQrs - about S. 9. a 8/2
   Centre   —"—   - 1/4 London Regt   - HQrs - about S. 9. b. 10/4
   Left   —"—   - 57th Rifles   - HQrs - about S. 10. a 6/6

   129th Baluchis, less Machine Gun Section, will be in Brigade Reserve in billets to be notified later about CROIX BARBEE.

   The Machine Guns, 129th Baluchis, under Lieut H.J.D. O'Neill, will be in the Right Subsection and will occupy the prepared positions in the Communication Trench leading from the HQrs, SEAFORTH HIGHLANDERS, to R6. They will be under the orders of the O.C. Right Subsection.

   The rest of the Machine Guns of the Brigade will remain with their Battalions.

4. Representatives of Units and Officers commanding Machine Gun Sections will visit their Subsections of the trenches today and arrange all details of relief direct with Battalion Commanders, but will first meet the Brigade Major at the HQrs, Connaught Rangers (M 14 c 4/2) at 8.0 a.m.

   Those of the Connaught Rangers and the Brigade Bomb Gun Officer will be met by a guide of the SEAFORTH HIGHLANDERS

4 WINDY CORNER (Cross Roads S.3 c) at 9.45 a.m.

Those of the 1/4 London Regt. and 57th Rifles will be met by guides of the GARHWAL RIFLES and 2/3 GURKHA RIFLES respectively at CROIX BARBEE at 9.15 a.m.

5. Reliefs will not pass CROIX BARBEE before 8.30 p.m. in the following order:—

   57th Rifles; Connaught Rangers; 1/4 London Regt.

6. O.C. Units will report today how they propose to occupy their Subsections and the positions of their Machine Guns, and will forward a rough sketch of their Subsections with the distribution of troops on the 1st June.

The Daily Distribution telegram of troops will be required as usual.

7. Only 200 rounds S.A.A. and belt boxes of Machine Guns will be taken into the trenches.

8. Subsections will report by 5.0 p.m., 1st June, what reserves of S.A.A. there are in the Front Trenches, Support Trenches and Local Reserve Trenches separately. These should be by boxes, or loose belts to the nearest 1000 rounds.

9. All fuzed bombs with battalions will be taken into the trenches.

10. There is an R.E. Depôt on the RUE DE BOIS at the ORCHARD.

11. Medical arrangements will be the same as with the relieved Units.

12. Brigade Reserve S.A.A, 1st Line Transport of Units, and No. 2 Company Train will remain in their present billets till further orders are issued.

13. The completion of relief will be reported.

14. Reports after 5.0 p.m. — to the RUE DES PUITS (Sq: M26 b 9/1).

Issued to Signals   E C Kensington Captain
at 1.0 a.m.   offg. Brigade Major
            Ferozepore Brigade

Garhwal Brigade

War Diary

Appendices - Operation Orders

Received Meerut Div d/- 6th May.
Dehra Dun Bde d/- 6th May.
Dehra Dun Bde d/- 7th May.
Bareilly Bde d/- 8th May.
Bareilly Bde d/- 9th May.
Meerut Divn d/- 14th May.
5th Infantry Bde d/- 14th May.
Sirhind Bde d/- 14th May.
Sirhind Bde d/- 15th May.
Bareilly Bde d/- 16th May.

S E C R E T.   No.G.405/26

                                   Headquarters, Meerut Division.
                                   May 6th 1915.

Memorandum.

        Enclosed copy of operation order (serial No. 10) is issued as a guide only, and may have to be modified on receipt of Corps Orders.

        The dates are suppositious only and correct dates and timings of bombardment will be forwarded later.

2.   Please acknowledge.

                                   P Davies
                                   Major,
                                   General Staff,
                                   Meerut Division.

To,
    Dehra Dun Bde
 ✓ Garhwal Bde
    Bareilly Bde
    C.R.A. Meerut
    C.R.E. Meerut.

SECRET

Copy No. 10

OPERATION ORDER No. 30,
by
Lieut:-General Sir Charles ANDERSON, K.C.B.,
Commanding MEERUT Division.

Reference maps:-   6th May 1915.
   Map of trenches - 1:10,000.
   BELGIUM & Part of FRANCE, Sheet 36, - 1:40,000, &
                        (Third Edition)
   FRANCE - BETHUNE Sheet - 1:40,000.

Information. 1.   The 1st Army is attacking on the 8th May 1915 with the object of breaking through the enemy's line and gaining the LA BASSEE - LILLE Road between LA BASSEE and FOURNES and then advancing on DON. *to the line BAUVIN - DON*

       The 1st Corps, retaining its right at GIVENCHY, will attack on a broad front in the vicinity of RICHEBOURG L'AVOUE with the object of advancing on RUE DU MARAIS, LORGIES and ILLIES.

       The Indian Corps will operate so as to cover the left of the 1st Corps, with the object of capturing the FERME DU BIEZ and of subsequently advancing to the line LIGNY LE GRAND - LA CLIQUETERIE FERME.

       The 4th Corps will operate so as to break through the enemy's line in the vicinity of ROUGES BANCS with the object of:-

         (i)   organising a defensive flank from the vicinity of LA CORDONNERIE FARM to FROMELLES.
         (ii)   Turning the AUBERS defences by an attack from the north-east.

       Its subsequent advance will be directed on LA CLIQUETERIE Farm with the object of effecting a junction with the Indian Corps.

       The 2nd Cavalry Division will remain in readiness near ESTAIRES to act as the situation developes.

       The Lahore Division will hold the front allotted to the Indian Corps, less that portion from which the attack is to be delivered by the Meerut Division. It will engage the enemy with rifle, machine-gun and trench-mortar fire, to assist in protecting the left flank of the Meerut Division from counter-attack from the north.

       Lahore Division will also open a communication trench from the advanced listening post at point 61 to connect up with our attack if this becomes desirable.

Intention. 2.   The Meerut Division will make the attack to be delivered by the Indian Corps.

       This attack is to be made on the enemy's trenches from the vicinity of the point V.6 to the vicinity of the point 56 as the first objective. On this front the enemy's wire will be cut by artillery fire.

       The second objective is the capture of LA TOURELLE and houses in the vicinity of point 50.

       The third objective is the capture of the DISTILLERY and FERME du BIEZ.

       Subsequent objectives will be the occupation of the BOIS DU BIEZ, LIGNY LE PETIT, LIGNY LE GRAND and LA CLIQUETERIE.

—ERIE so as to join up with the 4th Corps.

Bodies of infantry are not to halt if portions of the line are held up, but will press on to their further objectives without delay.

Artillery. 3. The Meerut Divisional Artillery, reinforced by that of the Lahore Division, one Section Mountain Artillery, one section of Hotchkiss Motor Battery and certain Heavy and Siege Batteries will support the attack.

The attack will be prepared and supported as follows:-

Ist PHASE.-

The assault of the enemy's first line trenches will be preceded by an artillery bombardment, guns being told off to:-
(a) Destruction of enemy's obstacles.
(b) Battering of enemy's trenches.
(c) Battering of enemy's strong points.
(d) Barrage against reinforcements advancing from the BOIS DU BIEZ; North-east, the East and the South-east.
(e) Engaging enemy's batteries by 1st Group Heavy Artillery.

IInd PHASE.

While the infantry are advancing on LA TOURELLE fire will be directed on:-
(a) LA TOURELLE and the Distillery South of it.
(b) Houses in vicinity of point 50.
(c) FERME DU BIEZ.
(d) South-west edge of BOIS DU BIEZ and approaches from LIGNY and LORGIES.

IIIrd PHASE.

Fire will be concentrated on the FERME DU BIEZ in preparation for the assault on that place.

Barranges will be continued to prevent the approach of reinforcements.

Teams of one Brigade Meerut Artillery will be brought up to a convenient locality in readiness for an advance in support of the infantry at short notice.

A second Brigade R.F.A. is also to be held in readiness to support this at longer notice.

Lines of advance within our lines are to be reconnoitred and spit-locked and bridges laid out before the day of attack. Light bridges for crossing ditches to be carried, and personnel of each battery must be prepared to rapidly repair roads and remove obstacles encountered in any advance beyond our present lines.

Both Brigades R.F.A. detailed as above will have four miles reserve telephone cable with each battery.

Ammunition to be expended during the bombardment will be dumped previously to avoid congestion of roads during the fight. Special attention will also be directed to ensure that the Brigades R.F.A. detailed to advance will do so with full supply of ammunition.

The section Mountain Artillery will, during the bombardment, operate from a position to be selected near LANSDOWNE POST and will afterwards advance in close support of the infantry attack, taking orders from the G.O.C. Dehra Dun Bde.

No.4 Trench Battery will remain in its present position in the Orchard. It will be at the disposal of the G.O.C. Dehra Dun Bde and will advance under his orders in support of the Brigade.

Dehra Dun Bde 4. Dehra Dun Bde will, as first objective, carry out the
Sect. Mtn.Art. assault on the enemy's front line trenches on a three
No.4 Trench battalion front.
Battery R.A. It will be formed up by 11.0 P.M. on the 7th May, as follows:-

The assaulting battalions in the front line trenches from the junction of the listening post communication trench to in front of the ORCHARD Redoubt inclusive, and in the CRESCENT Trench and ORCHARD Redoubt.

3.

The supporting battalions in BLACKADER Trench and ground in rear of ORCHARD.

The three assaulting battalions will form up in front of our advanced trenches after the wire cutting portion of the bombardment is completed at 5.20 A.M. and before the bombardment of the enemy's trenches ceases at 5.40 A.M.

The assaulting line will, during this bombardment, move up as close to enemy's line as our shell fire permits, and will reach the enemy's front line trenches at the earliest possible moment after this bombardment is lifted to more distant objectives at 5.40 A.M.

The first line will not delay at these trenches but will push on against their further objectives. The capture of the enemy remaining in the trenches, and bombing down the trenches to each flank, will be done under Brigade arrangements by succeeding lines.

After taking the first line trenches the battalion on the right will advance with its left on the LA BASSEE Road, capturing the houses on the right side of the road, and press on to the Distillery.

The Centre Battalion will advance with its right on the LA BASSEE Road taking houses on the left of the Road, and press on to the LA TOURELLE - FERME DU BIEZ Road

The left battalion, after crossing the trenches, will sieze the houses at points 52, 53 and on either side of the road leading thence to FERME DU BIEZ. It will also press on and sieze the FERME DU BIEZ.

The battalion in Brigade reserve will be moved up, under orders of G.O.C. Dehra Dun Brigade, into the front line trenches as the assaulting battalions clear them.

Assaulting battalions will, under brigade arrangements, leave such garrisons as may be necessary to hold them, in the following positions as they are captured. The localities will be strengthened, parties of sappers and pioneers being held in readiness at road junction in M.32.d to be sent forward under orders of C.R.E. to assist in this:-
(a) South end of LA TOURELLE Village
(b) DISTILLERY.
(c) Road junction in S.11.a (points 52 & 53)
(d) Group of houses near point 50.
(e) FERME DU BIEZ

The balance of units, after finding the above necessary garrisons, will push on to their further objectives.

Bombing parties will be organised by the G.O.C. Dehra Dun Brigade to bomb outwards along enemy's trenches.

5. The force as per margin will be organised by G.O.C.
Lieut. Col DRAKE-BROCKMAN, Garhwal Bde as a complete unit with staff,
The Garhwal Rifles, signalling arrangements and ammunition
2/8th Gurkha Rifles, supply.
Two bomb-guns of It will be formed up in the two eastern
Garhwal Bde Battery. blocks of assembly trenches immediately
north of RUE DU BOIS, by 4.0 a.m. on 8th
May. This force is detailed for the special purpose of securing the eastern edge of the BOIS DU BIEZ and capturing LA RUSSIE. It will move into the front line trenches as they are vacated by Dehra Dun Bde and carry out the above mission under orders of G.O.C. Dehra Dun Bde. It should not be used for the general support of Dehra Dun Bde.

Bareilly
Brigade. 6. Bareilly Bde will be formed up as below by 3.0 A.M. on 8th May:-

Three battalions in the three westerly blocks of assembly trenches north of the RUE DU BOIS, one battalion in LANSDOWNE POST and one battalion in breastworks east of that post on north side of FORESTERS LANE.

The Brigade, less 125th Rifles, but including machine gun section of that unit, will be in support of Dehra Dun Brigade, and will, under orders of G.O.C. Bareilly Brigade, occupy
assembly

assembly positions of Dehra Dun Brigade as they become available.

This forward move is to be made in communication with G.O.C. Dehra Dun Brigade as it may either follow, or precede, that of Lieut;Colonel DRAKE-BROCKMAN's detachment.

G.O.C. Bareilly Brigade will detail two Companies, 125th Rifles, as carriers for engineer working parties; to report to C.R.E. at road junction in M.32.d.7/7 at 8.0 P.M. on 7th May.

Hdqrs and two companies 125th Rifles will remain in LANSDOWNE POST till Garhwal Bde has moved into front line trenches, when it will move up into assembly trenches just north of the RUE DU BOIS and await instructions, the C.O. getting into communication with Divisional Headquarters through Dehra Dun Brigade Report Centre on RUE DU BOIS.

Garhwal Brigade.
7. Garhwal Brigade, less two battalions Indian Infantry, will be in Divisional reserve and will be formed up in the second line trenches about CROIX BARBEE by 3.30 a.m. on the day of the attack.

The Brigade will be brought forward by the Brigade Commander to the vicinity of ORCHARD Redoubt on the RUE DU BOIS as the forward movement of Bareilly Brigade makes assembly trenches available for them.

Nos 3 & 4 Coys, S.& M. 107th Pioneers Two Coys,125th Rifles.
8. The troops as in margin will be assembled in shelter trenches north of road junction in M.32.d.7/7 by 3.45 AM on 8th May and will be held in readiness to advance under the orders of the C.R.E..

Five separate working parties, complete with tools, sandbags and <u>carriers</u>, will be organised by the C.R.E. to put localities captured in a state of defence.

Strengths and localities for which required are as below; The balance will remain in reserve under orders of C.R.E. at position of assembly.

Locality for which required.	Strength.
North end LA TOURELLE Village and cross roads.	1 Section S. & M. 2 platoons,107th Pioneers
DISTILLERY	ditto.
Points 52 and 53	ditto.
FERME DU BIEZ	ditto.
Group of houses at points V.10, 50 & 51.	Half Coy., S. & M. One Coy, 107th Pioneers

4th Ind. Cav.
9. The 4th Indian Cavalry will rendezvous in RUE DU PONCH near cross roads in M.20.c.1/2 fields clear of roads, at 8.0 a.m. on 8th May, and will remain ready to move mounted at short notice.

Infantry Bde Bomb-guns.
10. Brigade Bomb-gun Batteries will be prepared to advance under orders to be issued by G.O.s C. Brigades.

That of Dehra Dun Bde will be assembled in the ORCHARD on the evening of 7th May.

3 pdr Hotchkiss Battery.
11. The two 3 pdr Hotchkiss guns on lorries will rendezvous at CROIX BARBEE cross roads at 10.0 P.M. on 7th May. The O.C. will report for orders at Divisional Report Centre RUE DU PUITS at 5.0 A.M. 8th May.

That on the trailer will be in position at the barricade at the cross roads at S.5.c.1/8 by the same hour. Its lorry to be concealed on the road about S.4.b.6/3 and the gun run into position by hand.

The motors will move by the ESTAIRES - LA BASSEE Road.

Any subsequent orders to the trailer will be communicated through Lahore Division.

Wire-cutting Bridging.
12. Our wire in front of our own trenches will be cut, and necessary bridges placed in position, during the hours of darkness

5/.

darkness on the night of the 7th/8th May, under orders of
G.O.C. Dehra Dun Bde.
(Moon rises at 2.7 A.M.)

S.A.A.Supply 13. The following advanced depots of S.A.Ammunition have been established.-
1640 boxes in RUE DU BOIS near R.E.Depot.
120 boxes each in dugouts in rear of front trench at junction of communication trenches:-
(a) from south-east corner of ORCHARD Redoubt,
(b) from North-east corner of ORCHARD Redoubt,
(c) from CRESCENT Trench.
To supplement such arrangements as Brigadiers may make for their own brigades, the supporting and reserve brigades will each detail their rear battalion to carry forward ammunition and establish further advanced depots in the fighting area at such localities as may be found suitable and possible.

Advanced 14. Advanced R.E.Depots will be formed at:-
R.E.Depot. (a) RUE DU BOIS.
(b) Form at M.32.d.7/7.

Bombs & 15. An advanced depot for bombs (trench gun) and hand-
Hand-grenades grenades has been established 100 yards in rear of the right of position of assembly of Bareilly Bde.
The Divisional Trench-gun Officer and Divisional Hand-grenade Officer will each arrange that an adequate supply of projectiles is collected.

Medical. 16. A collecting station will be established between LANSDOWNE POST and the tramway line where it crosses FORESTERS LANE. Route for wounded returning from the front will be by the ORCHARD communication trench which runs from RUE DU BOIS to FORESTERS LANE along the north-east side of the tramway and some 100 yards from it. This trench will be reserved for return of wounded only after fighting has commenced, and will be marked accordingly.
Route from collecting station to ST VAAST Corner where an advanced dressing station will be established, will be alongside the tramway line.
A wagon rendezvous in this vicinity will be established and will be marked by the RED CROSS Flag.
Field Ambulances will be opened at VIEILLE CHAPELLE and ZELOBES. Line of evacuation from wagon rendezvous is via OXFORD Road and WELLINGTON Road.

Distinguish- 17. Infantry battalions have been provided with red and black
-ing Marks. flags, 3' X 3', with a white ST Andrew's Cross (see annexed dia-
-gram) to assist in showing localities reached by our leading troops.
The distinguishing marks of the Divisions on our right and left, and of the Lahore Division, are as shown in annexure.

Sandbags. 18. Each man of the attacking infantry will carry two sandbags.

Masks. 19. Masks will be kept in readiness soaked in the soda solution by all troops in the front trenches and will be worn by assault-
-ing troops.

Prisoners. 20. Prisoners will be handed by capters to the Lahore Division at Dehra Dun Brigade Report Centre, RUE DU BOIS.

Road Traffic. 21. As per attached sketch.

22.

Supply Depot.	22.	An advanced emergency supply depot will be established at house at cross roads in M.32.d near head of tramway line.	
Aeroplane Report Centre.	23.	A station for receiving messages from aeroplanes will be established in the vicinity of the Divisional Hdqrs. R.15.b 4/5. The Camp Commandant will detail four men (British) to watch the station.	
Setting Watches.	24.	A Divisional Staff Officer will give the official time to all Brigades, C.R.A. and C.R.E. on the evening of 7th May.	
Report Centres.	25.	Meerut Division.	M.26.d.7/8 after 9.0 p.m. on 7th May.
		Dehra Dun Bde.	Ruined house on RUE DU BOIS S.10.a.8/7.
		Bareilly Bde.	In close proximity to that of Dehra Dun Bde on RUE DU BOIS.
		Garhwal Bde.	LANSDOWNE POST in S.4.a.2/3

Colonel,
General Staff,
MEERUT DIVISION.

Issued to Signal Coy for distribution,

Copy No. 1 to Indian Corps,
2   1st Division
3   7th Division
4   8th Division
5   Lahore Division
6   Meerut Divnl Arty
7   Lahore Divnl Arty
8   Meerut Divnl Engrs
9   Dehra Dun Bde
10 Garhwal Bde
11 Bareilly Bde

Copy No
12 4th Ind. Cavalry
13 107th Pioneers
14 Meerut Signals
15 No. 1 Group H.R.A.
16 Meerut Div. Ammn Col.
17 Wing, R.F.Corps
18 A.A. & Q.M.G. Meerut
19 A.D.M.S. Meerut
20 G.S. Meerut
21 to 24 War Diary and file
25 to 35 Spare

FLAGS FOR MARKING POSITION OF ADVANCED TROOPS

Secret Division
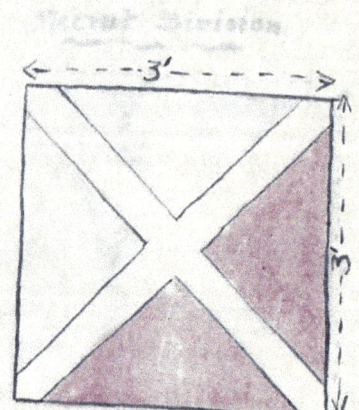

Eighth Division
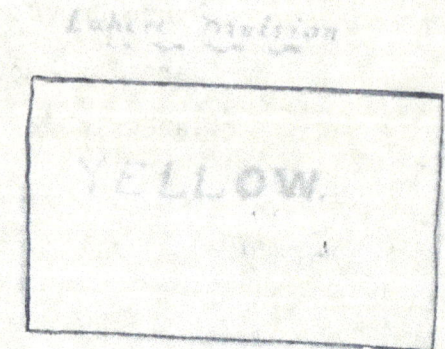
YELLOW

1st Division
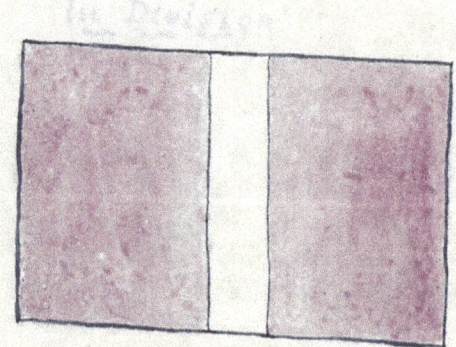

2nd Division
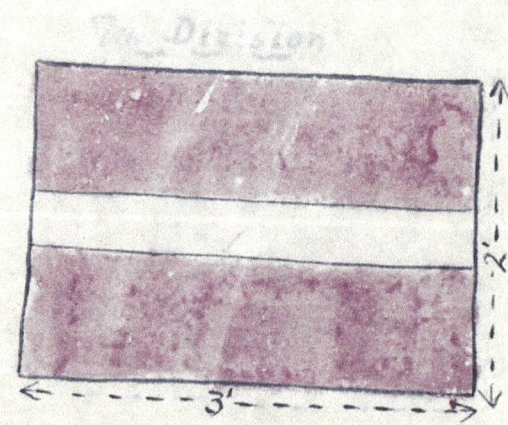

Infantry firing line

8th Division
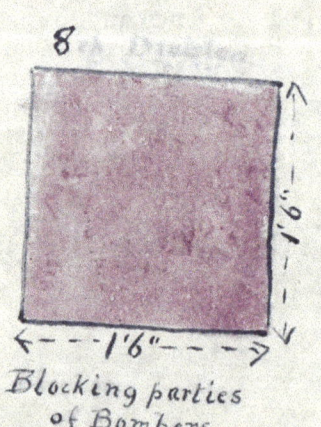

Blocking parties of Bombers

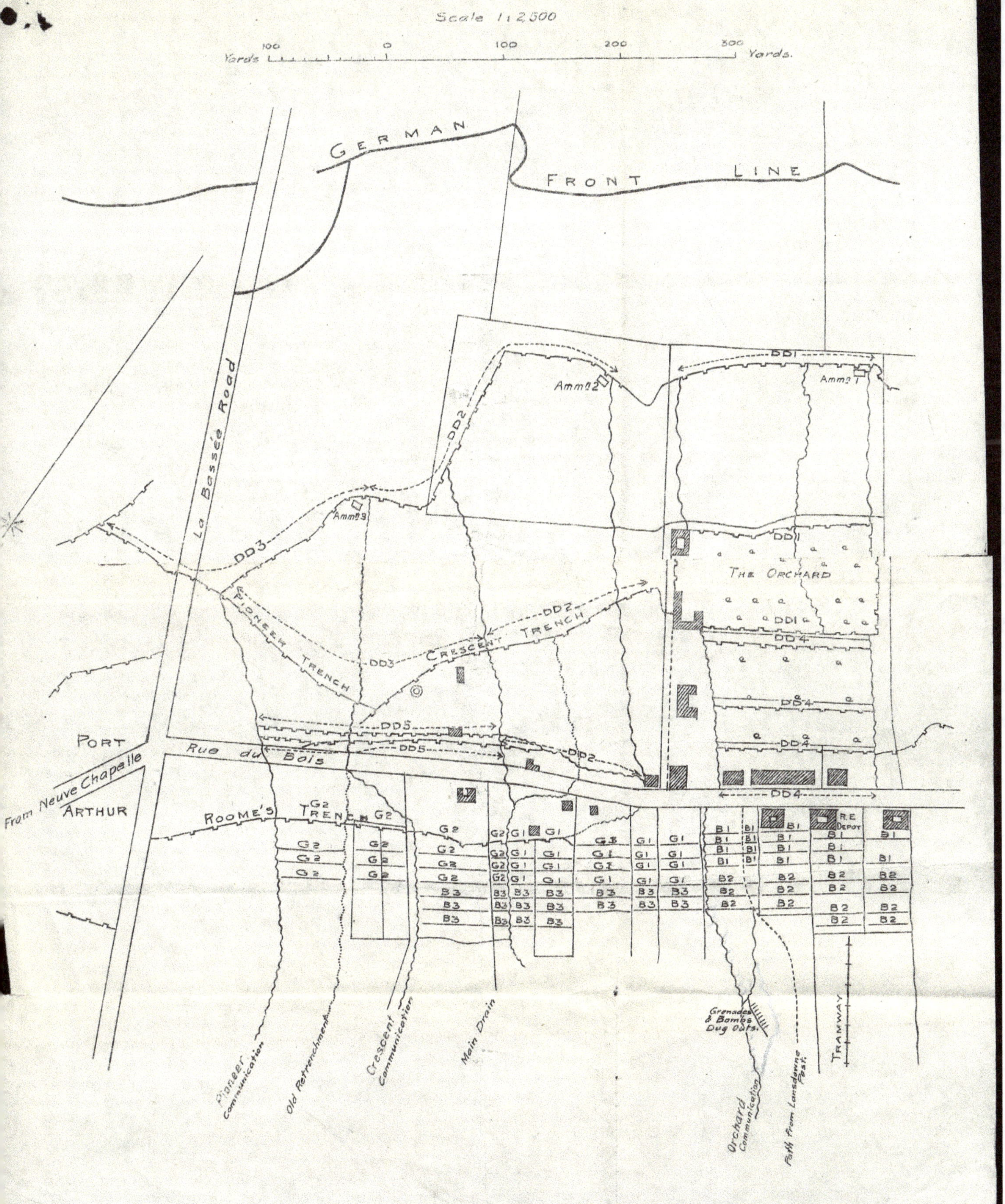

Scale 1:2,500
Yards 100 0 100 200 300 Yards.
GERMAN FRONT LINE
La Bassée Road
DD1
DD2
DD3
DD4
DD5
Amm.n 1
Amm.n 2
Amm.n 3
THE ORCHARD
PIONEER TRENCH
CRESCENT TRENCH
PORT ARTHUR
From Neuve Chapelle
Rue du Bois
ROOME'S TRENCH
G1
G2
B1
B2
B3
RE DEPOT
Grenades & Bombs Dug Outs.
TRAMWAY
Pioneer Communication
Old Retrenchment
Crescent Communication
Main Drain
Orchard Communication
Path from Lansdowne Post.

No. 405/45-G

SECRET

Headquarters, Meerut Division.

7th May 1915.

Memorandum.

Operations ordered for tomorrow are postponed. Division Hdqrs will not move to report centre tonight. Acknowledge by wire.

Garhwal Bde

Colonel
General Staff,
Meerut Division.

"A" Form.
MESSAGES AND SIGNALS.

Army Form C. 2121.

Prefix	Code	m.	Words	Charge	This message is on a/c of:	Recd. at _____ m.
Office of Origin and Service Instructions			Sent		_____ Service.	Date _____
			At _____ m.			From _____
			To _____		(Signature of "Franking Officer.")	By _____
			By _____			

TO Meerut Dn

Sender's Number.	Day of Month	In reply to Number	A A A
BM 304	7	405/45 G	

Reserved

From: Garhwal Bde
Place:
Time: 9 pm

The above may be forwarded as now corrected. (Z) M Stewart Major

Censor. Signature of Addresser or person authorised to telegraph in his name.

SECRET.

No. G.405/36

Headquarters, Meerut Division.

7th May 1915.

Memorandum.

The following corrections are to be made to Meerut Division Operation Order No. 30 issued to you yesterday:-

(i) INFORMATION. Para 1, line 4.   Alter "Advancing on DON" to read "Advancing to the line BAUVIN - DON"

(ii) Page 3, line 5.   Fill in time   -   5.20
              line 6,   ,,   ,,   5.40
              line 11,   ,,   ,,   5.40

              Line 37, for "North end" read "South end".

(iii) Page 4, para 8.   For "North end" read "South end".

(iv) Page 5, para 13, line 3 - for "164" read "1640"

(v) Page 4, para 9.   Alter to read:-

"9. The 4th Indian Cavalry will rendezvous in fields, clear of road, near cross roads in R.20.c.8/2 at 7.0 a.m. on 8th May, and etc. etc."

Note:-   The time given in para 5, line 7, is intended to read "1.0 A.M." Please make this clear in your copy, if not already so.

P. Davies

Major,
General Staff,
Meerut Division.

To,
Dehra Dun Bde
Garhwal Bde
Bareilly Bde
C.R.A. Meerut
C.R.E. Meerut
Lt.-Col. R.Drake-Brockman.

S E C R E T.   NOT TO BE TAKEN INTO TRENCHES OR INTO ACTION.

ARTILLERY TIME TABLE.

Line to be assaulted V6 - 56.

1st Phase.   Time ....:O - O.40.

Wire cutting.

Selected points shelled by heavy artillery and howitzers.

The trenches to be assaulted shelled.

Communicating trenches kept under fire.

Following barrages formed:- Along trenches from 140 to 63; along South-west edge of BOIS DU BIEZ; along roads leading from LIGNY LE PETIT and from LORGIES to the FERME DU BIEZ; along the LA BASSEE road South of LA TOURELLE; along support trenches in rear of line to be assaulted.

2nd Phase.   On the assault of the trenches the artillery fire will be lifted and a bombardment carried out from O.40 - 1.15.

This will prepare for the infantry capture of the line V7 - V11.

3rd Phase.   The artillery fire will be again lifted and a bombardment carried out from 1.15 to 1.45 which will enable the infantry to capture the DISTILLERY and FERME DU BIEZ.

The barrages will be maintained throughout the whole operation.

---

*
NOTE. - The figure 'O' represents the hour at which the bombardment is ordered to commence in Operation Orders.

SECRET. No. G.405/55

Headquarters, Meerut Division.

8th May 1915.

Memorandum.

The operations ordered in Meerut Division Operation Order No. 30 of 6th/7th instants, and postponed (vide my G.405/45 of yesterday) will be commenced as laid down in the above Operation Order, tomorrow morning 9th May 1915. Please acknowledge by wire.

Colonel,
General Staff,
Meerut Division

To,

Garhwal Bde

"A" Form. Army Form C. 2121.
MESSAGES AND SIGNALS.   No. of Message

Prefix	Code	m.	Words	Charge	This message is on a/c of:	Recd. at	m.
Office of Origin and Service Instructions.			Sent			Date	
			At	m.	Service.	From	
			To				
			By		(Signature of "Franking Officer.")	By	

TO: Meerut Dn

Sender's Number.	Day of Month	In reply to Number	
* Rm 310	8	G 405/55	A A A

Received

From Place: Garhwal Bde

Time: 2.30 pm

Signature of Addressee or person authorised to telegraph in his name.

"A" Form.
MESSAGES AND SIGNALS.
Army Form C. 2121.

SECRET

TO

Sender's Number.	Day of Month	In reply to Number	AAA
BM 309	8		

It has been decided that operations will take place tomorrow. If any further change in operation orders is required you will be informed.

From: Gatwal Bde
Place:
Time: 1.25 pm

OPERATION ORDER No 42 Copy No 1
by
Brigadier General C. G. Blackader D.S.O.
Commanding Garhwal Bde.

Reference Maps   15th May 1915
   FRANCE – BETHUNE sheet 1/40,000
   Trench map 1/10,000

Information   1. The 1st Corps and Indian Corps are to attack and to establish a line FESTUBERT – LA QUINQUE RUE – LA TOURELLE cross roads – PORT ARTHUR, and are thence to push on towards VIOLAINES and BEAUPUITS.

The 2nd Division is to assault on the right of and simultaneously with the Meerut Division, and the 7th Division on the right of the 2nd.

The SIRHIND Bde is to support the Garhwal bde; Bareilly bde in divisional reserve; DEHRA DUN bde in corps reserve.

Artillery   (6). A deliberate artillery bombardment is to precede the assault and is to cease on the front to be assaulted at 11.25 p.m. today.

The bombardment will continue on points 59 & 60 and on points east of a line 5g–V6E–V5E.

Intention   2. The GARHWAL B'de with machine guns of BAREILLY, with 6 guns of BAREILLY and DEHRA DUN and No. 4 trench mortar battery will hold the present front of the brigade & will attack the enemy's line between the ditches which run from S-E to N-W through the points V.5 and V.6.

Assaulting Battalions   3. The 2/Leicestershire Regt with 6 machine guns will assault with right on the ditch which runs through V6, having as objective the enemy's trenches mentioned in the tracing given to the O.C., & will get into touch with the 2nd Division on the right, clearing a double blocking beyond bombing distance any trenches leading to the front.

The Garhwal Rifles with 6 machine guns will assault with left on the ditch which runs through V6, having as objective the redoubt S.E. of V6, marked on tracing given to the C.O., & will form a defensive flank to the left, clearing a double blocking beyond bombing distance all trenches leading to front or flank.

Time of Assault   4. The assault will be delivered from the enemy's side of the ditch at 11.30 p.m on the night of the 15th 16th May.

Copy No 1

Supporting Battalions

5. The 3rd LONDONS in the eastern half of assembly trenches B1 & B2 will support the Garhwal Rifles.

Two companies 2/3rd GURKHA RIFLES under Major TILLARD in the western half of assembly trenches B1 & B2 will support the Leicesters.

These supports will keep filling up the trenches to the front as they are vacated.

The rear company of each body of supports will carry up ammunition from the depot in the RUE DU BOIS & from advanced depots in the captured position

Officers commanding supporting units will be with the officers commanding assaulting battalions.

Consolidation of Position

6. The objectives given for the attack will be consolidated before daylight.

Brigade Reserve

7. The 2/3rd GURKHA rifles (less 2 companies) in B1 & B2 assembly trenches in rear of the supporting companies of the 2/3rd G.R.

Defence of
the Line   8. Lt Col Morris v/s   will hold
                      Commanding   the line from the
         8th GURKHA rifles   LA-BASSEE - ESTA-
         Machine guns of GARHWAL   IRES road (exclusive)
         & BAREILLY rules   to but excluding the
         (less 12 guns)   centre communication
         N° 4 trench mortar batty   trench from the
         Bomb guns of BAREILLY   ORCHARD to the
         GARHWAL & DEHRA DUN   front line
         Brigades
                The machine guns & bomb guns will
         be disposed in accordance with instructions
         given to machine & bomb guns officers
         so as to cover the left flank of the attack.

Bombing   9. Assaulting battalions will organise
Parties &   bombing, blocking, sandbag & tool
                parties. These will be provided with
                flags to mark the position reached
                by them.

Sandbags   10. Every man will carry two sandbags
& Rations   & one days ration in addition to
               emergency ration

Depots for   11. Two depots in the front line, containing
Ammunition   in each case :—

    100 boxes S.A. Ammn
    200 bombs
    2000 sandbags
    2 boxes Very pistol Ammn

The bombs are not in carrying boxes; it is therefore imperative that units send back their boxes when sending for more bombs.

  There is also an ammunition depot at the R.E store in the RUE DU BOIS.

Masks   12. Masks will be kept in readiness soaked in solution prepared under direction of Medical Officers, and will be worn by assaulting troops.

Communication Trenches   13. The 1/Leicesters will have the use of the new HAZARA communication trench & the right orchard commⁿ trench.

  The Lincoln Rifles will use the centre & left orchard commⁿ trenches.

  The wounded will return by the commⁿ trench which leaves the front line 50 yards to the east of the ditch which passes the east side of the orchard, to the RUE DU BOIS and thence by the Orchard commⁿ trench parallel to & 100 yards east of the tramline, to the RUE DES BERCEAUX.

Medical   14. A collecting station will be established between LANSDOWNE POST & the point where the

Tramline to the RUE DES BERCEAUX — Copy No 1
crosses the RUE DES BERCEAUX

Distinguishing   15. The 2nd Div troops are wearing at night
Marks   showing both to front & rear.
                            The position of advanced or flank
                    bombing parties of the 2nd Div: will be marked
                    by yellow screens, 6' x 28" in the case of battalions
                    & yellow flags 28" by 28" for companies.
                            The 1st Div: red flags 3' x 3' with
                    white perpendicular stripe
                            London Div: sand bag cloth
                    disc, 2' in diameter with black cross in centre
                            LAHORE Div: Yellow flag 16" square

Communication 16. As soon as it is practicable
trenches to be   comn trenches will be opened up to
opened   the captured position.

Reports   17. To report centre on north side of RUE DU BOIS close to
                    and east of the R.E. DEPOT
Watchword 18. GARHWAL

Issued at 2pm through signal section   Bde Major
                                                                    Garhwal Bde
Copy No 1 — 2/Leicesters   Copy No 11 to War Diary
  "   2 — 3 Londons   "   " 12 retained
  "   3 — 2/3 Gurkhas
  "   4 — Garhwal Rifles
  "   5 — 2/8 G.R.
  "   6 — Bde M.G.O
  "   7 — " bomb E.O.
  "   8 — Meerut Div
  "   9 — Sirhind Bde
  " 10 — 6th Inf Bde

"A" Form. Army Form C. 2121.
MESSAGES AND SIGNALS.

| TO | 2 Leicesters |
| | Garhwal Rifles |

| Sender's Number. | Day of Month | In reply to Number | AAA |
| BM 157 | 15 | | |

After commencement of operations this evening you will utilise the ~~right~~ more westerly of the two communication trenches at your disposal for forward, and the more easterly one for rearward traffic except wounded who will follow route laid down in orders AAA Post sentries accordingly at entrances and exits

2 mins.

From   Garhwal Bde
Place
Time   1.05 pm

"A" Form.
MESSAGES AND SIGNALS. Army Form C. 2121.

TO: Leicesters, Garhwal Rifles
3 Londons 7/8
2/3 ~~Sirmoor~~

Reference Operation Order No 42 para 3. Cancel route for wounded North of RUE DU BOIS and substitute LANSDOWNE communication trench roughly parallel to and 50 yards west of the main drain, and leading into the centre of LANSDOWNE post

From: Garhwal Bde
Time: 5.15 p.m.

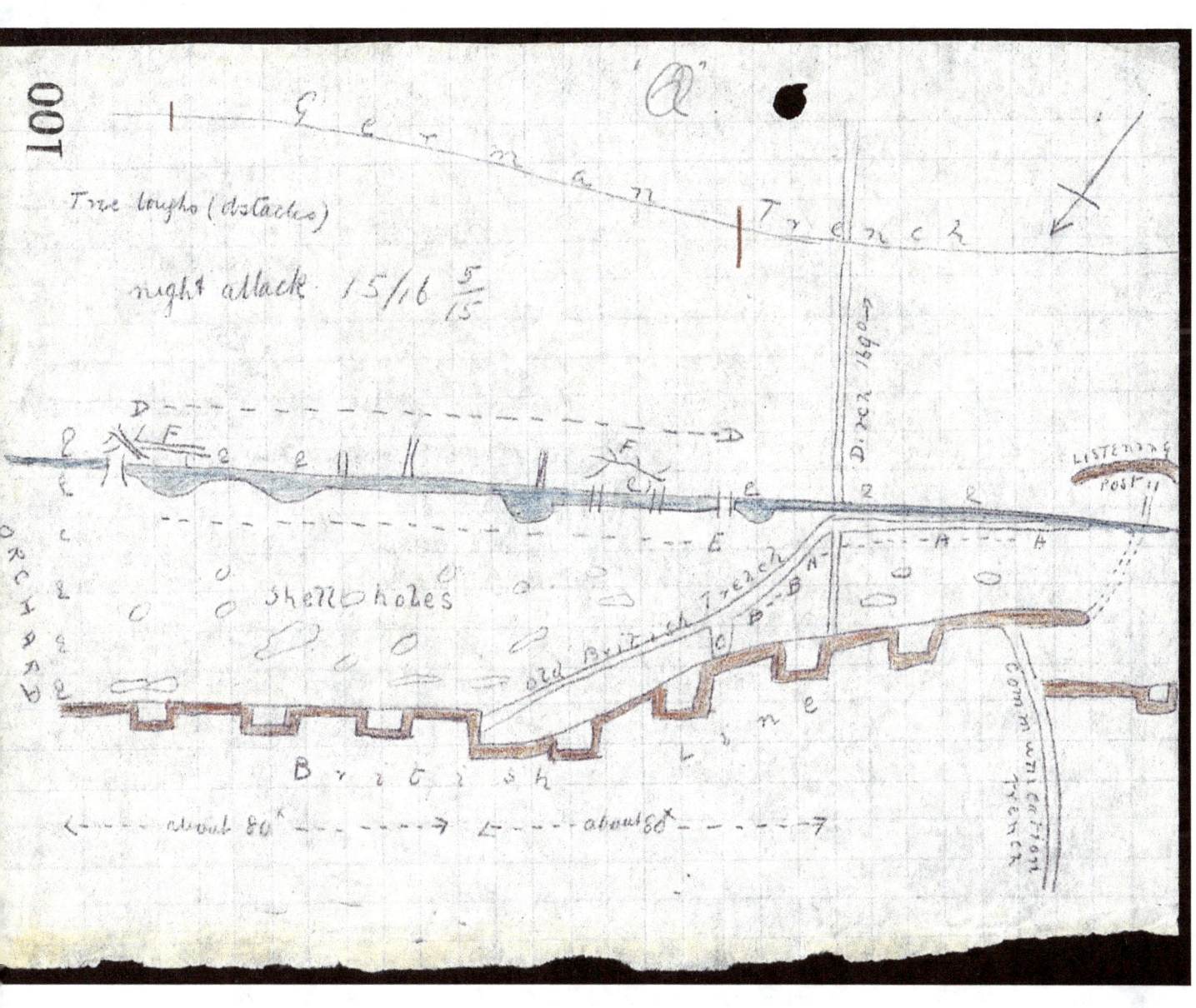

Operation Order No 31
by
Brigadier General C W Jacob
Commanding Dehra Dun Bde

M.31.d 6th May 1915

Reference map of assembly forwarded under Bm 22 of 5th

1. The Brigade will move into position of assembly by 11 pm on May 7th, preparatory to an attack at dawn.

2. All movements will be via ST VAAST corner M.32.d - track alongside trolley line - past LANSDOWNE Post to RUE DU BOIS. The only communication trench to be used between LANSDOWNE POST and RUE DU BOIS is that known as ORCHARD Communication trench.

3. The 1st Seaforths will pass ST VAAST POST, Companies at 10 minutes interval, commencing at 8 pm and will enter the assembly area from the RUE DU BOIS by the three first communication trenches crossing the RUE DU BOIS West of PORT ARTHUR cross roads i.e. PIONEER COMMUNICATION TRENCH — CRESCENT COMMUNICATION TRENCH and the trench leading to centre of CRESCENT TRENCH.

4. The 2nd Gurkhas will leave FORESTERS LANE by Companies at 10 minutes interval commencing at 9 pm. Companies marching from billets not to pass ST VAAST POST before 8-30 pm and will enter the Assembly area by the communication trenches leading into and through the ORCHARD.

5. The 4th Seaforths will pass St VAAST POST by Coys at 10 minutes interval, commencing at 9 pm and will enter the assembly area by the two communication trenches leading into centre of CRESCENT TRENCH and the new trench near West end of CRESCENT TRENCH.

6. The 9th Gurkhas will pass ST VAAST POST by Companies at 10 minutes interval. commencing at 9-40 pm and will enter the assembly area by the same communication trenches as

as 1st Seaforths.

7. The 6th Jats will pass ST VAAST POST in two parties at 10-20 and 10-30 pm and will enter the assembly area via the communication trenches leading from RUE DU BOIS towards North end of Orchard.

8. Ladders and Bridges will be carried up by Companies

9. The importance of absence of noise both during the march and when in assembly area is to be impressed on all ranks. Also the vital necessity of men keeping hidden from view as much as possible after dawn while the Artillery is registering and cutting wire.

10. Brigade Report Centre will be established at "96 Picadilly" after 8-30pm on May 7th.

Issued at 7 pm.

                     _____, Major
                Bde Major Dehra Dun Bde.

Copy No 1 to Meerut Div
" " 2 to Jullundur Bde
" " 3 to Garhwal Bde
" " 4 to Bareilly Bde
" " 5 to 1st Seaforths
" " 6 to 4th Seaforths
" " 7 to 6th Jats
" " 8 to 9th Gurkhas
" " 9 to 2nd Gurkhas
" " 10 to Bde Bomb gun Officer
" " 11 to No 4 French Battery RA
" " 12 to Section Mountain Artillery
" " 13 & 14 retained

SECRET

Operation Order 32   Copy No 6.
by
Brigadier General C W Jacob
Commanding Dehra Dun Brigade

7th May 1915

Information 1. (a). The 1st Army is attacking on May the 8th
(b). The 1st Corps retaining right on GIVENCHY is to advance on RUE DU MARAIS - LORGIES and ILLIES.
(c). The Indian Corps is to operate so as to cover the left of the 1st Corps capturing the FERME DU BIEZ and advancing on line LIGNY-LE-GRAND - LA CLIQUETERIE FERME.
(d). The 4th Corps is to turn the AUBERS defences by an attack from North East and subsequently to gain touch with the Indian Corps at LA CLIQUETERIE FE.
(e). The Meerut Division is to make the attack to be delivered by the Indian Corps.
(f). The Lahore Division is to hold the front allotted to Indian Corps less that portion from which the Meerut Division is to attack. It will assist the left flank of the Meerut attack by fire. It will also open a communication trench from the listening post at point 61 to connect up with attack if this becomes desirable.

Intention 2. The Dehra Dun Bde will break the enemy's line from point V.6 to 56 and establish itself on the front Distillery (square S.17. a-c) - FERME DU BIEZ - Point 53.

Orders to 3. (a) The 2nd Gurkhas will break the enemy's
Troops   line between point V.6 and the ditch which runs at right angles to the German trenches about point 59. Subsequently, working in conjunction with the right

right of the 4th Seaforths, the battalion will push on towards the line R.16-E — LE TOURELLE cross roads. The left flank should reach the ESTAIRES-LA BASSEE Road near point V.9.E whence it should push up the road clearing the houses on West side.

The battalion will establish itself on the above line but if circumstances permit will push forward a detachment to seize and occupy the DISTILLERY.

(b.) The 4th Seaforths will break the enemy's line from East of ditch mentioned in (a) and the LA BASSEE Road. Subsequently, working in conjunction with left of 2nd Gurkhas, the battalion will push on to the line LE TOURELLE cross road — point V.8 where it will establish itself. The main LA BASSEE road should be crossed in the vicinity of point V.9.E and the right flank should clear the houses on East side of road.

(c.) The 1st Seaforths will break the enemy's line between the LA BASSEE road and Point 56. Subsequently the battalion will push on towards Point V.8. and road junction immediately East of V.12. A protective flank is to be established facing the BOIS DU BIEZ along the road leading from point 53 to V.12. The battalion will establish itself in the above line but if circumstances permit will push forward a detachment to seize and occupy the FERME DU BIEZ.

(d) The 6th Jats will support the 2nd Gurkhas and as soon as the latter battalion has reached its objective will push forward and occupy the Distillery.

It will move forward to the trenches vacated by the 2nd Gurkhas as soon as the latter advance to the assault.

(e). Two Coys 9th Gurkhas will support the 1st Seaforths and as soon as the latter battalion has gained its objective will push forward and occupy the FERME DU BIEZ. They will move forward to the trenches W of LA BASSEE road vacated by 1st Seaforths as soon as the latter advance to the assault. 9th Gurkhas (less 2 Coys) will act as Brigade Reserve and will occupy the front line of trenches vacated by the 4th Seaforths as soon as the latter move forward, sending a British Officer to report to Bde Head Quarters to await any instructions.

(2). During night 7th/8th May Officers Commanding assaulting battalions will arrange to cut the wire in their front to allow of exit and will place bridges in position as far as possible. Every effort should be made to conceal the bridges. This work should be done before the moon rises 2·7 am.

(3) The three assaulting battalions will form up in front of our advanced trenches after the wire cutting portion of the bombardment is completed at 5·20 am and before the bombardment of the enemy's trenches ends at 5·40 am. The assaulting line will, during the bombardment, move up as close to enemy's line as our shell fire permits, and will reach the enemy's front line trenches at the earliest possible moment after the bombardment is lifted to more distant objectives at 5·40 am

(h). The following points as captured will be held by garrisons and strengthened. Parties of Sappers and Pioneers will be sent under orders of C.R.E to assist:-
   (a). South end of LE TOURELLE Village.
   (b) Distillery.
   (c) Road junction in S.11.a (Points 52 and 53).
   (d). Group of houses near point 50.
   (e) FERME DU BIEZ.

Ammunition 4. (a). Men will carry 200 rounds on the person.
   (b). Part of the Regimental Reserve SAA should be collected at convenient places in the forward line of trenches and Units should endeavour to have these carried forward behind the attack and to establish a forward Depot. This can be done either by detailing the rear Company to carry forward a certain number of boxes or by leaving parties from each Company with orders to follow some distance behind or when they see the distinguishing flag hoisted in certain localities.
   (c). A Depot of SAA has been established in the RUE DU BOIS near the RE Depot shewn on the assembly map. All Officers and N.C.O's should know where this is.
   (d) The two supporting battalions, 9th Gurkhas and 6th Jats will arrange to carry forward additional boxes of ammunition to some forward locality.
   (e). Depots of ammunition have been or will be established as shewn on assembly map at Head of communication trenches and also in the listening Post East of PORT ARTHUR.

Grenades & 5. A Reserve of grenades & bombs has been
bombs. collected in dug outs as shewn on the

the assembly map, and all concerned should know the exact locality

Sandbags 6. Every man will carry two sandbags.

Distinguishing Flags. 7. (a) Flags 3'×3' – Red and black divided diagonally and with a white diagonal cross have been issued and should be stuck up on the reverse side of prominent points gained to mark the progress of the attack.

(b). Troops of the 8th Division will show a red flag 2'-6" square with a white or yellow diagonal stripe. Blocking parties of bombers will show a red flag 1'-3" square.

(c) Troops of 7th Division will show a flag 3' long by 2' broad with three horizontal stripes two red and one white.

(d). Troops of 1st Division will show a red flag with white vertical stripe in centre.

(e). Lahore Division will show a yellow flag.

Masks 8. Masks will be kept in readiness soaked in the solution, by all troops in the front trenches and will be worn by assaulting troops

No 4 Trench Battery R.A. Bomb guns 9. No 4 Trench Battery R.A.; after the Artillery has cut wire and while the bombardment of trenches is going on will fire on V.6.

Brigade Bomb gun officer will detail two guns to proceed with each Assaulting battalion. These will be used to bomb localities which hold out obstinately.

Signals 10. Each Unit will carry two helios in addition to other Signalling Equipment.

Medical 11. A collecting station will be established between LANSDOWNE POST and the tramway where it crosses FORESTERS LANE. Route for wounded returning from the front will be be by the ORCHARD communication trench which runs from RUE DU BOIS to FORESTERS LANE along the North East side of the Tramway.

Prisoners 12. Prisoners will be handed over to LAHORE Division at Dehra Dun Bde Report centre

Official Time 13 Official Time will be given to Units at Bde Head Quarters after 5 pm on May the 7th - two watches to be sent by each representative.

Reports 14 RUE DU BOIS near communication trench leading into ORCHARD

Issued at 9 am. F. Walker
Bde Major Dehra Dun Bde Major

Copy 1 and 2 retained
Copy 3 to Meerut Division
Copy 4 to Jullunder Bde
Copy 5 to Bareilly Bde
Copy 6 to Garhwal Bde
Copy 7 to 1st Seaforths
Copy 8 to 4th Seaforths
Copy 9 to 6th Jats
Copy 10 to 9th Gurkhas
Copy 11 to 2nd Gurkhas
Copy 12 to Bde Bomb gun officer
Copy 13 to No 4 Trench Bty RA
Copy 14 to Section Mountain Bty

SECRET.

BRIGADE OPERATION ORDER No. 32
by
BRIGADIER-GENERAL W.M.SOUTHEY C.M.G.,

COMMANDING BAREILLY BDE.

Copy No.____

Reference Maps:-
FRANCE (BETHUNE) 1/40,000.
FAUQUISSART-AUBERS Sheet 1/10,000.

8th May 1915.

INFORMATION. 1. The DEHRA DUN BRIGADE has secured the line FME DU BIEZ - DISTILLERY, and Colonel DRAKE BROCKMAN'S Detachment has reached the BOIS DU BIEZ.

INTENTION. 2. The Brigade will attack the line HALPEGARBE - LIGNY LE LE GRAND.

POSITION OF ASSEMBLY. 3. Units of the Brigade will move at once and independently to positions of Assembly under cover as under facing EAST:-

(A) 2nd BLACK WATCH.) Along line of road running N.N.W.
    58th RIFLES.   ) from Road Junction Sq. S. 11. A. 8.6.
) Right of 2nd BLACK WATCH will rest
) on Road Junction.
) Each Battalion will be formed up on a
) front of 200 yards.

(B) 4th BLACK WATCH.   ) Along line of ESTAIRES - LA
    Machine Guns, 125th RIFLES.) BASSEE Road and on EAST of
    BDE TRENCH GUN DETACHMENT.) Road.
    41st DOGRAS.   ) Right of 4th BLACK WATCH will
) rest on CROSS ROADS.
) Each Battalion will be on
) a frontage of 200 yards.

The Maxims of 4th BLACK WATCH, 125th RIFLES, under the Brigade Machine Gun Officer, and the Bde Trench Gun Detachment will be formed up behind leading Coy. of 4th BLACK WATCH.

(C) BRIGADE HEADQUARTERS will move to vicinity of FME DU BIEZ.

ORDERS FOR THE ATTACK. 4. On receipt of orders to advance from Position of Assembly the attack will be carried out as follows:-

2nd BLACK WATCH - will move on a frontage of 200 yards with Right Flank on South edge of FME DU BIEZ - LIGNY LE PETIT Road.

1st OBJECTIVE:- LIGNY LE PETIT.
2nd OBJECTIVE:- ROAD JUNCTION Sq. T. 7. D.
3rd OBJECTIVE:- LIGNY LE GRAND - with Right directed on Farm near Point 23.

58th RIFLES - moving on left of 2nd BLACK WATCH, on a frontage of 200 yards. It will take its direction from 2nd BLACK WATCH.

1st OBJECTIVE:- Houses about Points 40 and 41.
2nd OBJECTIVE:- HALPE GARBE.
3rd OBJECTIVE:- LIGNY LE GRAND with Left directed on house

house close to Point 30.

BRIGADE RESERVE.

4th BLACK WATCH.
TRENCH GUN DETACHMENT,
MACHINE GUNS, 4th BLACK WATCH,
and 125th RIFLES.
41st DOGRAS.

) Will move under the orders
) of G.O.C. Brigade.
) The Trench Gun Detachment
) and Machine Guns of 4th
) BLACK WATCH and 125th RIFLES
) moving in rear of leading
) Company of 4th BLACK WATCH.
Each Battalion will move on a front of 200 yards and in the least vulnerable formation.

CO-OPERATION WITH TROOPS ON FLANKS. 5. The DRAKE-BROCKMAN Detachment will co-operate on our Left flank from the direction of LA RUSSIE and BOIS DU BIEZ, and Troops of the 1st Division will co-operate on our Right Flank immediately SOUTH of FME DU BIEZ - LIGNY LE PETIT Road. O.C. 2nd BLACK WATCH and 58th RIFLES will maintain touch by patrols with the 1st Division and DRAKE BROCKMAN DET. respectively.

The DRAKE BROCKMAN DET. will indicate its position by means of bombs emitting one or other of the following signals:-
(1) Green smoke and white stars.
(2) Yellow smoke.
(3) Single trail of yellow smoke falling downwards.

DISTINGUISHING FLAGS. 6. The distinguishing flags issued to Units for the purpose should be used freely to indicate the position of Battalions as they progress from one point to another, and should be conspicuous from the direction of the FME DU BIEZ.

SNIPERS, SPIES ETC. 7. All houses captured should be thoroughly searched for concealed Snipers, Spies, and telephones. All cellars should be cleared with hand-grenades before entering them.

8. No water from the wells found in any houses or villages should be drunk by Troops before an officer has satisfied himself that it has not been poisoned by the enemy.

AMMUNITION. 9. 200 rounds will be carried on the man.

The 4th BLACK WATCH will bring 100 boxes S.A.A. to Position of Assembly on ESTAIRES-LA BASSEE Road. From that point these will be brought forward by 4th BLACK WATCH and 41st DOGRAS, each carrying 50 boxes.

MASKS. 10. Each man will have ready a mask or other means of warding off the effect of asphyxiating gases.

Assaulting

REPORTS.

Assaulting Troops will wear these.

11. BRIGADE HEADQUARTERS will be established at first near Eastern boundary of FME DU BIEZ, and later on move forward to locality which will be notified.

W.R. Hamer
Captain,
Brigade Major.

ISSUED TO SIGNAL SECTION AT

Copy No. 1. 2nd Black Watch.
  "   " 2. 4th Black Watch.
  "   " 3. 125th Rifles.
  "   " 4. 58th Rifles.
  "   " 5. 41st Dogras.

"A" Form. Army Form C. 2121.
MESSAGES AND SIGNALS.

OPERATION ORDER No. 32
by
BRIG. GENERAL W.M. SOUTHEY C.M.G
COMMANDING BAREILLY BDE

Reference Map - FRANCE (BETHUNE) 1/40,000. 9th MAY 1915.

INTENTION. 1. The BAREILLY BDE will break the enemy's line from point V.6 to 56 and establish itself on the front DISTILLERY (Sq. S.17 a.c.) - FERME DU BIEZ - Point 53.

ORDERS TO TROOPS. 2.(a) The 2nd BLACK WATCH will break the enemy's line between Point V.6 and the ditch which runs at right angles to the German trenches about Point 59. Subsequently working in conjunction with the right of the 58th RIFLES the Battalion will push on

"A" Form.
MESSAGES AND SIGNALS.
Army Form C. 2121.

on towards the line R16 E – LA
TOURELLE cross roads the left flank
should reach the ESTAIRES – LA BASSÉE
Road near point V 9 E whence it
should push up the road clearing the
houses on WEST side.
The Battalion will establish itself
on the above lines but if circumstances
permit will push forward a
detachment to seize and occupy the
DISTILLERY
(c) The 58th RIFLES will break the enemy's
line from East of ditch marked in
(a) on the LA BASSÉE Road Subsequently
working in conjunction with left of 2nd
BLACK WATCH the battalion will push
on to the line LE TOURELLE cross roads

"A" Form.
MESSAGES AND SIGNALS.
Army Form C. 2121.

Prefix	Code	m.	Words	Charge	This message is on a/c of:	Recd. at	m.
Office of Origin and Service Instructions			Sent			Date	
			At	m.	Service.	From	
			To				
			By		(Signature of "Franking Officer.")	By	

TO

| Sender's Number. | Day of Month. | In reply to Number | AAA |

occupy the FERME DU BIEZ.
(d) 4th BLACK WATCH will be in Brigade Reserve in CRESCENT Trench and BLACKADER'S Trench
(e) The Rifle Bomb Guns will cover the attack of the 2nd BLACK WATCH and 58th RIFLES from positions between the ORCHARD Redoubt and the Front trench.
(f) The Artillery bombardment of the enemy's trenches will commence at 3-20 p.m. and last till 4 p.m. when the Infantry assault will take place. The assaulting Infantry should form up outside the Front trenches and push forward as close to the enemy's line as ——— is safe under cover of our Artillery bombardment.

From
Place
Time

The above may be forwarded as now corrected.   (Z)

Censor.   Signature of Addressor or person authorised to telegraph in his name.

* This line should be erased if not required.

"A" Form.
MESSAGES AND SIGNALS.

Army Form C. 2121.

(g) The following points, when captured will be held by garrisons and strengthened. Parties of Sappers & Pioneers will be sent under orders of C.R.E. to assist :-
 (a) South end of LE TOURELLE village.
 (b) DISTILLERY.
 (c) Road junction in S.II.A. (Points 52 and 53)
 (d) Group of houses near point 50
 (e) FERME DU BIEZ

4. 4th BLACK WATCH when ordered to move forward to support any portion of the attack will take with it 100 boxes S.A.A. as far forward as possible where it will be dumped under a Sentry

5. The distinguishing flags issued to Units should be stuck up on the reverse side

"A" Form. MESSAGES AND SIGNALS. Army Form C. 2121.

Point V.8 where it will establish itself. The [left?] LA BASSEE road at it be [crosses?] in the vicinity of Point V.9.E. and the right flank [close?] along the [houses?] on [East?] side of road.

(c) The 41st DOGRAS will [hold?] the enemy's [line?] [between?] the LA BASSEE road and Point 56. Subsequently the battalion will push on towards Point V.8 and road junction immediately East of V.12, a [protective?] flank in the meanwhile facing the BOIS DU BIEZ along the road leading from Point 53 to V.12. The battalion will establish itself in the above line but if [opportunity?] [occurs?] [commandant?] will push forward a detachment to seize and

"A" Form. Army Form C. 2121.
MESSAGES AND SIGNALS.

Prefix	Code	m.	Words	Charge	This message is on a/c of:	Recd. at	m.
Office of Origin and Service Instructions			Sent			Date	
			At ... m.		..................Service.	From	
			To				
			By		(Signature of "Franking Officer.")	By	

TO				

Sender's Number.	Day of Month.	In reply to Number	AAA

side of prominent points to mark
progress of attack

6. Masks soaked in solution will be
worn by the assaulting troops

7. All houses captured to be thoroughly
searched for concealed snipers, spies
and telephones

8. No water from wells to be drunk by
troops before an officer has satisfied
himself that it has not been poisoned
by the enemy

9. Brigade Head Quarters situated on
RUE DU BOIS.

Christmas Capt.
Brigade Major.

From
Place Issued to Signal Section at 1.20 PM
Time Copy No. 1. 2nd Black Watch   Copy No. 4. 59th Rifles
                                    5. 41st Dogras

Censor. Signature of Addressor or person authorised to telegraph in his name.
*This line should be erased if not required.

SECRET

Copy No. 9

OPERATION ORDER No. 31
by
LIEUTENANT - GENERAL Sir Charles ANDERSON, K.C.B.,
Commanding MEERUT Division.

Reference maps:-
 FRANCE - BETHUNE Sheet - 1:40,000.
& Special Map 1:10,000.

14th May 1915.

Information. 1. The 1st and Indian Corps are to renew the attack and to press forward toward VIOLAINES and BEAU PUITS and to establish a defensive flank along the LA BASSEE Road on the left, maintaining the right at GIVENCHY.
 The line to be established in the first instance is the general line of the road FESTUBERT - LA QUINQUE RUE - LA TOURELLE cross roads - PORT ARTHUR, which position is to be consolidated.
 The 1st Corps is assaulting with the 2nd Division on the right of the Meerut Division with the object of securing the line R.1 - R.3 - R.5 - R.7 - V.4. The assault of this Division will be simultaneous with that of the Meerut Division. Its subsequent advance will be with the object of securing the FERME D'AVOUE and the line of road P.14 to R.13.
 The 7th Division is assaulting the German front trenches between N.1 and P.5 in the early hours of the 15th May.

Intention. 2. The Meerut Division less Dehra Dun Brigade and one Brigade R.F.A., and plus the Sirhind Brigade will make the attack to be delivered by the Indian Corps.
 This assault is to be made against the enemy front line trenches included between the ditches running from South-south east to North-northwest through points V.5 and V.6. The first objective is the capture of the enemy's front line of V.6 redoubt and of the trenches behind the first line lying west of the north corner of the redoubt as far as the ditch running through V.5. Communication trenches will then be opened connecting captured trenches with our own line. The easterly one of such trenches will be turned into a fire trench facing east. Every endeavour will be made to accomplish this task and consolidate our position before daylight, getting touch on our right with the 2nd Division troops and bombing outwards along enemy trenches on our left flank to the east and south-east. A fire front facing east will thus be formed with V.6 redoubt as its centre. The second objective is to attack outwards in an easterly direction and secure the line 5.V.E - V.6.E - 59. The third objective; when the above line has been secured, and as the attack of the 2nd Division progresses, our attack is to push on and secure the road from PORT ARTHUR to LA TOURELLE Cross roads inclusive and consolidate itself thereon.

Artillery 3 A deliberate artillery bombardment will precede the assault (it commenced at 12 noon today) and will be maintained for 36 hours. This bombardment will deal with:-
  (a) Wire cutting on front of attack both in front of and behind the German front line parapet.
  (b) The first and second German lines on the front of attack.
  (c) The redoubt at V.6.
  (d) The German front line parapet from just north of point V.6 through points 59 and 60 to a point 30 yards east of the LA BASSEE Road.
  (e) The keep in rear of point 59.
  (f) The group of houses around point V.9.E on the LA BASSEE Road.
  (g) The covered way connecting V.9.E with the south-east corner of V.6 redoubt.
  (h)

(h) The houses alongside the LA BASSEE Road about V.10.E and V.7.
(k) The houses about the following points:- R.16.E R.17.E - R.17 - R.19 - R.16 - R.18 including the DISTILLERY.

This bombardment will cease on the front to be attacked at 11.25 P.M. on 14th May, i.e., five minutes before the infantry assault at 11.30 P.M. 14th May, but will continue steadily on points lying east of a line passing immediately west of points 59 - V.6.E and V.5.E. Point 59 itself is to be fired at during and after the assault, also point 60. The maintenance of an accurate fire on these two points during the assault is of great importance.

Section Mountain Artillery. The Section Mountain Artillery will be held in a state of readiness in the vicinity of ST VAAST to advance if required

No.4 Trench Battery. No.4 Trench Howitzer Battery is placed at the disposal of G.O.C. Garhwal Bde for the operations.

INFANTRY Garhwal Bde 4. The Garhwal Bde will carry out the assault on the enemy front line trenches as in para 2.

The assault will be made on a two battalion front under detailed arrangements to be made by G.O.C. Garhwal Bde.

The assault will be delivered at 11.30 P.M. on the 14th May.

In order to keep under the enemy's fire from his trenches on the left of our attack, the marginal force will be detailed under the command of Lieut:-Colonel G.MORRIS, 2/8th Gurkhas, to hold the front line parapet east of the communication trench running forward from centre of ORCHARD Redoubt. The trench howitzers, bomb-guns and machine guns will be established close to, or in, our front line trenches. Fire will be

---
1 Battn Ind. Infantry,
Machine gun sections of Bareilly Bde.
No.4 Trench Battery
Bomb-gun batteries of Dehra Dun, Garhwal & Bareilly Brigades.
---

distributed along the enemy's front from point 60 on the LA BASSEE Road towards V.6. Great caution is to be exercised to avoid firing into the left of our own attacking line. Fire is to commence as soon as the assault starts.

No.2 Trench Battery. No. 2 Trench Howitzer Battery is assisting in this bombardment from a point in the Lahore Division trenches and will fire on points 56 and 60 and their vicinity.

SIRHIND Bde 5. Sirhind Bde will be in support to Garhwal Bde. It will be formed up by ten P.M., 14th May in assembly positions as follows:-
  Two battns RUE DU BOIS,
  remaining battns in LANSDOWNE POST and the breastwork in the vicinity.

BAREILLY Bde 6. Bareilly Bde is in Divisional Reserve and will be held in a state of readiness in second line trenches at CROIX BARBEE from one A.M. on 15th.

Machine gun sections will be put at disposal of G.O.C. Garhwal Bde and will get into position as in para 4 during night 13th/14th May.

In communication with the C.R.E., one battn Indian infantry will be detailed to proceed on 13th May to tram-head at ST VAAST where it will be held in readiness:-
  (a) to provide two companies as carrying parties for engineers; &
  (b) two companies to proceed along the tram lines to carry ammunition and receive prisoners etc:, on receipt of orders to do so.

S E C R E T.   G-439/34.

CORRECTION TO OPERATION ORDER No 31.

MEDICAL. 15. Cancel line 4 from "ORCHARD communication trench" to "some 100 yards from it" in line 6 and substitute :-

"Trench east of the ORCHARD and thence by LANSDOWNE communication trench. This trench runs roughly parallel to and 50 yards west of the main drain and leads into centre of LANSDOWNE POST".

15th May 1915.

Major,
General Staff Meerut Division.

To:-

3/.

Dehra Dun Brigade.	7. Dehra Dun Brigade is in Corps reserve.
Brigade bomb-gun Batteries.	8. Bomb-gun Batteries of Dehra Dun and Bareilly Brigades will be placed at the disposal of the G.O.C. Garhwal Bde ~~and will go into the trenches on night 12th/13th May.~~
4th Cavalry	9. 4th Indian Cavalry will rendezvous at 5.0 a.m. 15th May in fields and orchards between VIEILLE CHAPELLE and LA COUTURE, and send a liaison officer to Divisional Report Centre RUE DU PUITS.
S. & M. Pioneers 2 Coys Ind.Inf.	10. Nos 3 and 4 Companies S. & M., 107th Pioneers, will rendezvous at ST VAAST on the evening of 14th May at 7.30 p.m. The C.R.E. will organise the following working parties:- (i) A small barricading party which will report to G.O.C. Garhwal Bde in the RUE DU BOIS at 10.0 p.m. (ii) A party for the opening of communication along line of ditch passing through V.5, will be despatched from ST VAAST by the C.R.E. as soon as information is received that the German first line has been carried. (iii) A party for the opening of communication along ditch passing through V.6 will follow as soon as situation is reported such as to admit of their working. (iv) A party for the consolidation of V.6 when taken will similarly follow when demanded. All these parties will, on arrival in the RUE DU BOIS come under the orders of the G.O.C. Garhwal Bde.
Wire cutting, bridging.	11. G.O.C. Garhwal Bde will arrange for wire to be cut and bridges to be put in position over the ditch in front of our parapet.
S.A.A. supply.	12. A depot of 840 boxes of S.A.A. has been established in RUE DU BOIS at R.E.depot, and 500 at ST VAAST. The G.O.C. Garhwal Bde will also place two advanced depots of 100 boxes each, in the forward trench from which the assault will be launched. To supplement such arrangements as Brigadiers may make for their own Brigades, the supporting and reserve brigades will each direct their rear battalion to carry forward ammunition, and establish further advanced depots in the fighting area as may be found suitable and possible.
Advanced R.E.depots.	13. Advanced R.E.Depots are formed at (a) RUE DU BOIS (b) Farm at M.32.d.7/7.
Bombs & Hand-grenades	14. The depots of bombs and hand-grenades 100 yards in rear of assembly trenches north of R.E.depot, RUE DU BOIS, have been restocked.
Medical.	15. A collecting station will be established between LANSDOWNE POST and the tramway line where it crosses FORRESTERS LANE. Route for wounded returning from the front will be by the ~~ORCHARD Communication trench which runs from RUE DU BOIS to FORRESTERS LANE along the northeast side of the tramway and some 100 yards from it.~~ This trench will be reserved for return of wounded only after fighting has commenced, and will be marked accordingly. Route from collecting station to ST VAAST Corner, where an advanced dressing station will be established, will be alongside the tramway lines. A wagon rendezvous in this vicinity will be established and will be marked by the RED CROSS Flag.

Field

4/.

Field ambulances will be opened at VIEILLE CHAPELLE and ZELOBES: Line of evacuation from wagon rendezvous is via OXFORD Road and WELLINGTON Road.

Sandbags 16. Each man of the attacking infantry will carry two sandbags.

Masks. 17. Masks will be kept in readiness, soaked in solution prepared under the direction of medical officers of units. Assaulting troops will wear theirs.

Disting-
-uishing
marks. 18. 2nd Division troops, at night, are wearing a white bib showing both to front and rear.
By day, position of advanced or flank bombing parties of Meerut Division will be shown by a three feet square flag, the top and left portion being black and the bottom and right portion - red, with a white ST ANDREW's CROSS.
Those of 2nd Division will be marked by a yellow screen, 6' by 28" in case of battalions, and yellow flags 28" x 28" in case of companies.
    1st Division:- Red flags - 3' x 3' with white perpendicular stripe.
    London Divn - Sandbag cloth disc, 2' in diameter with black cross in centre.
    Lahore Divn. - yellow flag 16" square.

Emergency
Supply
Depot. 19. An advanced emergency supply depot has been estab--lished at house at cross roads in M.32.d, near head of the tramway line.

Advanced
Report
Centres. 20. Meerut Divn.   RUE DU PUITS.
    Garhwal Bde.   9694 PICCADILLY, RUE DU BOIS.
    Sirhind Bde.   LANSDOWNE POST
    Bareilly Bde.   CROSS Roads CROIX BARBEE.

Colonel,
General Staff,
MEERUT DIVISION.

Issued to Signal Company
for distribution, at 12.30 p.m.

Copy No. 1 and 2   to Indian Corps,
        3   Lahore Division
        4   2nd Divn
        5   7th Division
        6   Meerut Divnl Artillery
        7   Lahore Divnl Artillery
        8   Dehra Dun Bde
        9   Garhwal Bde
       10   Bareilly Bde
       11   Sirhind Bde
       12   Meerut Divnl Engineers
       13   4th Indian Cavalry
       14   107th Pioneers
       15   Meerut Signals
       16   No. 1 Group H.A.R.
       17   A.D.M.S. Meerut
       18   A.A. & Q.M.G.
       19   Garhwal Bde (duplicate copy) by separate orderly
       20   G.S.
     21 to 26   War Diary and spare.

SECRET G-439/43

FOSSE - NOON 15/2/15

G.O.C. Garhwal Brigade.

In accordance with a conversation which I have just had here with the Indian Corps Commander, you will understand that the attainment of the first objective as laid down in para 2 of Operation Order No. 31, has for its object the establishment of a fire front facing east, based on V.6 redoubt, and its consolidation before any advance for the attainment of the second objective is made, with the exception that bombing parties should work out along enemy trenches toward the east and block them. These bombing parties must work in the trenches and avoid masking the fire of your own men from the line you take up.

The advance against the 2nd objective will only be made after we are firmly established on the V.6 redoubt line, and will also be dependent on the simultaneous progress of the 2nd Division. The troops of the 2nd Division will not be advancing from the enemy's 2nd line trenches until daylight comes and the attack of the 7th Division on their right is in progress.

You will thus give the fullest attention to a thorough consolidation of the position before any advance to the east of V.6 redoubt is inaugurated.

C. Noon, Col

for L.G.C. Meerut Division.

S E C R E T.

5TH INFANTRY BRIGADE.

SPECIAL INSTRUCTIONS.

1. The 5th Brigade will attack the German trenches on their front from the bend in the German line (exclusive) between R.6 and V.1 to the N.W. corner of the salient between V.3 and V.2.

   1st Objective. The 1st and 2nd line of German parapets from R.7 (inclusive) to a point N.W. of V.3 and to get in touch with MEERUT Division at that point.
   A further advance will not be made till after daylight.

2. The detail of the attack will be as follows:-
   (a) **Frontage** - 870 yards - two battalions front.
       INNISKILLING FUSILIERS from communication trench W. of CINDER TRACK (exclusive) to ditch 180 yards East of CINDER TRACK. Frontage 350 yards.
       WORCESTERS from this point to ditch just E. of communication trench running through COPSE. Frontage 320 yards.
   (b) The attack is to be carried out by successive lines at intervals of about 100 yards. Especial care must be taken to ensure adequate support being given.
   (c) Working parties will be supplied by supporting battalions OXFORDS and GLASGOWS. The working parties for the 1st line will go as a third line. They will each consist of a platoon made up to 50 men with 1 N.C.O. and 4 men R.E.
   (d) When the first line has been taken, the second line will be assaulted, the INNISKILLINGS assaulting from the line - their right to V.1, the WORCESTERS from the line - V.3 Northwards to the N.W. corner of the salient.
       Between V.1 and V.3 no further advance will be made until the 2nd line trenches facing West and running South from R.7 and from about V.4 have been captured. The attack on these will be supported by machine gun fire from the captured German front line just W. of V.3 and by a bombing attack up the communication trench running South from near V.3. Four machine guns will accompany the WORCESTERS 2nd line for this purpose.
   (e) The successful capture of R.7 and V.4 will be shown by lighting torches at these points.
       The two flank attacks will then drive the enemy from the trench between them by bombing attacks up the trench. This bombing attack will then be supported by a frontal attack from the line V.1 - V.3.
       Bridges must be carried to bridge the stream between the two lines and these must be placed in position as soon as the torches denote the arrival at R.7 and about V.4. Special parties to carry the bridges must be detailed for this purpose.

Forming up.

3. The two battalions allotted to the attack will form their men up on the front line and in the two cover trenches 90 and 100 yards in rear of the front line.
   The OXFORDS and GLASGOWS will form up on B, C, and D lines.
   The H.L.I. will be formed up H.Q. and 2 Coys in dug-outs at house S.9.a.91 and remainder in dug-outs and breastworks about house S.9.a.89.
   The two first lines should be deployed in front of our parapets in the old trench before the time for the assault, their places in the breastworks being taken by succeeding lines. As one line goes forward the succeeding one should take its place.

Timing of Attack.

It is essential that the start of the attack be simultaneous. Watches will be accurately set.
The attack will be carried out in absolute silence and at a walk until the enemy's trench is approached when it will be rushed.
It must be strongly impressed on all ranks that no change in the fire of our artillery will be apparent either to the eye or the ear when the moment comes for assault. The attack to be simultaneous must start absolutely punctually at the hour named.
Although the Infantry cannot perceive it, the artillery range will also be lengthened at that hour.

(2)

Direction.
5. The maintenance of the correct direction of attack is very important. During the day the position of gaps in the wire must be accurately marked, so that leaders can guide straight to them.

Bombs and S.A.A.
6. Battalions will complete with bombs today.
Bomb reserve depots (each containing 500 bombs) are in front breastwork at exit of communication trench 180 yards East of CINDER TRACK and 260 yards East of CINDER TRACK.
Special parties must be told off from battalions doing the attack to carry up bombs, care being taken to show them beforehand where they are to take them to.
S.A.A. Stores. (each containing 100 boxes) exist at the same places.
A further reserve of bombs and S.A.A. is at house S.9.a.91 and about house S.9.a.88.
These reserve stores will be under guards furnished by H.L.I.

R.E.Stores.
7. Depots of R.E.Stores are near the bomb stores in the front line. Reserve Depot is in house on RUE DU BOIS next the FACTORY.

Medical.
8. Advanced Dressing Station will be established at X roads. S.3.C
Stretcher parties will only use the two new communication trenches. Sentries will be posted by H.L.I. on the exit of each of the communication trenches in the front breastworks.

Working Parties.
9. The OXFORDS and GLASGOWS will provide the following working parties:-
(a) One platoon OXFORDS to report to O.C.INN: FUS: at S.9.a.91 at 6 p.m. (For work on German 1st line).
(b) One platoon GLASGOWS (to be made up to 50 men) to report to O.C.WORCESTERS at S.3.c.58 at 6 p.m. (For work on German 1st line).
(c) One platoon OXFORDS to report to O.C.INN: FUS: at S.9.a.91 at 6 p.m. (For work on German 2nd line).
(d) One platoon GLASGOWS (made up to 50 men) to report to O.C. WORCESTERS at S.3.c.58 at 6 p.m. (For work on German 2nd Line).
(e),(f),(g) & (h) - 100 men each of H.L.I. to make 4 communication trenches up to German front line. To be detailed by O.C.,H.L.I., but to remain at S.9.a.91 till called for.
9. 1 N.C.O. and 9 men H.L.I. to report to Trench Mortar Officer at house S.9.a.91 at 4 p.m.

R.E.
10. O.C.5th Field Coy.R.E.,will detail one N.C.O. and 4 men for each of the above parties.
He will also tell off 1 N.C.O. and 3 men to accompany the front line of the INNISKILLINGS and WORCESTERS to look for mines or telephone communication in German trenches.
The above to report to O.C.WORCESTERS at S.3.c.58 at 6 p.m. and to O.C.INN: FUS: at house S.9.a.91 at 6 p.m.
11. Tacks must be dipped in solution during the day and be carried by all men.
12. **Communications.** Battalion Head Quarters have been wired up in dug-outs in the front line. Brigade Head Quarters will be on the RUE DU BOIS. Buried lines connect there.

G. Thorpe
Captain,
14th May, 1915.   Brigade Major 8th Infantry Brigade.

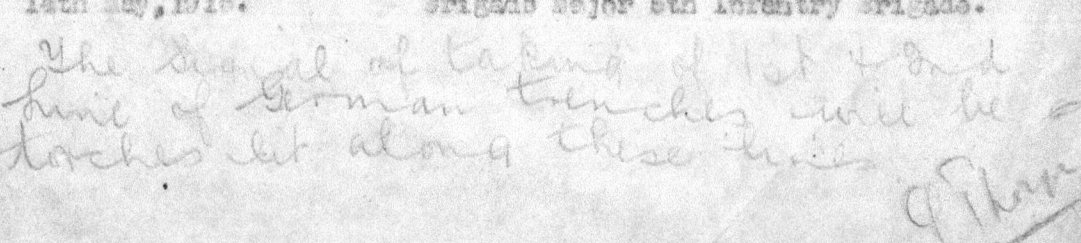

Operation Order No 42
by
Br gen W.G. Walker VC Comdg SIRHIND Bde.
Maps BETHUNE 1/40000 and Trench Map 1/10000.   14-5-15

1. The GARHWAL Bde will carry out the assault against the enemy's front line trenches included between the ditches running from SSE to NNW through points V5 and V6 - 1st objective is Capture of enemy's front line of & V.6 redoubt and of the trenches behind the 1st line lying West of the N corner of the redoubt as far as the ditch running through V5. Communication trenches will then be opened connecting Captured trenches with our own line - The Easterly one of such trenches will be turned into a fire trench facing East - Every endeavour will be made to accomplish this task and consolidate our position before day light, getting touch on our right with 2nd Div troops and bombing outwards along enemy trenches on our left flank to E and S.E. A fire front facing E will thus be formed with V6 redoubt as its centre - The 2nd objective is to attack outwards in an Easterly direction and secure the line V5 E - V6 E - 59 - The 3rd objective; when the above line has been secured, and as the attack of the 2nd Div progresses, our attack is to push on and secure the road from PORT ARTHUR to LA TOURELLE Cross roads inclusive and to consolidate itself thereon -

The assault will be on a 2 bn front at 11.30 p.m. 14th inst - A special force will hold the front line parapet East of Communication trench running forward from Centre of ORCHARD Redoubt; it will assist by fire action -

2. On arrival at LANSDOWNE POST the SIRHIND Bde will act as follows :-
1/HLI followed by 1/1 G.R will move via CRESCENT Com" trench to G1-2 and B3 & extensity assembly trenches respectively; as soon as B1 and B2 trenches are vacated by GARHWAL Bde, 1/HLI will move into B.1 and 1/1 G.R. into B.2. Reporting to GARHWAL Bde when they are in position - Units should be formed up in assembly positions by 10 p.m.
When required to advance from assembly trenches,

4 LI will use the two Western Commⁿ trenches reconnoitred by them and 1/1 G.R the two Eastern trenches also reconnoitred by them.

The remaining 3 bns will form up as follows
15th Sikhs in trenches North of road and East of LANSDOWNE Post. 4/Kings in trenches S of road and West of tram line. 1/4 G.R in LANSDOWNE POST.

3. 2 depots of S.A.A. are formed at R.E depot RUE DU BOIS and S VAAST - also two depots in forward trenches. 1/1 G.R will also arrange to carry forward 50 boxes S.A.A. These must be taken out of Ammⁿ Carts when they halt at S VAAST post.
Depots of bombs and hand grenades are near R.E. depot RUE DU BOIS.

4. Each unit will carry with it its battalion entrenching tools which will be taken out of the Carts at S VAAST Post. A supply of hand grenades ready fuzed will also be carried.

5. Collecting Station is between LANSDOWNE POST and the tramway line where it crosses FORRESTERS LANE. ORCHARD Commⁿ trench is reserved for wounded only after fighting has begun. 4/Kings will place a Sentry at Northern entrance to stop any one entering it except in this connection.
Should troops have to advance in rear entirely they will do so along the line of this trench keeping out of it.

6. O.C 1/HLI will place a Sentry at Northern entry to CRESCENT Commⁿ trench to regulate passage of troops.

7. From S VAAST Post onwards units not in possession of pack mules will man handle their guns. Mules can not be taken beyond assembly positions and should be collected at LANSDOWNE POST.

8. Masks will be kept ready for use soaked in Solution. Troops assaulting will wear them.

9. 2nd Div troops wear a white bib showing front and rear.
By day positions of advanced or flank bombing parties

of MEERUT DIV will be shown by a 3' Sq flag, the top and left portion being black and the bottom and right portion red, with a white Cross.

Those of 2nd Div will be marked by a yellow screen 6' by 28" for battalions, yellow flags 28" by 28" for Coys.

1st Div Red flags 3' by 3' with white perpendicular stripe

London Div Sand bag cloth disc with black Cross in centre

LAHORE DIV Yellow flag 16" Sq.

10. An emergency supply depot has been established at house at cross roads in M 32 d near tramway line.

11. Reports to LANSDOWNE POST (in farm)
 Each unit when in position in assembly position will report to Bde H.Q. Units will also report the position of their H.Q.
 Reports for GARHWAL Bde to 96 PICCADILLY RUE DU BOIS.

12. Above Operations have been postponed 24 hours. All dates are altered accordingly.

S. Ramsey
Brigade Major Captain
  Sirhind Bde

Copy 1 Bde H.Q.
 2 4th Kings
 3 1/5 R
 4 15th Sikhs
 5 1/4 GR
 6 Meerut Div } for information
 7 Garhwal Bde }
 8, 9, 10. War Diary
 2 Spare

No 239 BM   H.Q. Sirhind Bde
                                15/5/15

Memorandum
            Instructions received from MEERUT Divn
this morning entail certain modifications in Operation Order
No 42 of 14th instant

1 page 2 para 2 Only 3 communication trenches leading
from the Assembly trenches to the front line are now
available for use of the Bde.
            These are ① Trench through Centre of Orchard
                       ② Trench up Western edge of Orchard
                       ③ HAZARA trench about 100 yds
                             west of ②
In case of both battns being required to advance simultaneously
from the Assembly trenches, H.L.I would use ③ and
1/1 G.R would use ① and ②. The 1/1 G.R advancing
from the left of B1 and B2 trenches, the 1st H.L.I.
advancing from the right. This also applies to Battns
occupying B1 and B2 after the H.L.I. and 1/1 G.R
have advanced.

2 page 2 para 2 The 4th Kings will form up in the
Orchard Communication trench with the Head of the
Battalion at the junction of this trench with the
rear of B2 Assembly trenches - as soon as B1 and B2
trenches are cleared of 1st H.L.I and 1/1 G.R they will
move into B1 trenches

3 page 2 para 5 The trench running along the main
drain from LANSDOWNE POST will be reserved
for wounded and not in ORCHARD Communication
trench - both these trenches will have sentries
placed at the Northern entries by 4th Kings
ORCHARD trench is therefore available for use by
our troops.

4. Parking ground for wagons will be just S.W.
of CROIX BARBÉ no ground being available
at SPRAEST Post. All Carts will be under O.C.
Bde Resve Ammn

                                    F. Ridgeway
                                    Captain
                              B.M. Sirhind Bde

SECRET.   Operation Order No 43   Copy No 67
         by
     Br General W G Walker, V.C. C.B. Comdg Sirhind Bde
                                    d/- 15.5.15

Reference Map BETHUNE 1/40,000.

1   In supercession of Order No 41.
    The Bde will march this evening to LANSDOWNE POST
    via FOSSE - LES 5 MAISONS - CROIX BARBÉ - St VAAST POST
    to support the GARHWAL Bde in a night attack (vide
    Operation Order No 42, d/- 14.5.15.)

2   The head of the Column will pass the junction of the
    FOSSE Road Sq R 20 a 7.0 at 5.30 p.m.
        Order of March :-   1st H.L.I.
                            1/1 G.R.
                            15th Sikhs
                            4th Kings
                            1/4 G.R.
                Bde Reserve Ammn   } will park
        Ammn Wagons of units (in order of units) } near St VAAST
                                                   POST
    Only tool wagons and medical carts will accompany units.
    Tools will be unloaded on arrival at St VAAST POST and
    the tool carts will remain there with the Ammn Carts.
    Tools will be carried up by hand.   Medical carts may
    proceed as far forward as "Windy Corner" thence they
    will return and join the carts at St VAAST - with this
    exception no transport except pack mules will proceed
    in front of St VAAST.
    All other 1st Line Transport will remain at Depôts

3   The Staff Captain will issue instructions re formation and
    location of Depôt of units.

4   O.C. units will arrange the detail of kit to be
    carried but each man must have :-
        ① 1 complete days ration & iron ration
        ② 200 rounds S.A.A.
        ③ 2 Sand bags
        ④ Respirator or mask

5   Reports to head of Column on March.

                                Ringway
                                    Captain
                            B.M. Sirhind Brigade

Copy 1 to H.L.I, 2. 4th Kings, 3 to 1/1 G.R. 4 to 15 Ss
5 to 1/4 GR 6 Meerut Divn, 7 Garhwal Bde, 8,9,10 War Diary
2 Spare.

Copy No 6

BRIGADE OPERATION ORDER No 34
BY
BRIGADIER GENERAL W H SOUTHEY C.M.G.
COMMANDING BAREILLY BDE.

Reference trench map and
barrage of trenches 16th May 1915

INTENTION 1. The Brigade will relieve the GARHWAL
Brigade tonight in the front line V3 C and
inclusive of ESTAIRES – LA BASSÉE Road.
Troops of the 2nd Division will be holding the ground
on our Right flank and those of the JULLUNDUR
Bde. that on our Left flank.

DEFENCE   2. The front will be divided into three
ARRANGEMENTS. Subsections A, B, and C commencing from
the Right.
Limits of Subsections are marked by the
following South South western and edges
and their lines from Points C5(?) to
D9 D15.

"A" Subsection – Along the ditch running
down from Point V.5, and a line of
unmetalled along the western edge of the
ORCHARD Redoubt.

"B" Subsection – along the ORCHARD Redoubt
Right communication Trench and
immediately West of the Sub-point of the
CRESCENT Communication Trench.

"C" Subsection – along the line of the Southern
part of the CRESCENT communication trench and
drain and the Easterly edge of
ESTAIRES – LA BASSÉE road.
The garrison of Subsections will be as
follows –

"A" Form.
MESSAGES AND SIGNALS.
Army Form C. 2121.
No. of Message

Prefix	Code	m.	Words	Charge	This message is on a/c of:	Recd. at	m.
Office of Origin and Service Instructions.						Date	
			Sent		..........................Service.	From	
			At	m.			
			To		(Signature of "Franking Officer.")	By	
			By				

TO {

| Sender's Number. | Day of Month. | In reply to Number | A A A |

From
Place
Time

The above may be forwarded as now corrected.   (Z)

Censor.   Signature of Addressor or person authorised to telegraph in his name

* This line should be erased if not required.

	COMMANDER	GARRISON
"A" Subsection	Lt. Col. Davidson Macfie DSO 59th RIFLES	59th RIFLES
"B" Subsection	Lt. Col. G.T. Hervey 2nd BLACK WATCH	2nd BLACK WATCH
"C" Subsection	Lt. Col. Dening 125th RIFLES	125th RIFLES (less 2 Coys) 41st DOGRAS

2. Brigade Trench Gun and Machine Gun Officers will arrange the distribution of the Trench guns and Machine Guns of the Bde in the three Subsections.

2nd BLACK WATCH and 2 Coys 125th RIFLES will be in Brigade Reserve in breastworks EAST and WEST of LANSDOWNE POST

RELIEFS 3. The reliefs will be carried out at the following hours:-

"A" Subsection Head of Column to reach RUE DU BOIS at 8.30 p.m.

"B" Subsection Head of Column to reach RUE DU BOIS at 8.30 p.m.

"C" Subsection Head of Column to reach RUE DU BOIS at 8.30 p.m.

Guides will be provided to front line & support line for A Subsection over the open line between Rum Lane and ORCHARD communication trench, and for B Subsection by the ORCHARD communication trench, and Rose for C Subsection by PIONEER communication trench.

4. The reliefs will be carried out after the line of the SAMBRE GARHWAL BDE has been relieved and a service report by BAREILLY BDE

till operation is complete.

REPORTS 5 Brigade Headquarters will be at Farm opposite LANSDOWNE POST.

Mashbourne Captain,
Brigade Major

Issued to Signal Section at 5.25 P.M.

Copy No 1. 2nd Black Watch
       2. 4th Seaforth
       3. 125 Rifles
       4. 58th Rifles
       5. 41st Dogras
       6. GARHWAL BDE
       7. MEERUT DIVN
       8. War Diary
       9.
      10. file

"A" Form.
MESSAGES AND SIGNALS.
Army Form C. 2121.

No. of Message _____

Prefix _____ Code _____ m.
Office of Origin and Service Instructions.
_____

Words | Charge

Sent
At _____ m.
To _____
By _____

This message is on a/c of:
_____ Service.
(Signature of "Franking Officer.")

Recd. at _____ m.
Date _____
From _____
By _____

TO {

Sender's Number.	Day of Month.	In reply to Number	A A A

From
Place
Time

The above may be forwarded as now corrected.   (Z)

Censor.   Signature of Addressor or person authorised to telegraph in his name.

* This line should be erased if not required.

Garhwal Brigade

War Diary

Appendices – Operation Orders
issued 7th, 13th and 15th May

OPERATION ORDER No. 40   COPY No. 12
by
Brigadier General C.G.Blackader, D.S.O.
Commanding GARHWAL BRIGADE.

Reference Maps.   7th May, 1915.
Trench map, 1/10/ 1/10,000.
Map of France & Belgium, Sheet 36 (3rd edition) 1/40,000
Map of France, Bethune sheet, 1/40,000

Information. 1. The 1st Army is attacking on the 8th May with the object of breaking through the enemy's line and gaining the LA BASSEE-LILE road between LABASSEE and FOURNES and then advancing on DON to the line BAUVIN-DON

The 1st Corps, retaining its right at GIVENCHY advances on the RUE DU MARAIS, LORGIES and ILLIES.

The Indian Corps will operate to cover the right of the 1st Corps, capture the FERME DU BIEZ, and subsequently advance to the line LIGNY LE GRAND,- LA CLIQUETERIE FERME.

The 4th Corps operate through AUBERS with a view to effecting a junction with the Indian Corps at LA CLIQUETERIE FERME.

LAHORE Division holds the line front except that portion from which the attack is to be delivered.

MEERUT Division is to deliver the attack.

ARTILLERY of the MEERUT Division, reinforced by that of LAHORE Division one section HOTCHKISS motor battery, one section mountain artillery and some heavy batteries will prepare and support the attack.

The DEHRA DUN Brigade is to assault the enemy's front line trenches from the point V6 to the vicinity of the point 56 and push on against further objectives, leaving garrisons at SOHERN end of LA TOURELLE, DISTILLERY, road junction S1.X.a, (points 52 & 53.), houses near point 50 and the FERME DU BIEZ.

BAREILLY Brigade (less one battalion) in trenches north of RUE DU BOIS, and in and east of LANSDOWNE Post is to occupy the assembly positions of DEHRA DUN Brigade as they are vacated and to support that brigade.

One battalion BAREILLY Brigade (less two companies with S & M) will remain in LANSDOWNE Post and follow the Garhwal Brigade into the assembly trenches just north of the RUE DU BOIS.

Intention. 2. Garhwal Brigade (less two battalions) will be Divisional reserve

Detachment. 3 Lt.-Col. De-Brockman   will pass road junction M.
                  commanding   27. d. at 10 p.m., and march
               Capt.Ethel, staff offr.   via PONT LOGY and the area
               GARHWAL Rifles.   between the main drain on the
               3/8th GURKHA Rifles.   west and the ESTAIRES- LA
               Machine guns of above.   BASSEE road on the east to
               Two trench guns.   the two eastern blocks of a
                                          assembly trenches north of
                                          the RUE DU BOIS, to be in
               position by 1 a.m., reporting arrival to G.O's.C DEHRA DUN
               and GARHWAL Bdes.

Infantry   4. The Garhwal Brigade (less two Battalions, machine
movements.   gun sections trench gun battery) will occupy trenches
             pointed out t's. C., moving as under:-

	Unit.	Position of assembly.	To march off at.
	---------------	--	------------------
	2/3 Gurkhas.	North and clear of cross roads in CROIX BARBEE.	2.30 a.m.
	2/Leicesters.	CROIX-BARBEE - RICHEBOURG ST VAAST track.	2.15 a.m.
	3/ Londons.	East and clear of cross roads in CROIX BARBEE.	2!15. a.m.

  Main roads are not to be blocked; troops will form up off the roads for filing into their trenches.
  All units will report by 3 a.m. that they are in their allotted positions.

Machine & trench guns.   5. The Brigade machine gun detachments (less 6 guns) and the brigade trench gun battery (less 2 guns) will march at 2 a.m., via RUE des PUITS and ESTAIRES-LA BASSEE road to trenches at S.4.a.8.7., and will report when in position.

S.A.Ammn.   6. Two hundred rounds per man will be carried.
  S.A.A. depots have been established at R.E. depot, RUE du BOIS, and dug outs in rear of front trench, as shown on sketch of RUE DU BOIS in vicinity of PORT ARTHUR, which have been sent to O'S. battalions.
  The 3/ Londons, when ordered to advance, will carry up one box of S.A.Ammn. per two men from breastwork east of LANSDOWNE Post to the front line trenches and on from thence.

R.E.Depots.   7. Advanced R.E. depots will be at RUE DU BOIS and FARM at M.32.d.7.7.

Hand grenades and Bombs.   8. Each battalion has been provided with approximately 150 hand grenades in carrying boxes. An advanced base for bombs (trench gun) and hand grenades has been established 100 yards in rear of the right of the assembly position of the BAREILLY brigade.

Rations.   9. One day's cooked or tinned rations in addition to the unexpended portion of the day's ration and the emergency ration will be carried by each man.

Medical.   10. A collecting station will be established between LANSDOWNE Post and where the tramway line crosses the RUE des BERCEAUX. The route for wounded returning from the front will be by the "orchard" communication trench, which runs from the RUE du BOIS to the RUE des BERCEAUX along the north east side of the tramway line and some 100 yards from it. This trench will be reserved for the return of the wounded only after fighting has commenced.

Sandbags.   11. Every man will carry two sandbags.

Masks.   12. All masks will be kept in readiness and soaked in soda solution.

Flags.   13. All ranks should know the distinguishing flags for marking the positions of advanced troops of the various divisions.

Prisoners.   14. Prisoners will be handed over to the LAHORE Division at DEHRA DUN report centre in the RUE du BOIS.

Time.
Time. 15. An officer from brigade head quarters will give the official time to all units about 8 p.m.

First line 16. First line transport will march via WELLINGTON Road in accordance with orders issued separately, and will be parked at R.35.b.2,2. It will be ready to move at half an hour's notice from from 10 a.m. tomorrow onwards.

Report
Centre. 17. Brigade head quarters will be at LANSDOWNE Post from 9 p.m. tonight.

J.H.R. Stewart Major,

Brigade Major, GARHWAL Brigade.

Issued through signal section at   p.m.

Copy No, 1 . . . . .2/ Leicesters.
        2 . . . . .2/ Londons.
        3. ,,,,,,,,,2/3 G.R.
        4. . . . . . . .Garhwal Rifles.
        5. . . . . . . .2/8th G.R.
        6. ,,,,,,,,,Bde. M.G.O.
        7. . . . . . . .Bde. TRENCH GUN Offr.
        8. . . . . . . .MEERUT Division.
        9. . . . . . . .DEHRA DUN Bde.
        10. . . . . . . BAREILLY Bde.
        11. . . . . . . Col Drake-Brockman.
        12. . . . . . . War Diary.
        13 to 15 . . . Staff.   (14+15) destroyed

"A" Form.
Army Form C. 2121.

MESSAGES AND SIGNALS.

No. of Message

Prefix	Code		Words	Charge		This message is on a/c of:	Recd. at	m.
		Office of Origin and Service Instructions.						

		Sent			Service.	Date.
		At		m.		
		To				
		By			(Signature of "Franking Officer.")	By
						From

TO	Ludendorff London	9/8 1 pm 90	84 Threadm
		93	

Sender's Number.	Day of Month	In reply to Number	AAA
9am 9.5	7		

Rges OO N° 40 para 1 line 4 der
advancing on DON read "advancing to the
line BAVVIN – DON

Para on Guard Recce has been
and orders thing orders above.

From Ludendorff Pq

Place

Time 2.30 pm

(Z)
The above may be forwarded as now corrected.

Censor.   Signature of Addressor or person authorised to telegraph in his name.
                  Ludendorff

*This line should be erased if not required.
(832) — McC. & Co., Ltd., London. — W 11400/2045. 100,000. 2/15. Forms O 2121/10.

"A" Form.
MESSAGES AND SIGNALS.
Army Form C. 2121.

SECRET

TO Colonel Drake Brockman

Sender's Number.	Day of Month	In reply to Number	AAA
Rm 307	7		

Operations are postponed.

From Cadwacell
Place
Time

"A" Form.
MESSAGES AND SIGNALS.
Army Form C. 2121.

| TO | Leicesters 3 Londons | 2/3 | |

Sender's Number: RM 302
Day of Month: 7
AAA

Operations are postponed
First line transport will remain
where it now is

From Place: Rathernal Hill
Time: 6.25 p

Signature: J.M.C. Stewart

"A" Form.　　　　　　　　　　　　　Army Form C. 2121.
MESSAGES AND SIGNALS.

SECRET

TO: 3 London
    2/3
         2/4   Bde HQ 6

Sender's Number: M 311

AAA

The operations ordered in Fauquissart
Bde Operation Order No 4 and postponed
will be carried out as detailed in the
above order tomorrow the 9th May.
The preliminary moves will therefore
be made tonight 8/9.

From: Fauquissart Bde
Time: 3.35 pm

Operation Order No 41   Copy No 6
by
Brigadier General C. G. Blackader D.S.O.
Commanding Garhwal Brigade

13th May 1915.

1. The following reliefs will take place tonight. At 8.30 p.m. the 2nd Leicesters will relieve the 2/9th Gurkhas in front line and support and reserve trenches, moving by the front of the Assembly trenches N of the RUE DU BOIS.

2. At the same time the companies of the 2/8th Gurkhas at present in support and reserve will be moved past the rear of the Assembly trenches and will relieve the 2/3 Gurkhas in the left subsection taking over at the same time from the 13th London Regt the front trench in front of the Orchard up to but excluding the centre communication trench.

3. After the 2nd Leicesters have filed past the block of B1 Assembly trenches the Garhwal Rifles will relieve the 1/3rd Londons in the front trench from the Centre Orchard Communication trench (inclusive) to the West, and in the Orchard.

4. The 1/3rd London Regt on relief will move into that part of the B1 and B2 Blocks of assembly trenches north of the RUE DU BOIS, which lie East of the track passing Brigade Headquarters

5. The 2/3rd Gurkhas on relief will move into the Assembly trenches now occupied and about to be vacated by the 2nd Leicesters

6. Officers Commanding will arrange details mutually.

J.J. Stewart
Major
Brigade Major, Garhwal Bde

Issued through Signal Section 4.30 p.m.

Copy No 1   1/3 Londons
" 2   2nd Leicesters
" 3   2/3rd Gurkhas
" 4   Garhwal Rifles
" 5   2/8th Gurkhas
" 6   War Diary ✓
" 7   Staff

OPERATION ORDER No 42   Copy No 11
by
Brigadier General C. G. Blackader D.S.O.
Commanding GARHWAL Bde

Reference Maps   15 MAY 1915
   FRANCE - BETHUNE SHEET $\frac{1}{40,000}$
   Trench Map $\frac{1}{10,000}$

INFORMATION   1. The 1st Corps and Indian Corps are to attack and to establish a line FESTUBERT - LA QUINQUE RUE - LA TOURELLE Cross roads - PORT ARTHUR, and are then to push on towards VIOLAINES and BEAU PUITS.

      The 2nd Division is to assault on the right of and simultaneously with the Meerut Division, and the 7th Division on the right of the 2nd.

      The SIRHIND Bde is to support the Garhwal Bde; BAREILLY Bde in Divisional reserve; DEHRA DUN Bde in Corps reserve.

ARTILLERY   (b) A deliberate artillery bombardment is to precede the assault and is to cease on the front to be assaulted at 11.25 pm today.

      The bombardment will continue on points 59 and 60 and on points East

Copy No 11

of a line 59 – V6E – V5E.

INTENTION. 2. The GARHWAL Bde with maxim guns of BAREILLY, trench guns of BAREILLY and DEHRA DUN and No 4 trench mortar battery will hold the present front of the brigade and will attack the enemy's line between the ditches which run from S-S-E to N-N-W through the points V.5 and V.6.

ASSAULTING BATTALIONS. 3. The 2/Leicestershire Regt with 6 machine guns will assault with right on the ditch which runs through V5, having as objective the enemy's trenches marked in the tracing given to the O.C., and will get into touch with the 2nd Division on the right, clearing and double blocking beyond bombing distance any trenches leading to the front.

The GARHWAL RIFLES with 6 machine guns will assault with left on the ditch which runs through V6, having as objective the redoubt S.E of V6, marked on the tracing given to the O.C., and will form a defensive flank to the left, clearing and double blocking beyond bombing distance all trenches leading to front or flank.

TIME OF ASSAULT 4. The assault will be delivered from the

Copy No 11

enemy's side of the ditch at 11.30 p.m on the night of the 15th–16th May.

SUPPORTING BATTALIONS. 5. The 3rd LONDONS in the eastern half of assembly trenches B1 and B2 will support the Garhwal Rifles.

Two companies 2/3rd GURKHA RIFLES under Major Tillard in the western half of assembly trenches B1 and B2 will support the Leicesters.

These supports will keep filling up the trenches to the front as they are vacated.

The rear company of each body of supports will carry up ammunition from the depot in the RUE DUBOIS and form advanced depots in the captured position.

Officers commanding supporting units will be with the officers commanding assaulting battalions.

CONSOLIDATION OF POSITION. 6. The objectives given for the attack will be consolidated before daylight.

BRIGADE RESERVE 7. The 2/3rd GURKHA RIFLES (less 2 companies) in B1 and B2 assembly trenches in rear of the supporting

Copy No 11

Companies of the 2/3" G.R

| DEFENCE OF THE LINE | 8. Lt Col MORRIS, 2/3 Commanding
8th GURKHA RIFLES
Machine guns of GARHWAL and BAREILLY Bdes (less 12 guns.)
No 4 trench mortar Batry.
Bomb guns of BAREILLY GARHWAL and DEHRA DUN Brigades | will hold the line from the LABASSEE - ESTAIRES road (exclusive) to but excluding the centre communication trench from |

the ORCHARD to the front line.
The machine guns and bomb guns will be disposed in accordance with instructions given to machine and bomb gun officers, so as to cover the left flank of the attack.

BOMBING PARTIES Etc.
9. Assaulting battalions will organise bombing, blocking, sandbag and tool parties. These will be provided with flags to mark the positions reached by them.

SANDBAGS and RATIONS.
10. Every man will carry two sandbags and one days ration in addition to emergency ration.

Copy No 11

DEPOTS for Ammn Etc. 11. Two depots in the front line, containing in each case
    100 boxes S.A. Ammunition
    200 bombs
    2000 sandbags
    2 boxes Very pistol ammunition

The bombs are not in carrying boxes; it is therefore imperative that units send back their boxes when sending for more bombs.

There is also an ammunition depot at the R.E Store in the RUE DU BOIS.

MASKS. 12. Masks will be kept in readiness soaked in solution prepared under direction of medical officers, and will be worn by assaulting troops

COMMUNICATION TRENCHES 13. The 2/Leicesters will have the use of the new HAZARA Communication trench and the right orchard communication trench—

The Garhwal Rifles will use the centre and left orchard communication trenches.

The wounded will return by the communication trench which leaves the front line 50 yards to the east of the ditch which passes the east side of the orchard, to the RUE DU BOIS and

COPY No 11

thence, by the Orchard Communication trench parallel to and 100 yards east of the tramline, to the RUE DES BERCEAUX.—

MEDICAL. 14. A collecting station will be established between LANSDOWNE POST and the point where the tram line crosses the RUE DES BERCEAUX.

DISTINGUISH-ING MARKS
15. The 2nd Division troops are wearing at night a white bib showing both to front and rear.

The position of advanced or flank bombing parties of the 2nd Division will be marked by yellow screens, 6' by 28" in the case of battalions, and yellow flags 28" by 28" for companies.

The 1st Division, red flags 3' x 3' with white perpendicular stripe.

LONDON Division, Sandbag cloth disc, 2' in diameter with black cross in centre

LAHORE Division Yellow flag 16" square

COMMUNICATION. trenches to be opened.
16. As soon as it is practicable communication trenches will be opened up to the captured position.

Ref 13   17   To report centre on North side
of RUE DU BOIS close to and east
of the ~~Sappers~~ R.E. DEPOT

Copy No 11

WATCH   18   GARHWAL
WORD

J.H. Stewart Major
Bde. Maj. Garhwal Bde.

Issued at 2 pm through Signal section

Copy No 1   2 Leicesters ✓
         2   3 Londons ✓
         3   2/3 G.R. ✓
         4   Garhwal Rifles ✓
         5   2/8 G.R. ✓
         6   Bde MGO ✓
         7   " Bomb GO ✓
         8   Meerut Dn ✓
         9   SIRHIND Bde
        10   6th Infy Bde
        11   War diary   } ✓ at 4.45/-
        12   Retained
        13   "   "
        14   "   " } destroyed

"A" Form. Army Form C. 2121.
MESSAGES AND SIGNALS.

TO	Leicesters	Rifles
	3 Londons	78
	2/3	

Sender's Number.	Day of Month	In reply to Number	AAA
BM 156	15		

Reference Operation Order No 42 para 13. Cancel route for wounded north of ROE AO BOIS and substitute LANSDOWNE communication trench roughly parallel to and 50 yards west of the main drain, and leading into the centre of LANSDOWNE post.

From: Garhwal Bde.
Place:
Time: 5.15 pm

1.6.1915
31.8.1915

Serial No. 184.

121/6/28

WAR DIARY
OF
2nd Lincoln
From 1st June 1915 To 30th June 1915.

7W
6 sheets

Army Form C. 2118.

WAR DIARY
INTELLIGENCE SUMMARY.
(Erase heading not required.)

Instructions regarding War Diaries and Intelligence Summaries are contained in F. S. Regs., Part II, and the Staff Manual respectively. Title pages will be prepared in manuscript.

Hour, Date, Place.	Summary of Events and Information.	Remarks and references to Appendices.
1.6.15	In billets at PARADIS. Bn moved at 4.30 p.m. to new billets S of PARADIS arriving there about 8.20 p.m.	H.
2 & 3.6.15	In billets S of PARADIS. War training.	H.
6.6.15	In billets S of PARADIS. War training. C.O. and Coy bombers proceeded early this morning to the trenches which we are to take over from the 1/Seaforths on night 7/8 June.	H.
7.6.15	Bn left billets S of PARADIS at 4.30 p.m. and marched to the trenches via X.3.a., X.3.c., X.4.a., X.4.d., X.4.b., S.2.C., S.8.a. ALBERT ROAD (BETHUNE Sheet 1/40,000). First Coy arriving at S.8.a. at 8.45 p.m. other Coys at 5 minute intervals. A&B Coys proceeded to reline Coys of 1/Seaforths in fire trenches and supports, extending as shown on the sketch. C&D Coys to bivouac in breastwork running EAST and WEST on other side of ALBERT Road.	H.
8.6.15	A&B Coys in fire trenches and supports, C&D in reserve. Enemy fired a few rounds of shrapnel at infrequent intervals during the day. Heavy rain commenced, trenches deep in mud and water which necessitated much baling out.	H.
9.6.15	Head Quarters and Communication trenches shelled by enemy Arty. Coys found out useful information by patrolling at night.	H.
10.6.15	Enemy shelled our approaches and approach roads and also sent a few ineffective shells over our front	H.

Army Form C. 2118.

WAR DIARY

INTELLIGENCE SUMMARY.

(Erase heading not required.)

Instructions regarding War Diaries and Intelligence
Summaries are contained in F. S. Regs., Part II,
and the Staff Manual respectively. Title pages
will be prepared in manuscript.

Hour, Date, Place.	Summary of Events and Information.	Remarks and references to Appendices.
11.6.15	Trenches doing little damage. More useful patrolling was done tonight.	
12.6.15	Enemy shelled our front trenches intermittently all day. Lieut F.C. Woodham 2nd Bn. joined. Farm Corner new trench was cut off before width at once built up trenches and sent Lieut. Wickinson with a telephone to the advanced post. Our front line had about 120 big shells into them today with only 1 casualty. By night all damage was repaired. Relieved By 1st Bde. withdrawn.	H. H.
13.6.15	Divisional General inspected our lines. Our own guns shot 3 Germans today. Enemy shelled our communication trenches and head Quarters with shrapnel. Our patrols from G.D. did useful work in locating enemy's wire and working parties. New trench dug parallel to Farm Corner.	H.
14.6.15	Farm Corner trench breached by enemy's heavy guns in 2 places. While working all wire in front tonight	H.

65

Army Form C. 2118.

WAR DIARY
INTELLIGENCE SUMMARY.
(Erase heading not required.)

Instructions regarding War Diaries and Intelligence Summaries are contained in F. S. Regs., Part II, and the Staff Manual respectively. Title pages will be prepared in manuscript.

Hour, Date, Place.	Summary of Events and Information.	Remarks and references to Appendices.
15.6.15	Numerous enemy flares disclosed our position and heavy rifle and machine gun fire was opened. Sepoy Sandu was severely wounded. Captain Romilly D.S.O assisted by Pte Page of D. Coy went out under heavy fire and carried Lieut Sanders in. A Coy (Reserve) was moved up closer to trench on South side of RUE DU BOIS.	N.
16.6.15	Operations on large scale by troops on our right and a minor operation by Lahore Division on our left began at 6 pm. Enemy replied to our bombardment and our trenches were heavily shelled. Our machine guns under Captain Le Fanu were co-operating in the attack of H.L.I. on our left. Similar operations took place today and our trenches were shelled for some hours and our parapet was blown in in 6 places. Capt Romilly had been sent up and was brought down to 10th Ind Bde Hd Qrs. About this time a new kind of fuse was developed exposed to the trench fires caused by he[?]	N.

Army Form C. 2118.

WAR DIARY
or
INTELLIGENCE SUMMARY.
(Erase heading not required.)

Instructions regarding War Diaries and Intelligence Summaries are contained in F. S. Regs., Part II, and the Staff Manual respectively. Title pages will be prepared in manuscript.

Hour, Date, Place.	Summary of Events and Information.	Remarks and references to Appendices.
	other parades. Capt Weir in 1st Aid Post also with fever and 30 to 40 men have gone sick with the same illness during the last fortnight. Afternoon Platoons were inspected by a Major outside seeing the celebrations of 30th anniv. of Capt. C Calfeel joining and modified a delight of 65 men. Enemy quiet all day but protective in evening two aeroplanes dropped from aeroplane said enemy was mastering at dusk behind this positions opposite RUE DU BOIS. Night passed quietly	
14.6.15		A.
18.6.15	Germans shelled our heavy trench also with heavy artillery been thing parapet in several places. Captain 10 Bm only moved his 3 maxims in time to prevent destruction of Light Wig help ammunition and emplacements were blown into the air. 3/ London relieved No at 9 pm and we went to Brigade reserve in trenches between RICHEBOURG and LA COUTURE.	A.
19 to 22nd.6.15	Battalion in Brigade Reserve in trenches at TOUR ST VAAST. War Training carried on. Working parties found each night. Enemy's Artillery dropped shells of all calibers near position daily.	A.
23.6.15	In Brigade Reserve. Draft of 30 other ranks arrived attached to Bareilly Brigade for a few days.	A.

Army Form C. 2118.

WAR DIARY
of
INTELLIGENCE SUMMARY.
(Erase heading not required.)

Instructions regarding War Diaries and Intelligence Summaries are contained in F. S. Regs., Part II, and the Staff Manual respectively. Title pages will be prepared in manuscript.

Hour, Date, Place.	Summary of Events and Information.	Remarks and references to Appendices.
24. 6. 15	Bn fell in at 6 a.m. to move into new positions at WINDY CORNER and LORETTA Road. 1½ Coys at WINDY CORNER, 2½ Coys and Head Quarters at LORETTA Road. New positions were taken up by 8 a.m. During day enemy dropped about a dozen large shells on left of position.	F.
25. 6. 15	In Bde Reserve at WINDY CORNER and LORETTA Road. Working party found at night. Enemy quiet, no shelling	F.
26. 6. 15	In Bde Reserve. Enemy sent heavies and shrapnel near position during afternoon.	F.
27. 6. 15	As for 26. Lieut. R.C. Woodburn was wounded at about 10 p.m. whilst out with working party	F.
28. 6. 15	Bn relieved by 2nd Black Watch 2½ Coys at LORETTA Road at 6 p.m. and 1½ Coys at WINDY CORNER at 8 p.m. Bn moved into Divisional Reserve in billets EAST of VIEILLE CHAPELLE when relieved.	F.
29. 6. 15	In Divisional Reserve E of VIEILLE CHAPELLE. Large working party found at night. Only one man 13 casualties (wounded) by enemy shell fire	F.
30. 6. 15	In Divisional Reserve E of VIEILLE CHAPELLE. War training.	F.

Serial No. 187.

12/1650 2

8 W sheets

WAR DIARY
OF
2nd Leicesters.

FROM — 1st July — 1915. TO — 31st July — 1915

Army Form 2118.

WAR DIARY

OR

INTELLIGENCE SUMMARY.

(Erase heading not required.)

Instructions regarding War Diaries and Intelligence Summaries are contained in F. S. Regs., Part II, and the Staff Manual respectively. Title pages will be prepared in manuscript.

Hour, Date, Place.	Summary of Events and Information.	Remarks and references to Appendices.
1. 1. 15	In Billets E of VIELLE CHAPELLE, War Training	F+R
2. 1. 15	In Billets E of VIELLE CHAPELLE. Reinforcement of 1 C.S.M. 1 Sgt. 2 to/Cpls and 36 men joined the Bn. 4 Casualties in working party of night 1st – 2nd. – 3 Shrapnel wounds – 1 Bullet.	F+R
3. 1. 15	In Billets E of VIELLE CHAPELLE. War Training – Large Working party found at night for Support Trenches. 2/Lieut M.W. BROWN joined the Battn.	F+R
4. 1. 15	In Billets E of VIELLE CHAPELLE – "D" Coy sent to D.S. ALBERT ROAD as Section Reserve to Brigade. The Germans shelled neighbourhood of Bn Billets with heavies from 4 pm to 5.30 pm. Lieut PHILLIPS joined the Bn.	F+R
5. 1. 15	In Billets E of VIELLE CHAPELLE. Large Working party found at night for Support Trenches.	F+R
6. 1. 15	In Billets E of VIELLE CHAPELLE. "E" Coy relieved D Coy in Section Reserve. Captain Le FANU, Machine Gun Officer went to hospital Sick. Captain ROLPH sent in Report.	F+R

Army Form C 2118.

WAR DIARY
of
INTELLIGENCE SUMMARY.

(Erase heading not required.)

Instructions regarding War Diaries and Intelligence Summaries are contained in F. S. Regs., Part II, and the Staff Manual respectively. Title pages will be prepared in manuscript.

Hour, Date, Place.		Summary of Events and Information	Remarks and references to Appendices.
7	15	In Billets E. of VIELLE CHAPELLE. Found a party of 100 men for work at night on Support Trenches. Casualties 1 man of C Coy in Section Reserve, ALBERT ROAD, - bullet wound	FMR
8	15	In Billets E. of VIELLE CHAPELLE. The Secretary of State for War inspected The Brigade at ZELOBES	FMR
9	15	In Billets E. of VIELLE CHAPELLE - War Training	FMR
10	15	In Billets E. of VIELLE CHAPELLE - War Training	FMR
11	15	In Billets E. of VIELLE CHAPELLE - War Training	FMR
12	15	Batn. marched to Rest Billets W. of MERVILLE near HAVERSKERQUE leaving Billets E. of VIELLE CHAPELLE at 8 P.M. arriving at new billets at about 11.30 P.M.	FMR
13	15	In Billets W. of MERVILLE - War Training	FMR
14	15	In Billets W. of MERVILLE - War Training - Lieut G.W. TANNER (3rd Battn.) joined Battn.	FMR
15	15	Batn. left Billets W. of MERVILLE at 6.45 P.M. to march to BOUT DEVILLE near to join SIRHIND Bde as a Temporary measure. Arrived at BOUT- DEVILLE at 9.30 P.M.	FMR
16	15	In Billets at BOUT DEVILLE - War Training	FMR
17	15	In Billets at BOUT DEVILLE - War Training	FMR

Army Form C. 2118.

WAR DIARY
or
INTELLIGENCE SUMMARY.
(Erase heading not required.)

Instructions regarding War Diaries and Intelligence Summaries are contained in F. S. Regs., Part II, and the Staff Manual respectively. Title pages will be prepared in manuscript.

Hour, Date, Place.			Summary of Events and Information.	Remarks and references to Appendices.
18.	7.	15	In Billets at BOUT DE VILLE - War Training	FWR
19.	7.	15	In Billets at BOUT DE VILLE - War Training	FWR
20.	7.	15	In Billets at BOUT DE VILLE - War Training - H.R.H. The Prince of Wales paying a visit and practical part of the Bn on parade. Accompanied by Capt. Lidell G.S.O. 1st A. Corps Staff. H.R.H. subsequently breakfasted with the C.O.	FWR
21.	7.	15	In Billets at BOUT DE VILLE - War Training - C.O. and Coy Commdrs. left Billets at 9.15 A.M. to visit trenches, Battn is to take over from CONNAUGHT RANGERS, FEROZEPORE Brigade, on night 22/23-7-15.	FWR
22.	7.	15	Bn. left billets at BOUT DE VILLE and PONT DU HEM and formed up at PONT-DU-HEM Cross Roads at 8.55 P.M. Bn. moved off at 9 P.M. and marched to relieve CONNAUGHT RANGERS (FEROZEPORE Bgde.) in Right Centre Sub section of The SIRHIND Bgde. Front. Relief Completed by 12.30 A.M. 23-7-15. Distribution - "A" Coy (less 1 Platoon) and "B" Coy in firing line; "D" Coy and 1 platoon of "A" coy in support, "C" Coy in Reserve; "D" Coy found garrisons of TILLELOY NORTH and GRANT'S POST.	FWR

WAR DIARY
or
INTELLIGENCE SUMMARY.
(Erase heading not required.)

Army Form 2118.

Hour, Date, Place.	Summary of Events and Information.	Remarks and references to Appendices.
23 - 7 - 15	Distribution of Bn. in Right Centre Sub-section Same as on 22nd. Enemy quiet all day. Occasional Sniping. Enemy opened fire with machine gun on road on right of Headquarters at about 8.45 P.M. Our Machine Gun Detachment opened fire at 11.45 P.M. on German working party who were using an electric torch. It is thought that Enemy must have suffered some casualties as great noise and commotion was made. Our snipers did good work among another Enemy working party, 2 direct hits was obtained and other men were seen to fall. Our casualties for the day were 2.1 wounded by bullet and one by bayonet, accidental.	FHR
24 - 7 - 15	Distribution as for 23rd. Lieut TANNER took a patrol close up to German line and was fired at by German patrol at about 8 yards. Enemy then ran away and our patrol could not catch them. Brig: General Walker V.C. C.B. inspected trenches.	FHR

Army Form C. 2118.

WAR DIARY
or
INTELLIGENCE SUMMARY.
(Erase heading not required.)

Instructions regarding War Diaries and Intelligence Summaries are contained in F. S. Regs., Part II, and the Staff Manual respectively. Title pages will be prepared in manuscript.

Hour, Date, Place.	Summary of Events and Information.	Remarks and references to Appendices.
25 - 7 - 15	Distribution same as for previous day. Enemy quiet until about 5 P.M. when he started shelling RUE - DU - BACQUEROT with high explosive shells. Machine Gun fire was again opened on road on right of Head Quarters at about 9 P.M. One Enemy aeroplane was seen over our lines at 6. P.M.	F.H.R.
26 - 7 - 15	Distribution of Bn as for previous days. Our snipers claim to have hit one German during day. A German aeroplane flew over our lines about 4.30 P.M. Brigadier General WALKER. V.C. C.B. inspected GRANT'S POST this morning.	F.H.R.
27 - 7 - 15	Distribution as for previous days Except that 26 men from The Reserve were sent to front line. Enemy quiet except for occasionally sniping. Our snipers accounted for 5 Germans from working parties during the day. 2/Lieut C.N.C. COPEMAN was wounded in the wrist and L/Cpl. W. POUGHER 8395 was killed while out on patrol in front of our lines.	F.H.R.

Army Form C. 2118.

WAR DIARY
or
INTELLIGENCE SUMMARY.

(Erase heading not required.)

Instructions regarding War Diaries and Intelligence Summaries are contained in F. S. Regs., Part II, and the Staff Manual respectively. Title pages will be prepared in manuscript.

Hour, Date, Place.	Summary of Events and Information.	Remarks and references to Appendices.
28-7-15	Distribution as for previous days. Enemy appears to have stopped the working parties behind their lines during the day, as no movement was observed. 14525 Pte Byrnes was killed during the afternoon and 11177 L-cpl Collings slightly wounded but returned to duty. TILLELOY NORTH was shelled at about 6 P.M. The north parapet being breached by a small percussion shell. No casualties.	J.M.R.
29-7-15	Distribution as for previous day. An Enemy Aeroplane flew over our lines at 5.45 A.M. and returned about 6.30 A.M. Our snipers accounted for 2 Germans between 10 and 11 A.M.. Enemy retaliated by shelling snipers post & hit it twice, but did very little damage. An enemy machine gun which opened at 11.30 P.M. was silenced by our bomb gun which fired very good practice. At about 11.45 A.M. Enemy opened fire with high explosive + shrapnel shell from field Guns on our Head Quarters + got three direct hits on the building. They opened again at 4 p.m. & again at 8.30 P.M. & twice hit the building but caused no casualties. Our bomb gun was got into action again at about 12 noon & dropped three shots into the German trench, blowing sand bags & earth into the air.	J.M.R.

Army Form C.2118.

WAR DIARY
or
INTELLIGENCE SUMMARY.
(Erase heading not required.)

Instructions regarding War Diaries and Intelligence Summaries are contained in F. S. Regs., Part II, and the Staff Manual respectively. Title pages will be prepared in manuscript.

Hour, Date, Place.	Summary of Events and Information.	Remarks and references to Appendices.
29-7-15 (continued)	Enemy replied with Lange bombs or Minnenwerfer but did no damage. Our casualties during the day were 1 to wounded, 2/Lieut J.F. SWAIN was sent to hospital sick.	F.H.R.
30-7-15	Distribution as for previous days. An Enemy working party was dispersed by our Snipers at 6.30 A.m. Remainder of day very quiet. Rifle fire & sniping by enemy spasmodically on — we had no casualties during the day.	F.H.R.
31-7-15	Distribution as for previous day. Our Snipers were again busy during the day accounting for 4 Germans. Enemy shelled our Support trenches at 12 noon & reached a small part of the parapet. At 5.35 p.m. Captain Sandford R.A. observed & directed a 9.2 gun (howitzer) on to German parapet opposite "A"Co wire Capt. Wilson suspected gas. 30 shells were fired and great damage done. 3 Large cylinders were exposed 15 ft long & 1 ft. in diameter. Gas extent gives opinion they were not gas cylinders. Enemy retaliated with 4.2's, 5.9's & Field guns and bombs. Very extensive work is going on in German lines.	F.H.R.

Serial No. 184.

Confidential

12/6948 Diary

of

The 2nd Bn. Leicestershire Regiment

FROM 1st August 1915. TO 31st August 1915.

Army Form C. 2118.

WAR DIARY
of 1st Leicestershire Regt.
INTELLIGENCE SUMMARY.
(Erase heading not required.)

Instructions regarding War Diaries and Intelligence Summaries are contained in F. S. Regs., Part II, and the Staff Manual respectively. Title pages will be prepared in manuscript.

Hour, Date, Place.	Summary of Events and Information.	Remarks and references to Appendices.
1st August	On the Gordoval Brigade taking over the front from SIGN POST LANE (inclusive) to WINCHESTER ROAD (inclusive) the Battalion was allotted the centre subsection from SUNKEN ROAD TRENCH (inclusive) to point "75" just South of MOATED GRANGE TRENCH, on a frontage of 780 yards. 'A' and 'B' Coys occupied trenches with two Companies of the 89th Garhwal Rifles, 'D' Coy going into the Support trenches behind the 58th Rifles at 2 p.m. at 9 p.m. 'C' Coy relieved 'A' Coy, who came back to Reserve trenches close to RUE du BACQUEROT and also finding the garrison for TILLELOY SOUTH POST with one platoon under Lieut BROWN. 'D' Coy relieved the Company of the 58th Rifles at the same time. Battalion HQ moved to dug outs on RUE du BACQUEROT at 9.30 p.m. Owing to the reliefs taking place the activity of snipers and enemy machine gun and rifle fire was opened by Germans working parties to minutes. No men of the enemy retrieved by bombing the front line trenches wounding 5 men. During the day the line was slightly shelled.	Companies were commanded as follows. A Coy Captain W.C. WILSON B " A.S. McINTYRE C " Dr. WEIR D " W. PICKEN (Vice Captain F.N. ROMILLY acting Adjutant from 31st July 1915.) F.M.R.
2nd August	In addition on the 1st 2nd but owing to work being returned to in front the new troops taken over little firing was done. Officers patrols reconnoitred the wire from left and	

76

Army Form C. 2118

WAR DIARY
or
INTELLIGENCE SUMMARY.
(Erase heading not required.)

Instructions regarding War Diaries and Intelligence Summaries are contained in F. S. Regs., Part II, and the Staff Manual respectively. Title pages will be prepared in manuscript.

Hour, Date, Place.	Summary of Events and Information.	Remarks and references to Appendices.
	~~Strongpoint~~ held by the Battalion, not mentioned his hostile potatoes. Enemy's snipers were active during the night. Pvt Warner and Willis being killed. A hostile sniper's post was located at 197.	JHR
2nd August	In same position. The German sniper's post at 197 was shelled by our artillery. The enemy snipers were again active. One man was wounded. Colonel Johnson 17 Manchester Regt arrived to stay three days with the Battalion for instructional purposes. General Blackader was CO the Brigade region under Brigadier General WALKER VC &c. The Battalion was attached to the SIRHIND BRIGADE from 15th July to 1st August and on rejoining the Garhwal Brigade again General Walker sent the following letter to Lt Colonel H. Garden ---- "I wanted to tell your Armourers and to tell you how much I had appreciated the honour of having your Battalion under my command, for even so short a time. I have never very pleased with the way the men worked and your General "Vandevecher in the trenches, which is as good as any I have seen. Would you please convey my appreciation to your officers and men ...."	JHR

Army Form C. 2118.

WAR DIARY
or
INTELLIGENCE SUMMARY.
(Erase heading not required.)

Instructions regarding War Diaries and Intelligence Summaries are contained in F. S. Regs., Part II, and the Staff Manual respectively. Title pages will be prepared in manuscript.

77

Hour, Date, Place.	Summary of Events and Information.	Remarks and references to Appendices.
4th August.	In same position as on 3rd. The enemy continuously fired on working parties putting up the barbed wire, causing much inconvenience. Sergeant TORKINGTON and Private WOOTTON being killed and one man wounded in front of the parapet. A german search light was turned onto our trenches the previous night at 9 p.m. and 12.30 a.m., being worked from the direction of B.202. The germans also tried rifle grenades at 8 p.m. which did no damage. At 8.30 p.m. three platoons of C Company, 10th & 13th Royal Warwickshire Regts. were sent into the trenches for instruction. One platoon being attached to each Company in the Firing line. At 5 p.m. the 4.2" Howitzer Battery R.F.A. fired 18 rounds at 197, getting six direct hits leaving up a number of planks and sandbags. The 73rd Battery R.F.A. then opened fire with percussion Shrapnel. The germans retaliated to this bombardment by firing about a dozen shells from small field howitzers and put 4 rounds at our trenches. Their snipers were active. 2/Lt. SWAIN reported to Hosp.	For R
5th August	Position same as on 4th August. The germans fired very with during the night but turned on a search light at frequent intervals from the direction of B.202 and fired a green rocket at about 10.30 p.m.	

WAR DIARY
INTELLIGENCE SUMMARY
(Erase heading not required.)

Army Form C. 2118

Hour, Date, Place.	Summary of Events and Information.	Remarks and references to Appendices.
	A working party who observed felling trees and carrying planks at 206 and were fired on, in which they retaliated by a few rounds from field guns. Another sniper's post was located firing a tree in rear of 197 and fired on, a German wearing a felt helmet being hit. Our usual wire entanglements in front and all companies took up usual war entrenchments during darkness. Throughout the day at intervals along our front. The 2nd Battery R.F.A. registered along our front. At 2.30 pm our trench mortars fired at Minto at 197 were a Maxim gun was the point to be silenced. Enemy shelled our trenches with a dozen shrapnel at 2.15 pm and down at 5. pm. Four German Regts relieved "B" Company in the trenches, the latter going back to billets on the ESTAIRES – LA BASSEE Road, North of PONT DU HEM. Major General Anderson and Brigadier General Blackader marked the Brigade sector. 2Lieut D SUTHERLAND took over command of B Coy vice Captain A S McINTYRE posted to C Coy.	F.H.P
6th August	As for 5th August. Enemy snipers were active by day and their field artillery registered along our front. The Germans used a search light probably mounted on a motor car so they illuminated our front from different points at intervals during the night. The usual work of wiring our front and strengthening parapets was done.	

WAR DIARY
or
INTELLIGENCE SUMMARY.

(Erase heading not required.)

Army Form C. 2118

Instructions regarding War Diaries and Intelligence Summaries are contained in F. S. Regs., Part II, and the Staff Manual respectively. Title pages will be prepared in manuscript.

Hour, Date, Place.	Summary of Events and Information.	Remarks and references to Appendices.
	The three platoons B. C. Coy 10th Royal Warwickshire Regt were relieved at 10.15 pm by "D" Coy of the Same Regt. Captain A.L. McINTYRE was sent to Hospital (sick). Captain C.C. ROLPH, commanding the M.G. Section, came back from the front line to go to WISQUES to join the 14th M.G. Course.	J.H.R.
7th August	In same Subsection. Reference to 6th August. Patrols having located Enemy's working parties, fire was opened on them at 1.30 and 2.30 am. Our French mortar fired eight rounds along the German trenches to our front, getting several into their trenches. Enemy replied by firing 4.2 howitzers which made good practice on shell tracking on our parados. During the morning they fired 10 Rifle Grenades, three bursting on our parapets, but no casualties occurred either from these or their shells. Their trench light was during alarm before at nights, and their patrols were heard. During the morning the Germans fired an high explosive shells at TILLELOY SOUTH POST ONE which landed in the middle of the work at 11.15 am, but no one was injured. Lt. SWAIN went out with a Patrol to ascertain what some white marking shown on an aerial photograph were. The Patrol went to 200 yards along the German trenches and went 50 yards from them, and could only assume that the white marks must have been the sheep creating the entanglement at that point.	J.H.R

Army Form C. 2118.

WAR DIARY
or
INTELLIGENCE SUMMARY.
(Erase heading not required.)

Instructions regarding War Diaries and Intelligence Summaries are contained in F. S. Regs., Part II, and the Staff Manual respectively. Title pages will be prepared in manuscript.

Hour, Date, Place.	Summary of Events and Information.	Remarks and references to Appendices.
8th August	In same trenches as on 7th. Nothing of importance occurred. The Battalion was relieved at 9.30 pm by the 1/9th Gurkha Rifles and marched back to vieux BERQUIN. At LA GORGUE.	J.H.R.
9th August	At LA GORGUE. War Training.	
10th August	At LA GORGUE. War Training.	
11th August	At LA GORGUE. War Training. The Battalion found a working party of 200 men to dig communication trenches near the RUE du BACQUEROT. This working party Subaltern Lieu Crawshaw, both wounded.	J.H.R.
12th August	At LA GORGUE. War Training.	
13th August	At LA GORGUE. War Training. Pte Reynolds died from wounds received on 11th August while digging.	J.H.R.
14th August	At LA GORGUE. War Training.	
15th August	At LA GORGUE. War Training.	J.H.R.

Army Form C. 2118.

WAR DIARY
or
INTELLIGENCE SUMMARY.
(Erase heading not required.)

Hour, Date, Place.	Summary of Events and Information.	Remarks and references to Appendices
August 16th	The Battalion left LA GORGUE at 7pm and relieved the 2nd Black Watch in B Subsection & IND. H.P. The Garhwal Brigade relieving the Bareilly Brigade in this sector. The Subsection extended from FAVUISSART - AUBERS Road to a point 750 yards South of it. Private DOWELLS was killed during the night. Major E.P. RIDDELL Rifle Brigade and Major L.L. WHEATLEY D.S.O. Argyll and Sutherland Highlanders were attached for instructional purposes. The Trenches were occupied as follows. Firing line A Coy (Capt. Cam M.C. Wilson) B Coy. (2/Lt. D. SUTHERLAND) Support Trenches ½ C Coy. (2nd H.H. PHILLIPS) Reserve D.Coy (2 Lt PICKIN) in Road Bend Post and ½ C Coy (Captain D.L. MEIR) in WANGERIE POST.	FKR
August 17th	In same position. Major Riddell and Wheatley left to go to Lahore Division. General Blackader visited the Battalion. The Germans sniped intermittently by day and fired five 5.9" shells	

Army Form C. 2118.

82

WAR DIARY
or
INTELLIGENCE SUMMARY.
(Erase heading not required.)

Instructions regarding War Diaries and Intelligence Summaries are contained in F. S. Regs., Part II, and the Staff Manual respectively. Title pages will be prepared in manuscript.

Hour, Date, Place.	Summary of Events and Information.	Remarks and references to Appendices
17th August	which exploded near our advanced Lewis post S.E. of ROAD BEND without doing any damage. Our snipers hit one German during the day. Our patrols went along our entire front at various points during the night and one Officer's patrol went along a ditch to within 20 yards of the German wire entanglements. A German aeroplane flew over our lines at 7 P.M. German snipers also active during the night. At 9 P.M. two platoons of the 6th WILTSHIRE REGT were sent to the front line to reinforce, one platoon to 'A' Coy and one to 'B' Coy, relieving a platoon of each mentioned Company, who in turn relieved half 'C' Coy in the Support trenches. The latter rejoined 'C' Coy H.Q. at WANGERIE POST.	F.J.P.
18th August	In same subsection as on 17th August. The Germans were very inactive and sniped very little. The 28th Battery R.F.A. did good practise, on three occasions knocking shrapnel into a working party, and another personal shrapnel burst directly on a loophole to a German who fired through it at one of our aeroplanes. Patrols under Lt M.W. BROWN and 2Lt TANNER went out during

Gulab Singh & Sons, Calcutta—No. 22 Army C.—5-8-14—1,07,000.

Army Form C. 2118.

WAR DIARY
or
INTELLIGENCE SUMMARY.

(Erase heading not required.)

Instructions regarding War Diaries and Intelligence Summaries are contained in F. S. Regs., Part II, and the Staff Manual respectively. Title pages will be prepared in manuscript.

Hour, Date, Place.	Summary of Events and Information.	Remarks and references to Appendices

| | the night, the former bringing in two newspapers which were retrieved to a stick between the opposing lines, probably placed there as an awning mark for malker gun or a point for german patrols to visit. 2/Lt Tarrer's patrol went to a german sap which ran out about 60 yards from their lines and climbed over the parapet to the T head and fell into it. They found it occupied by a german picquet, who fired on them and threw bombs at their party. To retirement, but they suffered no casualties and managed to withdraw to our trenches, effectively clearing up a moot point whether this sap was occupied by germans at night or not — | |
| 19th August. | In position as for 18th. Our patrols found an old german trench was occupied as a listening post. Shots being fired from it at our trenches. Two germans were shot by our snipers. In the late afternoon the Enemy bombarded the junction of our immediate left with heavy artillery and minenwerfer bombs. The cooperation being very good. On our trench mortars attempting to get into position to retaliate | |

84

Army Form C. 2118.

WAR DIARY
or
INTELLIGENCE SUMMARY.
(Erase heading not required.)

Instructions regarding War Diaries and Intelligence Summaries are contained in F. S. Regs., Part II, and the Staff Manual respectively. Title pages will be prepared in manuscript.

Hour, Date, Place.	Summary of Events and Information.	Remarks and references to Appendices
	The German field guns shelled them and prevented their action. A Coy's left was shelled and bombed as well but there were no casualties from this fire; our guns retaliated on the German trenches. Three German bomb throwers in A Coy's trench in the early part of the night. Aeroplane reconnaissance was over our lines in the morning. The two platoons of the 6th WILTS were relieved at 8 + 5. P.m by two other platoons of the same Regiment. From information received from a German deserter a relief was due to take place on the night of the 18th and the roads along where the reliefs would move were indicated. Our field batteries opened fire at various times commencing at 8.30 p.m onto certain cross roads, trolley lines and other points and also in direct machine gun fire was brought to bear on the same points and roads to harass and delay the German relief. Several 13 Lookouts visited the front trenches in the afternoon.	JHP

Gulab Singh & Sons, Calcutta—No. 22 Army C.—5-8-14—1,07,000.

85

Army Form C. 2118.

WAR DIARY
or
INTELLIGENCE SUMMARY.
(Erase heading not required.)

Instructions regarding War Diaries and Intelligence Summaries are contained in F. S. Regs., Part II, and the Staff Manual respectively. Title pages will be prepared in manuscript.

Hour, Date, Place.	Summary of Events and Information.	Remarks and references to Appendices
20th August.	In same subsection. The Germans showed considerable activity during the day and night. They shelled our trenches with field guns at noon and with 5.9" howitzers later in the afternoon. At 9.20 pm they fired two green signal rockets. They let with a pin ball. The Germans in front of our trenches (where the new single front) there lies to about 70 yards. They then began shelling our trenches with trench guns and light howitzers for about a quarter hour. They then after in have afterwards they opened heavy rifle and machine gun fire. Again at midnight preceded by Infantry and M.G. fire, My ____ shewed activity for about ten minutes. The casualties sustained by this fire were Pte PAYNE killed, five men wounded and three from D Co. 6" Wilts detached with other platoons in ourselves. A German Sausage Baloon was up in the afternoon opposite our subsection.	
21st August.	In Same subsection 1MD.H.B as on 20th inst. thereinup. Sniping became more pronounced from 10 pm onwards. The 28 Battery R.F.A. attained four direct hits on the enemys parapet	

Gulab Singh & Sons, Calcutta—No. 22 Army C.—5-8-14—1,07,000.

Army Form C. 2118.

WAR DIARY
or
INTELLIGENCE SUMMARY.
(Erase heading not required.)

Instructions regarding War Diaries and Intelligence Summaries are contained in F. S. Regs., Part II, and the Staff Manual respectively. Title pages will be prepared in manuscript.

Hour, Date, Place.	Summary of Events and Information.	Remarks and references to Appendices
22nd August.	Opposite the right of our Subsection. The enemy's Trenches at this portion of the line are from 300 to 400 yards away from our Trenches. Two Officers 6/WLTS returned their 2 platoons in our Trenches at 8.15 p.m. Major-General A. Wilson Commanding Meerut Division, visited the Trenches in the Section held by the Garhwal Brigade; the Brigadier of the 19° Division also came to our line to see the system of trenches &c — In same position. No opportunity for Offensive action received. The Germans were very quiet all day. In the late afternoon the German Anti-aircraft guns brought down one of our aeroplanes by gun fire and it fell heading toward the German lines. A German aeroplane was over the Section held by the Garhwal Brigade for half an hour in the evening. About 10 p.m. some Germans crept up a ditch and line of willow trees to our listening post found by B Coy. which was about 120 yards from our Trenches and a short distance from a German Sap. From a concealed position and unseen	F.J.P.

Army Form C. 2118.

WAR DIARY
or
INTELLIGENCE SUMMARY.
(Erase heading not required.)

Hour, Date, Place.	Summary of Events and Information.	Remarks and references to Appendices
23rd August	They threw two hand grenades into the listening post, killing Pte Mitchell, mortally wounding a private of the 6/WILTS and wounding the other two men of the post. Pte DAVIS, who was also one of the group but not lying with them, escaped unhurt, showed great courage and devotion to duty by remaining at his post on watermelon more men arrived. Sergeant BENTLEY, from whose platoon the post was found, also who displayed gallantry by at once going out alone to the post on hearing the explosion of the two bombs. Captain E.C. DEANE R.A.M.C., Medical Officer to the Battalion also showed conspicuous gallantry by climbing over the Parapet and running across the open under fire to the and the wounded. In same Trenches. One german was hit by one of our snipers. The germans again bombed our listening post which had been with drawn early in the evening, we retaliated immediately with M.G. and heavy rifle fire directed on to their listening post. At 10.30 p.m. our french mortars fired two salvos from four mortars onto the	

WAR DIARY
or
INTELLIGENCE SUMMARY.

Army Form C. 2118.

88.

Hour, Date, Place.	Summary of Events and Information.	Remarks and references to Appendices
24th August	German listening post, preceded by rifle fire and flares being sent up by us to hide the sounds of the machine. Great confusion followed and shouts and cries were heard. The enemy retaliated by firing four large bombs at 11.45 p.m. when did no damage, our four Trench mortars replying at once and extraordinary when silenced their fire. A German aeroplane, flying very high, passed over our lines in the evening. Two platoons 6/WILTS. relieved the two platoons of the same Regt in our trenches. Major R.V. Kealleh D.W.72 D.S.O. rejoined the Battalion from wounded. 2/Lt. V.E. ELLINGTON 9th Bn. Leicestershire Regt. joined for duty and posted to 'B' Coy. 2/Lt. A.E. Sturdy was sent to Hospital sick. Captain F. Lewis took over command of D Coy. 2/Lt Bailey and a reinforcement of 25 min arrived at LAPUGNOY and are temporarily attached to the Brigade Base. In same situation of trenches. C Coy relieved A Coy in the front line at 8.30am and D Coy relieved B Coy in the front line at 9PM and B Coy returning to Subsection reserve. Our 4.5" Howitzers and Field guns shelled the enemy's parapet opposite our Trenches and also shelled to shaking, our Machine	J.S.H.P

89.

Army Form C. 2118.

Instructions regarding War Diaries and Intelligence Summaries are contained in F. S. Regs., Part II, and the Staff Manual respectively. Title pages will be prepared in manuscript.

WAR DIARY
or
INTELLIGENCE SUMMARY.
(Erase heading not required.)

Hour, Date, Place.	Summary of Events and Information.	Remarks and references to Appendices
25th August.	Guns co-operated at German wire. During the night our Machine Guns opened fire at intervals where the Germans might be repairing their parapets and wire and also opened indirect fire onto RUE D'ENFER. The German sniper by day and this slackened considerably at night, only desultory M.G. fire being resorted to. Lt. Colonel WYLD. 16th Bn. K.R.R. arrived to stay three days with the Battalion for instructional purposes. The Commanding Officers 6/OXFORD L.I. and Company Commanders of the 6th OXFORD L.I. and 12th K.S.L.I. visited the Battalion prior to taking them over. Brigadier-General Stewart Commanding the 58th Brigade also visited the Battalion. Pte Bailey was killed and two men wounded during the last 24 hours. Two additional platoons 6/WILTS were attached in trenches for instruction. A quiet day except for the usual sniping day and night. A German carrying water from a house behind their line was hit by one of our snipers. We opened M.G. and rifle fire at German working parties during the night. Two platoons 6/WILTS attached for instruction rejoined their Battalion in the evening. 2 Lt. G.H. Salmon was sent sick to Hospital. 2 Lt Wilson P.'s joined in Hq 1st R.	

Army Form C. 2118.

WAR DIARY
or
INTELLIGENCE SUMMARY.

(Erase heading not required.)

Instructions regarding War Diaries and Intelligence Summaries are contained in F. S. Regs., Part II, and the Staff Manual respectively. Title pages will be prepared in manuscript.

90

Hour, Date, Place.	Summary of Events and Information.	Remarks and references to Appendices
26ᵗʰ August.	In same position. The Battalion, less 1 platoon of D Coy under 2Lt W.T. Pickin, was relieved at 8.15 pm by the 6ᵗʰ OXFORD and BUCKS. L.I. And the Posts in the Subsection by the 12ᵗʰ K.S.L.I. and marched back to billets one mile N.W. of ESTAIRES.	F.H.R.
27ᵗʰ August.	In billets N.W. ESTAIRES. War training. 2Lt WOODBURN returned from wounded. 1 Platoon D Coy was relieved in trenches by Bn Platoon 12ᵗʰ K.R.R. rejoined the Battalion.	F.H.R.
28ᵗʰ August.	In billets N.W. ESTAIRES. Major R.N. KNATCHBULL D.S.O. was sent sick to Hospital (old wound). The Battalion left billets at 4.30 pm to relieve the SIRHIND Bde in Subsection IND.H.B. halting for two hours en route. The garrisons for the relieved sept. at 12 noon. The Battalion was detailed to find garrisons for three posts and apart. garrison for a fourth. The remainder lay in Brigade Reserve. The Companies were thus detailed as follows:— PORT ARTHUR. 50 men D Coy under Captain Lewis HILLS Redoubt. 50 men D Coy under 2/Lt SWAIN. CHURCH REDOUBT 10 men B D Coy in addition. 5. 40 men 4ᵗʰ Cavalry. CHATEAU Redoubt. 50 men C Coy, 2ⁿᵈ Lt Wilson H.Q. and A Coy in LUDHIANA	

Army Form C. 2118.

WAR DIARY
or
INTELLIGENCE SUMMARY.
(Erase heading not required.)

Instructions regarding War Diaries and Intelligence Summaries are contained in F. S. Regs., Part II, and the Staff Manual respectively. Title pages will be prepared in manuscript.

91

Hour, Date, Place.	Summary of Events and Information.	Remarks and references to Appendices
	LODGE. 'C' Coy less 50 men and 1 Platoon D Coy in CURZON POST and B Coy at PONT LOGY, forming the three relief garrisons. Brigade Reserve. In the morning the photographer sent by the Government of India took several photographs and cinematograph films of men of the Battalion at their various duties, and in the afternoon took a film of the Battalion marching through LA GORGUE.	
29th		F.H.R
30th	In same position. 10 men at CHURCH REDOUBT were with drawn to CURZON POST. General Blackader visited the sub-section.	F.H.R
	In same position. A portion of the firing trenches were inspected to a fresh bombardment from 2 to 5 pm with heavy howitzers and field guns. The trenches retaliated onto the British trenches opposite that portion being from Vandel. Two German aeroplanes flew over our lines in the evening.	F.H.R
31st	In same position. The bombardment of the 30th was again repeated but in lesser degree. The German did not reply. Two German aeroplanes were over the lines in the morning.	F.H.R

Day	Date	Strength B.O.	ORB	Rejoined B.O.	ORB	Casualties K	W	M	S	Remaining Strength B.O.	O.R.B
Sun	1-8-15	21	951		3				2	21	952
Mon	2-8-15	21	952		1		6		2	21	945
Tues	3-8-15	21	945				2		1	21	942
Wed	4-8-15	21	942		8		1		5	21	944
Thur	5-8-15	21	944			2	1		5	21	936
Fri	6-8-15	21	936	1*	2		2		3	21	933
Sat	7-8-15	22	933						3	22	931

* Lieut J. P. Swain rejoined from sick

Day	Date	Strength B.O.	Strength ORB	Rejoined B.O.	Rejoined ORB	Casualties K.	Casualties W.	Casualties M.	Casualties S.	Remaining Str B.O.	Remaining Str O.R.B
Sun	8.8.15	21	931		3		3			21	931
Mon	9.8.15	21	931							21	931
Tues	10.8.15	21	931	1ˣ			3		3	22	925
Wed	11.8.15	22	925						3	22	922
Thur	12.8.15	22	922						1	22	921
Fri	13.8.15	22	921		2		2		5	22	916
Sat	14.8.15	22	916		2				5	22	913

ˣ Lieut A.E. Sturdy joined

Day	Date	Strength		Rejoined		Casualties				Remaining strength	
		B.O.	O.R.B	B.O.	O.R.B	K	W	M	S	B.O.	O.R.B
Sun	15.8.15	22	913						8	22	905
Mon	16.8.15	22	905						4	22	901
Tues	17.8.15	22	901		3	1			4	22	899
Wed	18.8.15	22	899				1			22	898
Thur	19.8.15	22	898		3				3	22	898
Fri	20.8.15	22	898				3		4	22	891
Sat	21.8.15	22	891				3			22	888

Day	Date	Strength B.O.	ORB	Rejoined B.O.	ORB	Casualties K.	W.	M.	S.	Remaining Strength B.O.	O.R.B.
Sun	22-8-15	22	888		2	1	4		3	22	849
Mon	23.8.15	22	849				1		2	22	846
Tues	24.8.15	22	846	⊗2	2	1	2		✻5	23	841
Wed	25.8.15	23	841			1	2		3	23	865
Thur	26.8.15	23	865	⊗2	1				✻2	24	865
Fri	27.8.15	24	865							24	865
Sat	28.8.15	24	865		2				2	24	865

Ⓠ Major R.N. KNATCHBULL Rej^d from wounded
    2/Lieut V.E. ELLINGTON Joined.

✕ Lieut A.E. STURDY Sick to Hosp^l

⊗ 2/Lieut C.C. BAILEY Joined
    2/Lieut W Wilson —"—

✻ 2/Lieut G H SALMON Sick to Hosp^l

Day	Date	Strength B.O.	Strength ORB	Rejoin B.O.	Rejoin ORB	Casualties K	Casualties W	Casualties M	Casualties S	Remaining strength B.O.	Remaining strength O.R.B.
	29.8.15	24	865				1		9	23	856
	30.8.15	23	856	a 1			2		7	24	847
	31.8.15	24	847		1					24	848

a 2/Lieut C.B. WOODBURN Rejoined from wounded

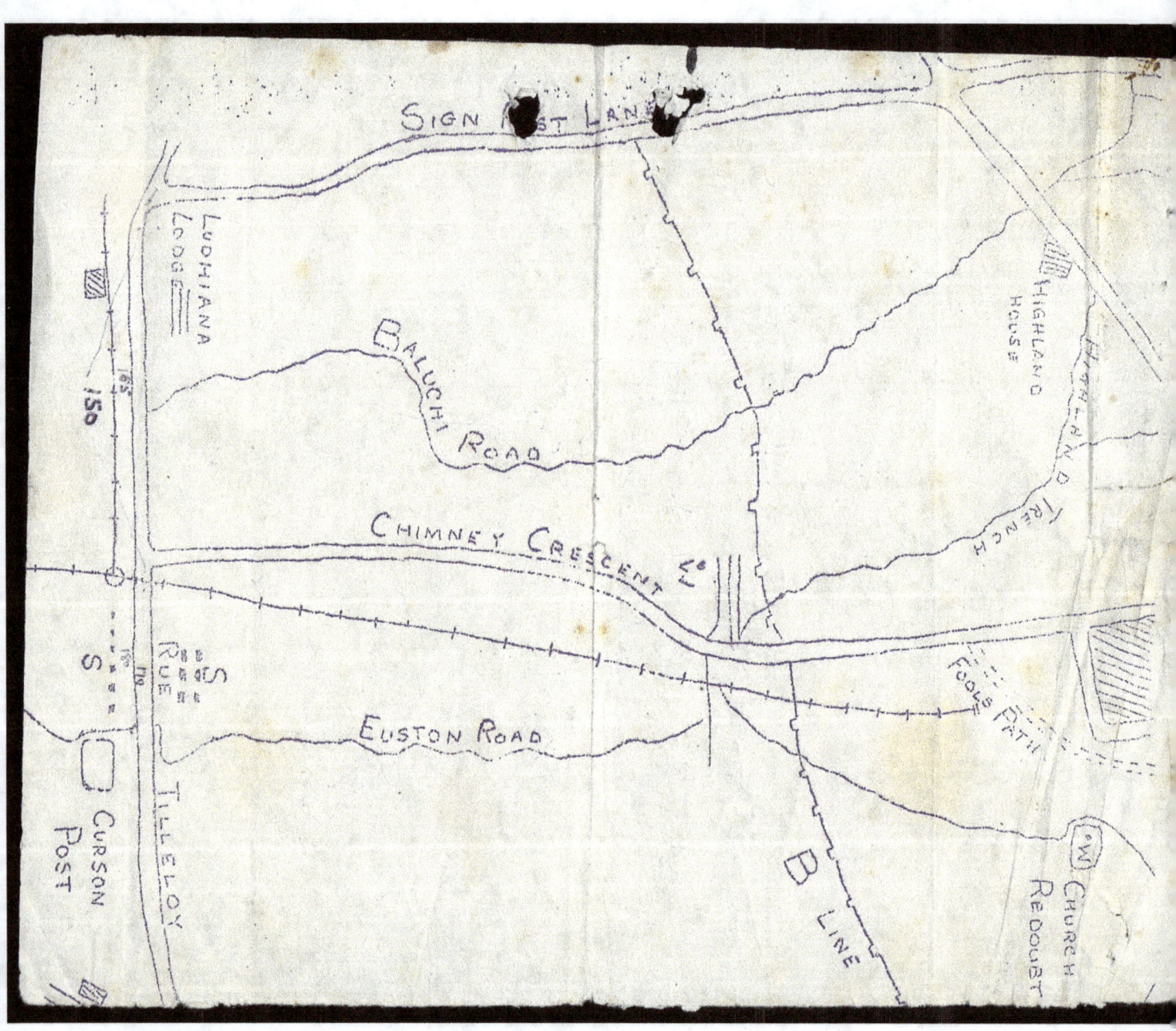

3705

were taken beyond Battn H⁰ 9/10
ing their front trenches
survived taken [in] Officers

4th St. Coln 19 ⅖

SECRET
SKETCH MAP.   1/ G.

This map must not
be seen by officers only when
when on patrol

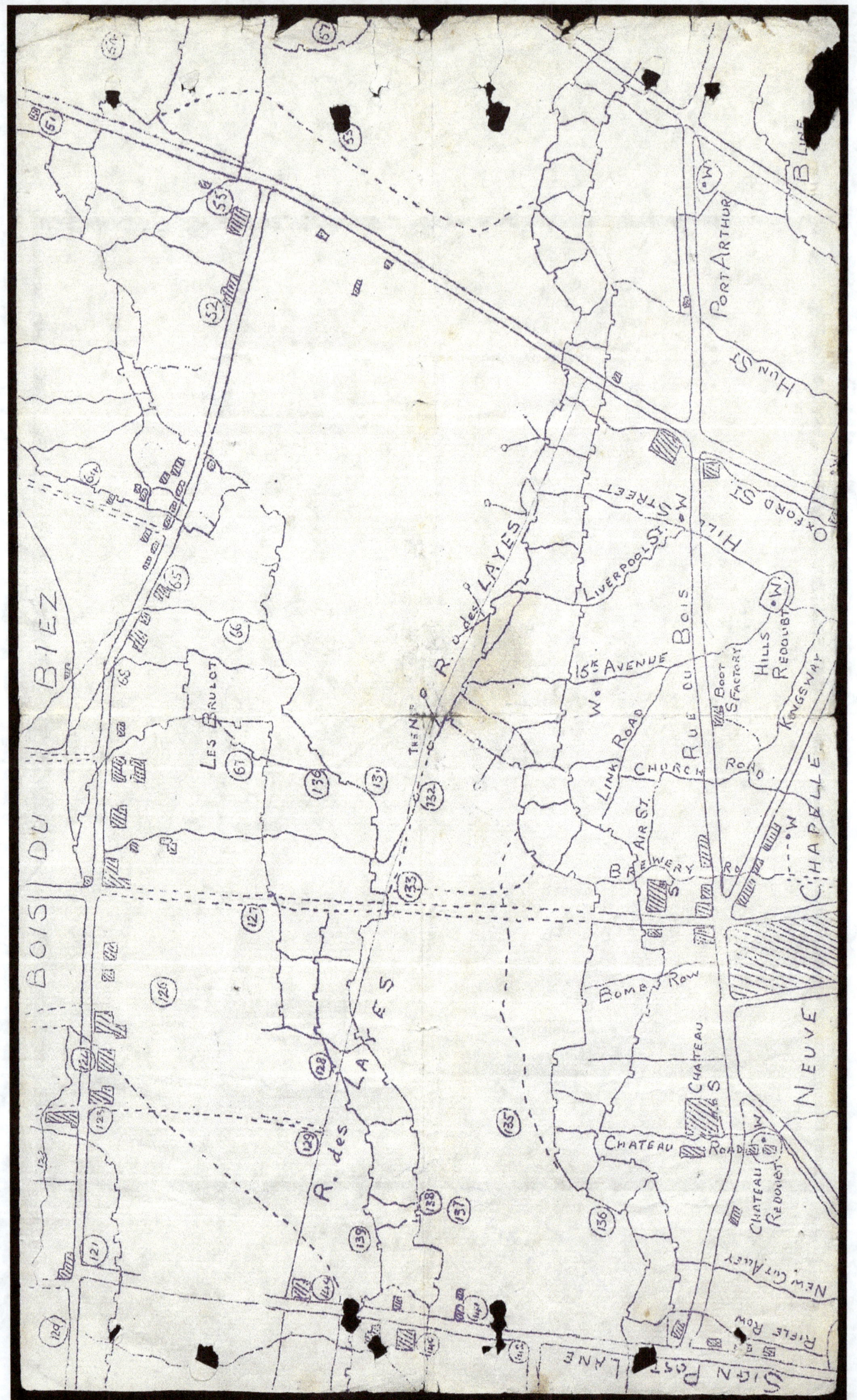

1. 9. 1915
30. 11. 1915

Serial No. 1807.

Gharwal Bde
Meerut

10 W
Extract

Confidential

121/7226

War Diary

of

2nd Battalion Leicestershire Regiment.

FROM 1st September 1915. TO 30th September 1915.

Army Form C. 2118.

WAR DIARY
INTELLIGENCE SUMMARY.
(Erase heading not required.)

Instructions regarding War Diaries and Intelligence
Summaries are contained in F. S. Regs., Part II,
and the Staff Manual respectively. Title pages
will be prepared in manuscript.

Hour, Date, Place.	Summary of Events and Information.	Remarks and references to Appendices
1st. September 1915	The Garrisons at PORT ARTHUR - HILL'S and CHATEAU REDOUBTS were relieved at 1 p.m. by men of the 59th. Rifles, 47th. SIKHS and 1st. Manchesters respectively. The remainder of the Battalion was relieved at 9 p.m. by the 4th Suffolks and 40th. Pathans, the former taking over LUDHIANA LODGE and the latter CURZON POST and PONT LOGY. The Battalion returned to billets at Bout De Ville.	
2nd. September 1915	In Billets. Every available man digging at night.	T.u.R.
3rd. September 1915	In Billets. Party of 50 digging at night.	T.u.R.
4th. September 1915	In Billets. Every available man digging at night.	T.u.R.
5th. September 1915	In Billets. Every available man digging at night.	T.u.R.
6th. September 1915	In Billets. Every available man digging at night.	T.u.R.
7th. September 1915.	In Billets. Every available man digging at night. One man slightly wounded when on patrol reconnoitring German wire.	T.u.R.
8th. September 1915	In same Billets.	T.u.R.
9th. September 1915	In same Billets. Every available man digging at night.	T.u.R.
10th. September 1915	In same Billets. 2nd. Lieuts TANNER and SWAIN reconnoitred the ground in front of our trenches.	T.u.R.
11th. September 1915	In same Billets. War Training. 2nd. Lieut Swain went to Hospital, Sick.	T.u.R.
12th. September 1915	In Same Billets. 100 men digging. The GARHWAL Brigade took over the trenches from the DEHRA DUN Brigade in that portion from SIGN POST LANE exclusive to SOUTH MOATED GRANGE STREET. The 3rd. LONDONS and 39th. GARHWAL Rifles in front line and supports "D" Coy formed part of the Local Reserve in HOME COUNTIES TRENCH The remainder of the Battalion remained in the same Billets as Brigade Reserve. A German areoplane was shot down and fell behind the German Lines opposite our section and was destroyed by our Artillery fire.	
13th. September 1915	In same Billets. 250 men employed digging. War Training.	T.u.R.
14th. September 1915	In sameBillets. Every available man digging.	T.u.R.
15th. September 1915	In same Billets. Digging parties were found by all Coys:	T.u.R.
15th. September 1915	In same Billets. Every man digging in front trenches.	T.u.R.

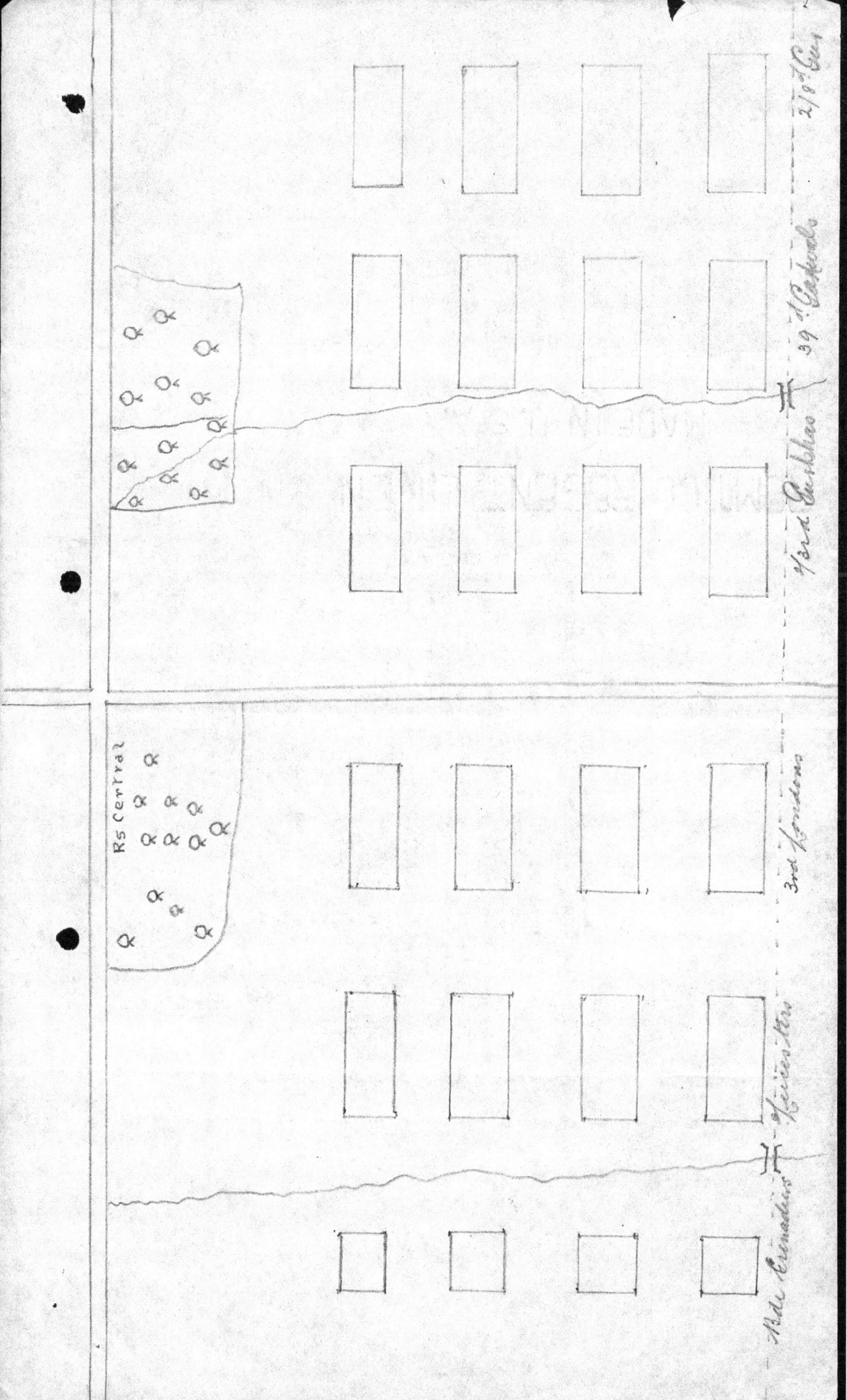

Army Form C. 2118.

WAR DIARY

INTELLIGENCE SUMMARY.

(Erase heading not required.)

Instructions regarding War Diaries and Intelligence Summaries are contained in F. S. Regs., Part II, and the Staff Manual respectively. Title pages will be prepared in manuscript.

Hour, Date, Place.	Summary of Events and Information.	Remarks and references to Appendices
17th. September 1915	In same Billets. Usual digging parties were found.	F.W.R
18th. September 1915	In same Billets. 50 men digging and 100 men carrying were found by the Battalion for front trenches.	F.W.R
19th. September 1915	In same Billets. 100 men digging and 100 carying were found by the Battalion.	F.W.R
20th. September 1915	The Hon'ble The Secretary of State for War, Earl KITCHENER of KHARTOUM K.G, etc. inspected the Brigades of the MEERUT Division. The GARHWAL Brigade was formed up according to the attached plan about 1 mile South of LA GORGUE. LORD KITCHENER and some Staff officers of the INDIAN Army Corps and MEERUT Division as well as the Commanders of the 1st Army, INDIAN Army Corps and MEERUT Division arrived on the ground at 11 a.m. The Battalion paraded 570 strong, all ranks, including officers. LORD KITCHENER Said that he had heard very good reports of the Battalion and was very pleased to see the men on parade as he had heard so much about their good work. He complimented the Battalion on their soldierlike apperaance on parade. At 7-15 p.m. at night all the Officers and N.C.Os. practiced an assembly rehearsal for taking over the trenches from the DEHRA DUN Brigade preparatory to an attack.	F.W.R " " "
21st. September 1915.	In same Billets. War Training.	
22nd. September 1915.	In same Billets. War Training.	
23rd. September 1915.	In same Billets. War Training.	
24th. September 1915.	The Battalion marched from concentration area PONT DU HEM at 7-10 p.m. to position of assembly in front and support lines M 36 d to M 30 c 15.15. which was completed at 10 p.m.	
25th. September 1915.	At 5-30 a.m. the Battalion was in positions of readiness in accordance with orders in four lines opposite their objective with bombing parties, sandbag parties and carrying parties all arranged and in position.	Ref: Trench Map1/10,000

Army Form C.

WAR DIARY
INTELLIGENCE SUMMARY

(Erase heading not required.)

Instructions regarding War Diaries and Intelligence Summaries are contained in F. S. Regs., Part II. and the Staff Manual respectively. Title pages will be prepared in manuscript.

Place	Date	Hour	Summary of Events and Information	Remarks and references to Appendices
	25th. September 1915.		At 6 a.m. the first line got over the parapet quickly followed by the second. The left had to right form to get in line with the right as the trench ran back from a salient near the centre. As the first two lines went out the third and fourth filed into the vacant positions in the firing line. The gas affected a number of our men and, the smoke caused a dense fog and direction was difficult. Casualties began at once and the third line was ordered out to fill up gaps. Owing to the thick smoke it seemed likely that gaps would occur on the flanks and at 6-7 a.m. the fourth line was sent out with special instructions to maintain touch with the units on either flank. At about 6-10 a.m. the left were over the German parapet and our flag was seen flying on their lines. The left went forward with such dash that they outstripped the 2/8 Gurkhas and came in for a lot of fire from rifles and maxim guns from our right, this caused a good many casualties including all the officers and most of the N.C.Os. of "A" Company which was the extreme left. Undeterred the men went on, got over the uncut wire and reached the road with parties of the 2/8 Gurkhas and gained their objective. In the meantime our right had not fared so well. They went forward in good line under a heavy fire till held up by the German wire. A number of our men here were collected in the ditch in front of the German wire waiting for devopments. Officer casualties:- Killed Captain F.H. Romilly D.S.O., Captain E.C. Deane R.A.M.C. Died of wounds 2nd. Lieut M.W. Browne, Wounded Lieut-Colonel H. Gordon D. S.O., Captain W.C. Wilson, Lieut H.H. Phillips, 2nd Lieuts G.W. Tanner, H.H. Hemphill, V.E. Ellingham, C.C. Bailey, G.W. Grossmith. Slightly wounded Major F. Lewis, Captain D.L. Weir. Gassed, 2nd. Lieut W. Wilson, Missing and believed killed Lieut W.T. Pickin, 2nd. Lieut R.E.S. Lodge. Missing and known th have been wounded 2nd. Lieut C.G. Woodbourn. Missing and no trace 2nd. Lieuts W.J. Wilkinson, E.A. Wilkinson, T.R. Longcroft. Rank and rile casualties Killed 72 Wounded 217 Gassed 42 Missing 96, Wounded slightly but did not quit Battalion 3. What was left of the Battalion were relieved from the front line by the 2/39th Garhwal Rifles at 6-30 p.m. and moved into support and local reserve just in rear. Before the operations began the Battalion worked for a week in strengthening the front line and preparing the defences behind. Four very strong lines were constructed capable of resisting the enemy's bombardment.	
	26th. September 1915		Relieved from support and local reserves by the 2/2 Gurkhas at 12 noon and went into billets near LA GORGUE	74
	27th. September 1915.		In Billets near LA GORGUE	74

Army Form C. 2118.

WAR DIARY
~~INTELLIGENCE SUMMARY~~

(Erase heading not required.)

Instructions regarding War Diaries and Intelligence Summaries are contained in F. S. Regs., Part II. and the Staff Manual respectively. Title pages will be prepared in manuscript.

Place	Date	Hour	Summary of Events and Information	Remarks and references to Appendices
	September 1915. 28th.		In Billets near LA GORGUE.	
	September 1915. 29th.		Left LA GORGUE and went into Billets at PARADIS.	
	September 1915. 30th.		In Billets at PARADIS.	

Serial No. 187.

Confidential

12/7601

War Diary

of

2nd Battalion Leicestershire Regiment.

FROM 1st October 1915. TO 31st October 1915.

Army Form C. 2118.

WAR DIARY
or
INTELLIGENCE SUMMARY.
(Erase heading not required.)

Instructions regarding War Diaries and Intelligence Summaries are contained in F. S. Regs., Part II. and the Staff Manual respectively. Title pages will be prepared in manuscript.

Place	Date	Hour	Summary of Events and Information	Remarks and references to Appendices
	1st. October 1915		In Billets at PARADIS	7.
	2nd. October 1915		In Billets at PARADIS	7.
	3rd. October 1915		Moved from PARADIS to billets in LOCON. The Brigade in Divisional Reserve. Lieut A. J. Boulter from 7th. Battalion joined for duty.	7.
	4th. October 1915		In Billets LOCON. Lieut M.C. Turionsky R.A.M.C. assumed Medical Charge of the Battalion.	7.
	5th. October 1915		In Billets LOCON. 2nd. Lieut Swindells C.G.R. from 7th. Battalion joinrd for duty.	7.
	6th. October 1915.		In Billets LOCON. 2nd. Lieut Gwytner G.L, 2nd, Lieut Seal J.R. 2nd. Lieut Buckinghen O.H., 2nd. Lieut Billings H., Lieut Howell A.H. 2nd. Lieut Byers H.D and 2nd. Lieut Chudleigh H.E.L. Joined Battalion for duty.	7.
	7th. October 1915		In Billets at LOCON. 2nd. Lieut Dowding L 2nd. Hassall, T.C.D. and Captain Ames R.H. and 242 other ranks joined the Battalion.	7.
	8th. October 1915		In Billets LOCON. Major Henderson M.F.S. rejoined the Battalion.	7.
	9th. October 1915		In Billets LOCON 2nd. Lieut Redwood J, 2nd. Lieut Muggeridge H.D. joined the Battalion.	7.
	10th. October 1915		In Billets LOCON.	7.
	11th. October 1915		In. Billets Locon. Moved from billets at 10-20 a.m. and with 1 Coy 3/London Regt attached releived 2nd. & 4th. Black Watch in front line IND B 1 Sub-Section (GIVENCHY RIDGE).	7.
	12th. October 1915		Front Line. No casualties. Received reinforcement of 1 Officer (2nd. Lieut A.E.Sturdy) rejoined from sick) and 124 other ranks.	7.
	13th. October 1915		Front Line. LAHORE & MEERUT Divns.made a smoke feint attack from 1 to 2 p.m. Enemy retaliated with guns. minnenwerfer, machine guns and rifle fire. Casualties Officer 2nd. Lieut Seal burns from our own smoke bombs, Other Ranks wounded 6, gassed by enemy's shells 4, burns from our own bombs 5.	7.
	14th. October 1915		Front Line. Casualties, 2nd. Lieut Redwood slight wound from splinters, did not leave unit.	7.
	15th. October 1915		Front Line. Casualties, Officers:- Killed Captain C.C. Rolph, Brigade Machine Gun Officer,killed by a Rifle Grenade.Other Ranks killed 1 by Rifle Grenade, wounded 4 by Rifle Grenade 2 by bullets, and 2 burns from our smoke bombs the day before.	7.
	16th. October 1915		Front Line. Casualties Officers 2nd. Lieut Hassall slight wound from rifle grenade 2nd. Lieut Billings burn from our smoke bombs on 13th. instant.	7.
	17th. October 1915.		Front Line. Casualties Other Ranks 2 wounded by bullets.	7.
	18th. October 1915		Front Line. Casualties Other Ranks 2 wounded by bullets.2nd. Lieut Muggeridge to Hospital suffering from shock.	7.

Army Form C. 2118.

WAR DIARY
or
INTELLIGENCE SUMMARY.
(Erase heading not required.)

Instructions regarding War Diaries and Intelligence Summaries are contained in F. S. Regs., Part II. and the Staff Manual respectively. Title pages will be prepared in manuscript.

97

Place	Date	Hour	Summary of Events and Information	Remarks and references to Appendices
	19th. October 1915.		Relieved by 3rd. Middlesex Regiment at 10-30 a.m. and went into billets at LOCON.	
	20th. October 1915.		Marched from LOCON at 4-30 p.m. To ALBERT Road in Brigade Reserve. Received a reinforcement of 65 other ranks.(ALBERT Road runs between RUE DU BOIS and RUE DES BERCEAUX.)	
	21st. October 1915.		In Brigade Reserve at ALBERT Road. The Battalion found a carrying party of 300 men at night to the front line.	
	22nd. October 1915.		In Brigade Reserve at ALBERT Road. 1 man wounded by bomb splinter at practice.	
	23rd. October 1915.		In Brigade Reserve at ALBERT ROAD.	
	24th. October 1915.		In Brigade Reserve at ALBERT Road . The Battalion found a carrying party of 300 men to the front line.	
	25th. October 1915.		In Brigade Reserve at ALBERT Road.	
	26th. October 1915.		In Brigade Reserve ALBERT Road.Battalion found a carrying party of 250 men to the front line.	
	27th. October 1915		In Brigade Reserve ALBERT Road.	
	28th. October 1915.		The Battalion relieved the 39th. Garhwal Rifles in the trenches south of the RUE DU BOIS "IND III-B" with 2/8th. Gurkhas on our right and BARIELLY Brigade on our left.We held the line from the salient BOAR'S HEAD (Which used to be known as V.(1) when we were last in this line in June) to about 150 yards South of"FARM CORNER" near FERME DU BOIS.	

2353 Wt. W2544/1454 700,000 5/15 D. D. & L. A.D.S.S./Forms/C. 2118.

Army Form C. 2118.

WAR DIARY
or
INTELLIGENCE SUMMARY.

(Erase heading not required.)

Place	Date	Hour	Summary of Events and Information	Remarks and references to Appendices
	29th October 1915		It was raining hard all day and the trenches were in a very bad state with mud which prolonged the relief till 10 p.m. Received re-inforcement of 65 other ranks. 2/Lieuts Belle and Martin joined the Battalion.	
			In IND III-B. Enemy quiet all day. Our casualties were one man killed. We threw bombs and rifle grenades at enemy trenches from BOAR'S HEAD during the day. By night an officer's patrol discovered a large German working party on their wire protected by a party of scouts. The patrol returned and we dispersed the Germans with rifle and machine gun fire.	
	30th October 1915		In IND III-B. Enemy shelled front line with shrapnel and the support line with 4.2 howitzers but did no damage the majority of the shells being blind. Our casualties were three men wounded.	
	31st October 1915		In IND III-B. Enemy shelled support line with 4.2 howitzers but did no damage the majority of the shells were again blind. Lieut Colonel H.Gordon rejoined and took over command of the Battalion. It was raining hard all day and the trenches were getting worse and in many parts so undermined that the parapet and parados fell in. The men were kept hard at work repairing them with sand bags. We were told today that the Indian Corps would be embarking shortly from Marseilles for an unknown destination.	

SERIAL NO. 187.

Confidential

War Diary

of

2nd Bn. Leicestershire Regiment.

FROM 1st November 1918 TO 30th November 1918.

12 W
8 sheets

Army Form C. 2118.

WAR DIARY
or
INTELLIGENCE SUMMARY.
(Erase heading not required.)

Place	Date	Hour	Summary of Events and Information	Remarks and references to Appendices
	1st November 1915		In the same section "IND III-B". Still raining and communication very difficult. "Pall Mall" Trench the only possible communication from Rue du Bois to our line was knee deep in water most of the way and large parties were put to work on repairing the sides which fell in in sections. All the "dug-outs" were wet including the Headquarters which was three or four inches deep in water. We kept up the usual fire at the enemy. They sent a few shells at us without damage. Our snipers were busy and accounted for one German killed and one wounded.	
	2nd November 1915		A very wet night followed by drizzling rain all day. No sleep possible for the men and all morning they were hard at work on front line which had fallen in in many places and in keeping open "Pall Mall" Communication. In the afternoon we got ready to be relieved by 1st Seaforths of the Dehra Dun Brigade. They started from Rue du Bois at 5.15 p.m. and it took their 1st Company 2 hours to reach our front line such was the state of the ground. At 10 p.m. the relief was complete and we marched to billets at L'Epinette - the last Company only arriving there at 3 a.m. on the 3rd. This was our last day in the trenches in France. From October 29th 1914 till today I do not remember ever having held such bad trenches	

Army Form C. 2118.

WAR DIARY
or
INTELLIGENCE SUMMARY.
(Erase heading not required.)

107

Place	Date	Hour	Summary of Events and Information	Remarks and references to Appendices
	3rd November 1915		or seeing such bad conditions of ground and climate. The men were covered with mud which was made all the worse by many falls on the way back through the communication trenches. Rested at L'Epinette and cleaned as far as possible. At 11.30 p.m. received orders to march to THIENNES at 8 a.m. following day.	A
	4th November 1915		Marched to THIENNES about 8½ miles - but a good many men fell out owing to feet troubles and the weight of wet packs and clothes.	A
	5th November 1915		Cleaning up and getting ready for entraining.	A
	6th November 1915		Cleaning up and getting ready for entraining.	A
	7th November 1915		Lieut Colonel H.Gordon D.S.O. to temporary command of the 70th Infantry Brigade Major F.Lewis D.S.O. took over command of the Battalion from this date. The Battalion entrained at Thiennes Station, en route for Marseilles, in three parties. The 1st party consisting of 2/Lieut Martin & 100 other ranks under the Command of Captain R.H.Ames entrained at 4.25 p.m. with the 39th Garhwal Rifles. The 2nd party consisting of 2/Lieut Buckingham & 100 other ranks under the command of 2/Lieut Swain entrained at 8.25 p.m. with the 2/3rd Gurkha Rifles. The remainder of the Battalion left billets at 10 p.m. and marched to the Station where they entrained in a troop special which left at 12.25 a.m. on 8th inst.	B

Instructions regarding War Diaries and Intelligence Summaries are contained in F. S. Regs. Part II. and the Staff Manual respectively. Title pages will be prepared in manuscript.

Army Form C. 2118.

WAR DIARY
or
INTELLIGENCE SUMMARY.

(Erase heading not required.)

Sheet No: 101.

Instructions regarding War Diaries and Intelligence Summaries are contained in F. S. Regs., Part II. and the Staff Manual respectively. Title pages will be prepared in manuscript.

Place	Date	Hour	Summary of Events and Information	Remarks and references to Appendices
	7th November 1915 (continued)		The following commendatory letter was received today from Field Marshal Sir J.D.P. French, O.M. etc, Commanding-in-Chief, British Army in France:- GENERAL HEADQUARTERS, BRITISH ARMY IN THE FIELD. 7th November, 1915. "As the Garhwal Brigade is now leaving my Command to take part in operations elsewhere, I wish to send it my personal thanks for the services it has rendered to the King-Emperor since reaching France more than a year ago. The behaviour of the Brigade in action and its discipline have been excellent throughout, and it has always maintained its fighting spirit in spite of heavy losses and under the most trying weather conditions. I wish the Garhwal Brigade all good fortune wherever its duty may take it, and feel sure it will everywhere maintain the excellent reputation it has earned in France. SD/ J.D.P.French Field Marshal. Commanding-in-Chief, British Army in France.	

Army Form C. 2118.

WAR DIARY
or
INTELLIGENCE SUMMARY.
(Erase heading not required.)

Place	Date	Hour	Summary of Events and Information	Remarks and references to Appendices
	8th November 1915.		In the train en route for Marseilles.	
	9th November 1915		In the train en route for Marseilles	
	10th November 1915		Arrived Marseilles about 11 a.m. Major F.Lewis D.S.O., Major E.F.S.Henderson, Captain D.L.Weir, Captain R.H.Ames, Lieut A.H.Howell, 2/Lieuts A.E.Sturdy, A.C.L.Chudleigh, L.Dowding, J.Redwood, C.G.R.Swindells, C.B.Godfrey, G.L.Gwyther, H.D.Byers, H.Billings, J.P.Swain, T.S.D.Hassall, A.Belle, Lieut J.G.Waine, (R.A.M.C.) 899 other ranks with baggage and vehicles embarked on S.S. Clan MacGillivray at about 1 p.m. and sailed at 5.30 p.m. 2/Lieut D.W.Sutherland & 25 other ranks with 12 Officer's chargers 1 riding horse and 54 mules embarked on S.S. Urlana and sailed at 2/Lieuts Martin & Buckingham embarked on S.S. Oranda as there was not sufficient accommodation on S.S. Clan MacGillivray.	
	11th November 1915		At sea. Nothing of note occurred. The usual ship's routine was carried out.	
	12th November 1915		At sea. Nothing of note occurred. The usual ship's routine was carried out.	

Sheet No: 103

Army Form C. 2118.

WAR DIARY
or
INTELLIGENCE SUMMARY.
(Erase heading not required.)

Hour, Date, Place.	Summary of Events and Information.	Remarks and references to Appendices
13th November 1915	At sea. The usual ship's routine carried out.	
14th November 1915	At sea. The usual ship's routine carried out.	
15th November 1915	At sea. The usual ship's routine carried out.	
16th November 1915	Arrived Port of Alexandra & anchored in the Bay.	
17th November 1915	Moved along side quay about 12.30 p.m. The Battalion disembarked in two parties. The first at 10 p.m. & second at 12.30 a.m. 18-11-15.	
18th November 1915	First party Major Henderson "A" & "B" Coys, M.G.Section and 30 of 1st Line & half 1st Line wagons left at 12.30 a.m. and arrived at Tel-el-Kebir at 6.30 a.m. The 2nd party Major F.Lewis D.S.O., Hd Qr Party, "C" & "D" Coys, remainder of 1st Line & 1st Line wagons left at 2.30 a.m. & arrived at 8.30 a.m. Pitched Camp on N side of Railway Station about 1 mile from Tel-el-Kebir.	
19th November 1915	In Camp at Tel-el-Kebir.	
20th November 1915	In Camp at Tel-el-Kebir.	

Army Form C. 2118.

WAR DIARY
or
INTELLIGENCE SUMMARY.
(Erase heading not required.)

Instructions regarding War Diaries and Intelligence Summaries are contained in F. S. Regs., Part II, and the Staff Manual respectively. Title pages will be prepared in manuscript.

Hour, Date, Place.	Summary of Events and Information.	Remarks and references to Appendices
21st November, 1915	In Camp at Tel-el-Kebir	
22nd November, 1915	In Camp at Tel-el-Kebir. Orders received that the Battalion would entrain for Port Suez 23-11-15, in two parties. The majority of baggage & transport vehicles & eight mules were loaded on the trains that night.	
23rd November, 1915	1st Party: Major E.F.S.Henderson, "A" & "B" Coys, M.G.Section and 24 N.C.O's & men 1st Line, half 1st Line wagons & eight mules entrained at 6.15 a.m. & arrived at Port Suez at 9.40 a.m. The 2nd Party - Major F.Lewis, D.S.O., Hd Qrs Party, "C" & "D" Coys, the remainder of 1st Line & 1st Line wagons at 7.20 a.m. & arrived at 10.45 a.m. The following re-embarked on H.M.T. Clan MacGillivray:- Major F.Lewis D.S.O. Major E.F.S.Henderson, Captains D.L.Weir, A.S.McIntyre & R.H.Ames, Lieut A.H.Howell, 2/Lieuts A.E.Sturdy, A.C.L. Chudleigh, L.Dowding, J.Redwood, C.G.R.Swindells, C.B.Godfrey O.H.Buckingham, H.Billings, J.P.Swain, A.Belle, D.C.Royce	

Army Form C. 2118.

WAR DIARY
or
INTELLIGENCE SUMMARY.
(Erase heading not required.)

Instructions regarding War Diaries and Intelligence Summaries are contained in F. S. Regs., Part II, and the Staff Manual respectively. Title pages will be prepared in manuscript.

Hour, Date, Place.	Summary of Events and Information.	Remarks and references to Appendices
24th November, 1915	Lieut & Qr Mr H.C.Brodie, Lieut J.G.Waine R.A.M.C., 896 other ranks & the 1st Line vehicles & sailed at 3 p.m. Lieut H.N.H. Grimble, 2/Lieuts G.L.Gwyther, H.D.Byers, H.E.Martin, T.C.D. Hassall & 5 other ranks, 3 native mule drivers & 8 mules embarked on H.M.T. "Janus".	
25th November, 1915	At Sea. Usual ship's routine carried out.	
26th November, 1915	At sea. Usual ship's routine carried out.	
27th November, 1915	At sea. Usual ship's routine carried out.	
28th November, 1915	At sea. Usual ship's routine carried out.	
29th November, 1915	At sea. Usual ship's routine carried out.	
30th November, 1915	At sea. Usual ship's routine carried out.	
1st December, 1915.	At sea. Usual ship's routine carried out.	
2nd December, 1915	At sea. Usual ship's routine carried out.	

www.ingramcontent.com/pod-product-compliance
Lightning Source LLC
Chambersburg PA
CBHW080825010526
44111CB00015B/2608